Chicken Soul
for the Soul®

Grieving, Loss
and Healing

Chicken Soup for the Soul: Grieving, Loss and Healing
101 Stories of Comfort and Moving Forward
Amy Newmark

Published by Chicken Soup for the Soul, LLC www.chickensoup.com
Copyright ©2022 by Chicken Soup for the Soul, LLC. All Rights Reserved.

The publisher gratefully acknowledges the many publishers and individuals who granted Chicken Soup for the Soul permission to reprint the cited material.

Front cover image courtesy of iStockphoto.com/RomoloTavani (©RomoloTavani)
Back cover and Interior photo courtesy of iStockphoto.com/aldomurillo (©aldomurillo)
Photo of Amy Newmark courtesy of Susan Morrow at SwickPix

Cover and Interior by Daniel Zaccari

Distributed to the booktrade by Simon & Schuster. SAN: 200-2442

Publisher's Cataloging-In-Publication Data
(Prepared by The Donohue Group, Inc.)

Names: Newmark, Amy, compiler.
Title: Chicken soup for the soul : grieving, loss and healing : 101
    stories of comfort and moving forward / [compiled by] Amy Newmark.
Other Titles: Grieving, loss and healing : 101 stories of comfort and
    moving forward
Description: [Cos Cob, Connecticut] : Chicken Soup for the Soul, LLC,
    [2022]
Identifiers: ISBN 9781611590876 (print) | ISBN 9781611593266 (ebook)
Subjects: LCSH: Grief--Literary collections. | Grief--Anecdotes. | Mental
    healing--Literary collections. | Mental healing--Anecdotes. | LCGFT:
    Anecdotes.
Classification: LCC BF575.G7 C45 2021 (print) | LCC BF575.G7 (ebook) | DDC
    155.937--dc23

Library of Congress Control Number: 2021948079

PRINTED IN THE UNITED STATES OF AMERICA
on acid∞free paper

28 27 26 25 24 23 22   01 02 03 04 05 06 07 08 09 10 11

Grieving, Loss and Healing

101 Stories of Comfort and Moving Forward

Amy Newmark

Chicken Soup for the Soul, LLC
Cos Cob, CT

Changing your life one story at a time®
www.chickensoup.com

Table of Contents

❶

~Oh, How It Hurts~

❷

~Saying Goodbye~

3
~Let It Out~

4
~The New Normal~

5
~Honoring and Remembering~

❻

~Moving Forward~

❼

~It Takes a Village~

8

~Words of Wisdom~

9

~Finding New Purpose~

10

~Love That Doesn't Die~

⑪

~Creative Coping~

Oh, How It Hurts

Writing Through the Aftermath

Our writing can transform us.
~Sandra Marinella, The Story You Need to Tell

It was bad. Horrifically bad. Bullet to the brain. Sudden death delivered in a heartbeat. One shot from a sheriff's deputy after a brief and wild car chase. My daughter had handed a note to the teller while her partner, a brainless thug, unzipped his jacket to reveal the authentic-looking, BB-gun pistol tucked into his belt. The report of a weapon was all deputies needed to open fire on the getaway vehicle, ending my daughter's life in less time than it takes to say her name: Sarah Kate. She would have felt no pain, the medical examiner informed us. We took comfort in that.

The aftermath was brutal. The story, as they say, had legs. There's a bizarre fascination to the story of a runaway wife, a mother of two, fatally shot after a bank heist. Reporters kept calling. A local news crew knocked on the door. We had to avoid TV. The robbery was not the couple's first. There had been other banks in other parts of the country, as far away as Oregon. Newscasters compared the duo to Bonnie and Clyde. Charges were filed against the survivor. Sarah's body was transported home. Her mother hugged her goodbye at a local mortuary. A few days later, she went back to retrieve the ashes.

I read all the newspaper reports I could find on the Internet until I was certain I had read them all. I studied the photos: a crashed car riddled with bullet holes, its tires flattened by spike strips; police and rescue personnel standing around; my daughter's body on the asphalt, covered by a plain white sheet.

I jotted notes, recording all the unpleasant details, straining to make some sense of the narrative. There were too many gaps and plot twists I didn't know. No logic beyond "One thing always leads to another," and "So it goes."

Was my daughter the casualty of a crime gone wrong or a life gone haywire? Was she a victim of mental illness or a drug addiction? Would anyone believe the deceased had been a kind, goodhearted human being, a little mixed up, a little insecure, but a loving mother and wife until her marriage broke, an affectionate daughter before she took a horribly wrong turn?

I made more notes. I admit I didn't know what I was doing or what I expected to accomplish. I may have been distracting myself, instinctively trying to work through my devastation, my grief, my sense of universal disturbance, all the while counting and adding up all my remaining blessings.

Writing had saved my life before. Over the years, my vocation had become a directing force and a guiding light. So, maybe if I concentrated, head down, nose to the grindstone, I could capture some part of my grief, scratch out some portion of our collective anguish. All our hearts were wrecked. God, we were hurting.

When you're a writer, you write. When you're a parent, you love. And when you lose a child, no matter what the cause or reason, the world and everything in it is thrown out of whack. You don't stop being a parent or loving your child. And, every minute, you expect the moon and the stars to start tumbling from the sky.

So, I wrote. The days crept by. The pages added up.

It was a fool's game. A grieving father's pastime. I pushed myself, extending my workday and isolation. I persuaded myself that it remained my solemn duty to record the aftermath of this event, that my primary responsibility remained as always to the reader.

I made regular attempts at finding the edge of whatever lesson or truth lay at the heart of this sustained agony. I wanted the story inside the story. I wanted my daughter alive. I wanted my old life back. And, most of all, I wanted the suffering I saw in those around me — in my wife, in my son, in my grandchildren — to stop once and for all. This went on and on like a bad dream.

One morning, being a tenacious reporter, a spy in my own life, I asked my wife how she had slept.

"Same," she said.

I inquired about her dreams, and she said she'd stopped having them.

"Everybody dreams," I said.

She shook her head. "Not in months."

"You must," I said.

"I don't," she insisted.

I did not mention my own nightmares or grumble how her goodnight kisses had turned cold. She was worn out from working, meditating, exercising, and taking care of the children, housing them in their mother's old room, comforting them, and coordinating her schedule with their father's to make sure the children were always safe and secure.

"You know we'll get through this," I said. "You understand that, right?"

She looked at me as though I was speaking an old and forgotten language.

"In time, we'll all move past this," I said. "You'll see."

Her lips tightened, and she breathed deeply through her nose, while she shook her head slowly in disagreement.

I reminded her again that life is for the living, that calamities touch us all, that gumption and endurance are essential. I went on and on.

"Please stop," she said. "There's no getting past this."

I gave her a sour look, mainly because I felt her declaration included me. I was tired of waiting. I didn't want to row this boat anymore, not with this heavy load, not with storm clouds threatening and the chance of surging tides.

Her eyes shone wet. I expected her to start weeping again.

I would not have been surprised if she'd peeled away her shirt and torn open her chest to reveal how her beautiful heart had been displaced by an emptiness, an immeasurable void, a space nothing would ever fill.

"Tell me something," she said softly. "What are we now, you and me? Can you tell me? You're so good with words." Her eyes expanded, widening to reflect all the light contained in the room. "Tell me what we've become, you and me," she said. "Because when a woman loses her spouse, she is a widow. When a husband loses his wife, he's a widower. And when a child loses his parents, that child is an orphan. But what are we? What's the word for a mother or father whose child has died? Why is there not even a name for people like us?"

That question still lingers, hovering nearby. What are we now? Is it established taboo not to say aloud what a grieving parent becomes?

Life constantly pulls you forward. It pulled us. Our alliance continued to hold. Our relationship would not only endure but flourish and become stronger. Gradually, our anguish would ease as new joys seeped in, and happy experiences (particularly those magical moments spent with our grandchildren) washed gently over us. But one fact persists: We are the bereaved, and the degree of our grief remains nameless.

So, I wrote about that, as though it were the consequence of some unfortunate event that had happened to other people: a story about two inconsolable strangers, routinely recorded by someone else.

— Bob Thurber —

Intersection of Grief

Sometimes, only one person is missing,
and the whole world seems depopulated.
~Alphonse de Lamartine

The long, silver necklace chain swings lightly from the rearview mirror, the heart pendant at the end keeping time as we pass buildings and cars on the rainy street. It is just after 4:00 on a rainy Thursday, and the Earth is shrouded in gray.

"You ever go to the Outer Banks?" the driver asks, meeting my eyes in the rearview mirror. She fiddles with the knobs on the dashboard, attempting to warm up the car.

"No," I sigh. "I'm not much of a beach person."

"We're going next week. Leaving Sunday. I need a break. After everything I've been through, I told myself I'm taking a break. So, we're going to the Outer Banks."

I nod and look out the window. So much for a quiet Lyft ride. After a long day at work, I have been eagerly anticipating the silence that will take me home to where cozy pajamas and ibuprofen await me. You've been gone a month, and although I am no stranger to loss, a pervasive emptiness resides in my chest. I'm not quite sure how to understand my feelings. You — my first love, the father of my child — are gone, and I am left behind to witness the fullness of a life that you are no longer a part of. Simple things like going to work have been hard, and I just crave the quiet. I want to be alone.

"Yeah, I've really been going through it lately," the driver continues, slamming on the brakes to avoid rear-ending a Jeep that abruptly stops in front of us. Turning her dyed-blond head over her shoulder, underneath her bangs, she raises her eyebrows. "You know, Mama died ten days before Christmas."

I mumble my condolences and sigh. No, I don't know, and I really don't want to. I just want to be home.

"Yeah, I moved down here nine and a half years ago to take care of her and Daddy. Now Daddy, he was my rock. It was harder because he died first. But Mama died ten days before Christmas, and my son and me, we didn't want to do it, but we opened up her Christmas presents. We had to, you know, because she was gone. Broke our hearts to do it."

I nod, silently, and avert my eyes. The sweater you gave me for Christmas is wrapped around my shoulders, keeping me warm in the back of the small car. It is a beautiful black-and-white marbled poncho, very classy — like you. You always did know how to buy the perfect gift. It will forever be one of the last things you gave me. I wonder how long it will last, how I can keep it nice so I can hold on to a shred of you, of something you touched and intended for me.

"It's taken me all this time to get her stuff together. And we just sold her house," the driver continues. "So, I've traveled this area all up and down, running her errands and tending to all her papers and bills." She laughs and looks back over her shoulder again. "It was harder on me when Daddy died, but then I had to start paying Mama's bills. She was old-fashioned, you know. Couldn't use the Internet and wanted to pay her bills with cash and checks. So, I had to help her do everything. Been here nine and a half years helping them both, and now they're both gone." The driver chuckled. "How's your day been?"

"Fine," I say, not elaborating. It's been exhausting. I've called banks, lawyers and your mother all day long, trying to figure out how the benefits for our daughter will be routed because she's only thirteen. I've cried because I have to get a court-appointment letter that states I'm my own child's legal guardian. I've laughed because I have imagined you watching me, an English teacher trying to deal with numbers and accounts, in my own personal hell without you. I've smiled at co-workers, pretending to be fine, even cracking a few jokes. I've laid my head down on my desk and closed my eyes, pretending all of this isn't real and is just some bad dream I'll eventually wake from.

"Now, Mama lived in Fort Mill. Are you close to there?" the driver asks.

"Yes," I reply.

"Oh, lots of new houses over there," the driver says, checking the GPS map on her cell phone as she verifies the next turn off the highway. "It's only been a few months, but a lot of that land over there is being built up."

I long to cocoon inside my sweater and hide myself from the rain, from the driver, from the world. I want to sleep and pretend everything is some ugly, muddy lie. I don't care about Mama or her Christmas presents or her house. All I can think about is you. You and your warm little house with the yellow door and the snowflake wreath. Your little, old dog that barks like clockwork when a car pulls into the drive. Your built-in bookshelves with pictures of you and our daughter, and your colorful treasures from travels around the world. You, and how you'll never come home from work again, like I am doing now.

The clicking of the turn signal is impertinent as we sit at the red light surrounded by cars. "Looks like we're almost there," the driver says, smiling widely. I smile back, falsely, and nod my head in agreement. I thumb through text messages on my phone, scrolling to the thread between you and me:

You: "Do you think she knows the gravity of the situation?"

Me: "No, I don't think so."

You: "I haven't used the word 'dead' yet. I've said 'deteriorate' and 'go quickly' and 'spend time with her before I can't.' And I've said that I'm going to keep fighting until I can't anymore because she's my reason to be here."

"Here we are. Are these new?" the driver asks, gesturing to my apartment building.

"We've been here three years," I say numbly, gathering my belongings.

"They sure weren't back here when Mama first moved here, I can tell you that," the driver laughs. "None of this stuff was."

I thank the driver and step out of the car. "You have a great evening now!" She waves cheerfully.

I'm overcome with pangs of guilt because I didn't enjoy the ride, or the driver, or the car, or anything. I'm wounded inside, and the driver opened up my wounds with her own grief. I feel sorry for myself but also have the awareness that she, too, had experienced great loss and pain. She wanted to talk about hers; I didn't.

As I walk toward my apartment, I know today is not the last time I'll think of you. There are many more long roads ahead for our daughter and me. I turn my key in the lock. Our daughter runs to greet me. She looks so much like you that it hurts. As I pull her to me to embrace, I remember your words: She's my reason to be here.

Finally, I'm home.

— Stephanie Tolliver Hyman —

My Breath Stops Short

We rise by lifting others.
~Robert Ingersoll

My breath stops short. That's right. I try to inhale deeply, but it seems to get stuck. Stuck somewhere on top of my pounding heart that I am sure is two times its normal size. Maybe that is why I just can't seem to get that breath in. My chest feels heavy, as if I am carrying around significantly more weight than before and it all seems to be in my chest.

Sit down for a few moments, I tell myself. *Everything is going to be okay. It's okay to feel the heaviness of grief. It's okay that the pain I am feeling is stopping me in my tracks. It's okay.*

Anyone who has struggled with deep inner pain and suffering knows the sensation of the breath stopping short. It's as if the heartbreak is so big and takes up so much space that there just isn't enough room for the breath to go any further. *Hold on,* I tell myself, *hold on.* Pain ends. That's the acronym for hope after all, right? So, if that's true, then surely this broken heart won't kill me. I will find my way through and to the other side of this pain.

I have felt an abundance of heartbreak in recent years, but this was different. I can literally *feel* my heart breaking. I feel the flood of tears streaking down my face, but at first I am not even sure I am crying. I look up to be sure that this downpour isn't coming from the sky. I try again to take another deep breath and another until what seem like short gasps of air fill me up enough to let it go. It's okay to cry it out. It's cleansing, right? There it is: the ugly cry. It's okay. I'm all alone, so I give myself permission to cry and cry until I feel cleansed. At least for the time being. Take another breath. Clean myself up. Give my head a little shake. It's time to live my life today.

Carrying around this heavy grief is like being cloaked in a heavy, weighted blanket as I try to put on a face that won't drop others to their knees when they see me. Surely, others won't be able to see my heartbreak, my deep pain and suffering. Surely, I can hide it all from the world. Well, maybe most of the world.

It really doesn't matter what has caused my deep pain and suffering. The point is that I am suffering such heartbreak that I feel like I am carrying the weight of the world around with me everywhere I go. So, I make a decision to stay home for a few weeks and manage my grief in private. I spend endless hours drawing and colouring in an attempt to clear my mind and live in the moment, always with a box of tissues close by. The people closest to me can feel the darkness of my pain, so I know that I need to work through the hardest stuff before I can resume my day-to-day life, which includes teaching yoga.

So, I draw and I colour. I cry and I draw. I colour and I cry. And I continue this way for over a month. I even drew and coloured and cried in my favourite local cafe just so I could get out of my house and be in the company of others. I think people just got used to seeing me this way during this time and let me be.

Then, one day, I got up and looked at myself in the mirror. I decided that I must move on. I gave myself permission to cry as hard and loud as I wanted every morning in the shower, and that would be it. I would practice breathing as normally as possible, and I wrote my affirmation on a card I carried in my purse in case I needed a reminder. "I can do this." I repeated this mantra over and over for the first few days when out, and soon it became easier. I started feeling lighter and finding someone or something that made me smile and almost forget my pain, even for a few moments.

I got brave enough to go grocery shopping. While out, I heard a familiar sound: the sound of someone behind me. It sounded like their breath was stopping short, the sound of a deep gasp for air. I couldn't help but look behind me and saw a woman around my own age wearing sunglasses indoors. I could feel her pain from a few feet away. It's like my heart knew hers. Without thinking, I reached into my purse and took out my card that read, "I can do this." I looked at her, reached out my hand and passed her the card. Tears streamed down her face from behind her glasses. I said, "I see you. We are going to be okay." We both stood there in silence, crying. She touched my hand and said, "Thank you." We both took a deep breath that stopped short and continued our shopping.

I don't know what her grief was about, and she didn't know what mine was about. It didn't matter. We were both cloaked in the heaviness of grief and sadness of our own, but we were the same — two people out there trying to manage our heartbreak who were not alone.

— Trish L. —

Lost

No matter what age... I'll always need you mom.
~Author Unknown

"I lost my mommy,"
Was what I wanted to say
To the woman I met in the supermarket.
But I would have sounded like a four-year-old,
Lost in a very scary place,
Separated from the love that most wanted to protect me.
And then the tears would have started.
And I really didn't want that.
Not next to the smiling bananas. Or anyplace.
So, I just said, "My mother passed away."
But, in truth,
Missing the warmth,
Of those lingering hugs,
I am pushing a shopping cart,
Passing the freezer section,
Looking like an adult,
But feeling, as I turn down each new aisle,
I lost my mommy.

— Bracha Goetz —

Grief Tantrum

God could not be everywhere,
and therefore he made mothers.
~Rudyard Kipling

The small child rages. She kicks; she screams; she throws things. She lies on the ground, her face red, her fists clenched, her toes flexed. Her hair is wild around her face as she shakes her head back and forth and beats at the carpet. She will scream at anyone who comes near her. They won't, though; they don't know how to deal with her. I don't know how to deal with her either, but I cannot leave her. She is mine.

Others don't believe that it is what it is. For some reason, they can't see it: visceral, indescribable pain. They can't face that pain, and they think it's inappropriate, so they stay away. They want to go on being appropriate. They don't want to admit that this great injustice, DEATH, is real.

She's only seven. She hasn't learned what is appropriate and what isn't. She hasn't learned the words to say, "I'm sad because I miss Daddy."

Why would she know that? What mommy would think to teach her child how to act appropriately about the sudden death of her daddy? It doesn't flow easily off the tongue like the ABCs.

She thinks she is all alone. Her eyes are clouded with tears of rage, and she can't see anything else. She is not alone. Sitting next to her, lying beside her, is Mommy.

I hand her another toy.

"Here, throw this one."

We rip pieces of paper to shreds. We hit our pillows. She kicks her toys. She stomps through the house, screaming. I follow her. I will not leave her like this; I will not leave her the way she feels Daddy did.

She slams the door in my face, and I silently wait; I know she didn't mean it. The door opens, and she is there, a tiny heap on the floor, crying uncontrollably now, not raging, just crying. I try to scoop her up in my lap, but she won't let me, so I push some toys out of the way and lie down beside her. I let her cry. There is nothing else to do. There is no fixing this, and there is no bringing Daddy back. If I stay beside her, at least she knows she is not alone.

I call these episodes "grief tantrums." In the three years since my husband died, she has had more grief tantrums than I can count. For a while, they happened every day: giant tantrums that you would see in a two- or three-year-old, complete with crying, screaming, kicking, and throwing things.

Except she's not two. Two-year-olds do that because they haven't learned to focus their emotions and put them into words. Once they learn those skills, they grow out of tantrums. My daughter has grief tantrums for the same reason. She doesn't know how to put her emotions into words. At seven she has no words to explain the emotions that come with her daddy dying. She doesn't know how to focus or control this massive grief. This isn't a "didn't get her way" tantrum. This isn't a "you won't give me ice cream" tantrum. This is a terrifying "my daddy is gone, dead, never coming back, and I can't grasp that" tantrum.

To outsiders, it looks like she is having an "I didn't get my way" tantrum. It starts as something small and innocuous. She can't find the pink crayon; she doesn't want to go to school; she doesn't want spaghetti for dinner. It's not about that. It's never about that. The pink crayon reminds her of the time she and Daddy drew a garden of pink flowers. Not wanting to go to school is because she's afraid that if she leaves her side, Mommy will die, too. Not wanting spaghetti is because Mommy doesn't make it the way that Daddy used to.

Her therapist explained it very clearly to me the other day. He said to imagine that you're walking down a road. If somebody bumps you, it's just a little bump. You shake it off and keep going. But kids who have had trauma are walking on the edge of an emotional cliff. If they get bumped, even a little bit, they are now falling off a cliff.

That describes my daughter exactly. Every little emotional bump is huge to her, and she doesn't know how to handle it. No wonder she's screaming and kicking. Somebody bumped into her, and because she was already on the edge, she's now holding on to a cliff by her fingernails.

She can't say, "I had so much fun with my friends' daddies this weekend. It made me really miss all the fun things I used to do with my daddy, and that makes me really sad, so I'm going to cry about Daddy for a little bit. Will you hold me while I do that?"

Seven-year-old children don't have those words. Many adults can't verbalize those emotions. So, she rages; she kicks; she throws things.

Every night, her daddy and mommy tucked her into bed after reading her a story. We said our prayers together. We sang the "Mommy and Daddy Love You Song." I kissed her goodnight and said, "I'll see you in the morning!" Then I walked out of the room.

He kissed her goodnight and said, "I'll see you in the morning!" leaving the door opened a crack as he left the room. She didn't see him in the morning. She never saw him again.

Before her daddy died, her biggest worry was whether or not we would be having ice cream for dessert. That should be a child's biggest worry. But overnight, her worries went from ice cream to who was going to take care of us, what was going to happen to us, and what if Mommy dies, too. She shouldn't have that on her shoulders.

When the grief tantrums come, I can be there by her side. I can hand her another toy to throw. I can rip paper into shreds with her while she screams in pain. I can lie there on the floor, holding her foot while she cries in anguish. I can be with her in her pain and sorrow. I will not leave her. I will not be scared away by her grief like everyone else. I am her mother, and she is my child.

— Jennifer Stults —

The Reality of Grief

*I cried endlessly when you died but I promise,
I won't let the tears mar the smiles that
you've given me when you were alive.*
~Author Unknown

I never understood the word "grief" until we met face-to-face. On July 2, 2020, I lost my ray of sunshine, my absolute world, my best friend. My mother lost her battle to cancer at a young age, something I never thought I would see at the age of twenty.

Growing up, I knew a few people who had lost a loved one, but never once did I think that it could happen to me. Parents are supposed to be superheroes, right? Nothing is supposed to be able to hurt them; after all, aren't they supposed to protect us? We know that one day we will lose our parents, but we never expect it to happen so prematurely. Why did I become the unlucky one? Why did I have to become the protector of my mom? I ask myself these questions every single day. As a result, I have had to come to terms with the simplest but most brutal reality: Life simply isn't always fair.

This concept is such a hard pill to swallow, almost equivalent to a hard punch in the gut. But grief, I learned, is not a one-time stage in life. It follows you every day, always. But through all this, there is a brighter side. I can't simply say it gets easier because I know it never does. But, with time, it becomes more bearable.

Time passed so slowly after I lost my mom, but I have seen for myself that the cliché that "time heals all wounds" is somewhat true.

Our wounds will never truly heal, but I believe that, in a sense, they develop into scars. Sometimes, more often than not, we are reminded of these scars, but they reiterate to us that we are so much more than the bad cards we have been dealt in life.

It's been a little over a year since my mom passed away. Sometimes, I just like to think she's on vacation (which was her favorite activity) and I'll see her when she comes back. I know this may seem silly, but for some reason it helps me ignore the harsh reality that she's really gone. I am not sure that I have completely come to terms with her death. It is such a hard concept to understand.

When my mother passed, she wasn't a typical cancer patient. My mother was the epitome of strength and working hard as a nurse, doing what she loved on her very last day. Even though my mother was sick, she didn't look like it. I believe this made her passing even harder on me because it was so sudden. One second, she was perfectly fine at work; the next second, she wasn't. Just like that, my life changed forever.

After her passing, I kept wondering when it would be okay to feel happy again. It just felt wrong to be happy. To be honest, it was hard to do anything after she passed. It was hard to eat because I knew she couldn't eat. I know it probably sounds odd, but like I said, death is a hard concept to understand and accept. I couldn't accept that she couldn't sit and eat with me anymore. I had to be carried into our house after coming home from the hospital without her because I physically could not get myself to go in the house.

The passage of time while grieving is different for everyone. I am, for the most part, past the gut-wrenching despair. With each day that passes, my memories of her become more and more distant. Since her passing, I have spent more time at home and by myself, even though I am aware that I need to get out more.

I often wonder if my friends are looking at me with pity. Are they waiting for me to be happy again? I didn't see it at first, but now I do. The unbereaved naturally wait for the bereaved to be happy again, as they simply do not understand the process it takes to get there. But through this I have learned that I have four amazing friends who have stuck with me through the entirety of my grieving process. The nights

I wanted to stay at home, they stayed with me. The nights I was alone and didn't ask for company, they still came to check on me. It requires a great deal of empathy and patience to remain by someone's side through it all. I did not see it then, but I surely do now. I will never forget those who did not abandon me when I was so vulnerable. In the future, I will do the same for another.

Growing up, I was always the happy-go-lucky kid, and I hated anyone to see me upset. I am still that way. Many see me as always smiling, uplifting others, and never showing that I'm depressed. Truthfully, I hate attention when I am upset and will do anything to avoid letting someone know I have been crying or am sad. I grieve alone.

I cry during my morning showers in peace. Some days, I cry while having morning coffee or driving to work. Some nights, I burst into tears before bed. But as time has passed, I do these things less and less.

I still have my rough days and nights, but I am here to say it is okay to do these things. What is not okay is bottling up one's emotions and pretending they don't matter. Emotions matter. Grief is not something to avoid; it is something one must learn to accept and cope with. As Jamie Anderson once said, "Grief, I've learned, is really just love. It's all the love you want to give but cannot."

— Mackenzie Gambrill —

The Monty Dinner

The bond with a dog is as lasting
as the ties of this earth can ever be.
~Konrad Lorenz

The silence in the car is oppressive as we drive home on Thursday night. It's just the four of us and an empty collar. The absence of a tiny dog is crushing us. Glancing at my husband behind the wheel, his eyes fixed on the road ahead, I turn to Max and Emma in the back seat. "Okay, tomorrow night we're having dinner in the dining room. Your job is to find your favorite picture of Monty and bring it with a story that goes with it." They stare vacantly ahead. I'm not even sure they have heard me.

Dinner in the dining room is usually reserved for Sundays and holidays. It's a chance to set a proper table and expose the children to more formal dining and etiquette that they'll likely need later in life. But this is a Friday night dinner made special because of Monty. He deserves it, and I think we need it. I throw nutritional caution out the window. It is not my finest culinary hour, but I prepare a meal that will elicit no complaints or refusals. By early afternoon, with the table set (including a box of tissues), I go in search of a picture of Monty to put at my place, mentally crafting a story to go with the photo.

That afternoon, I think about deaths I experienced in childhood. They are memories of family members or close friends, all sad and confusing experiences, often punctuated by awkward silences. I can hear my mother cautioning, "Don't mention so-and-so; it will make them sad." But Monty's death is the first grief experience for my children, and I want something more healing, more helpful for them. I don't know for certain how we will accomplish that. I place my trust in whoever put the idea for this dinner in my mind on the way home from the vet's office last night.

At dinnertime, as I bring the first plates into the dining room, I stop and stare at the sight on the table. Max and Emma have not brought just one favorite picture of Monty. The table is covered with pictures, spanning all the years of the children's lives in which Monty was a part. Mercifully, dinner progresses with no whining about food or fighting between siblings. As we finish, I pick up the photo of Monty I had selected earlier. "I'll go first," I venture, not exactly sure where I am going but determined to start the process.

"Monty was my walking buddy," I say. "Every morning, he came with me, and we had to stop so he could sniff what seemed like every bush. Everyone on our route knew him, and they would smile and wave, calling his name. I remember needing to pick him up, all seven pounds of him quaking in my arms, when we came across a coyote during our walks near the desert wash. He was a fearless protector of me when it came to human strangers, but I think he knew he was outmatched when facing a coyote."

And so, it begins, each of us taking a turn. Eventually, all four of us interrupt each other's stories with forgotten details or gentle corrections. There is a picture of Monty in the doll carriage, being pushed around the back yard. Monty tolerating being sprayed with Febreze when his wet-dog smell offended someone. Recollections of Monty's queasy stomach making car rides a dangerous proposition for whoever had him in their lap. Monty cagily managing to slip onto the foot of the bed once the lights went out each night, only to disappear before anyone woke in the morning.

As the dinner and storytelling come to a close, I feel the crushing weight from last night's car ride lifting. We used some of those tissues while telling our tales tonight, and we will use more of them in the days and weeks to come. But a light has come on. We see we have so many reasons to remember and celebrate our time with Monty. He had a good life with us, and we were enriched by having him in our family. That will be our focus.

We still continue the tradition of The Monty Dinner whenever death intrudes in our lives. Our children learned from their first grief experience that it is an act of healing to speak, remember and appreciate the gift of loving someone, human or pet, for whatever length of time we're allowed to know them. Max still has Monty's collar. It brought him such sadness on that dark Thursday with death and grief so very raw. Now, he can smile and say, "Monty was a good dog. Smelly sometimes, but still good." And with that, I know I am giving my children a more positive path to grief.

— Sheila Roe —

Losing My Words

Grief is the healing process of the heart, soul, and mind;
it is the path that returns us to wholeness.
~David Kessler

Shortly after losing my father in a horrific accident, I lost my words. It felt like I lost my mind, too, but that seemed understandable and, oddly, less disconcerting. I am a storyteller; I needed my words. A friend sat holding my hand. I stammered, trying to relay the tragedy to her. My racing thoughts exited my mouth in slow motion. My voice did not sound like my voice. Grief narrowed my vision. I had to squint to see what was in front of me. The image of my elderly father, sitting in his kitchen chair, accidentally setting himself on fire, expanded in my brain until I thought I heard it snap in half.

My brain broke.

I told this to my husband, friends, children, and rabbi. I said this, not in hysteria, but matter-of-factly, as a way of explaining the mess of this person standing before them who could no longer string together coherent sentences. I needed to get my brain fixed.

It is a Jewish custom not to leave one's home during the seven days of mourning a parent's death. This was fine with me. I had nowhere I wanted to go except to bed, but there I was on a November afternoon, in the car, my husband driving me to see a therapist. I remember struggling to get the words out to tell the doctor how my world had turned upside down in an instant, and then spun again and again as details of the accident unfolded. How I flew to Florida thinking my father was still alive, and then learned of his death from a text message as the plane landed. How I couldn't breathe as I pushed through the people standing in the aisle, and then ran crying through the airport terminal.

Maybe I told the doctor about how my mother's eyewitness account of the horror seared into my brain as if I'd been there myself. I was haunted by the screams of pain I never heard. Did I tell him about seeing the singed yellow papers on my father's desk, the burned spot on the kitchen floor, and how, as I walked across the room, ashes stuck to my bare legs?

I asked the doctor to fix my brain. He told me that I was in shock — my body was shutting down as a way of protecting myself. There is no medication to take away the pain of my devastating loss, but he prescribed something to ease anxiety and help with sleep. The doctor said that I would recover from this seemingly "unrecoverable" event. I did not believe him.

Over the next few weeks, my mental timeline warped. Days lost their shape. Past and present events co-mingled. I tried assembling fragments of those lost days into a story. Nothing made sense. Rage rose from the pieces of this broken narrative. Why did my father light the match? How was my mother not able to douse the flames? Why did they airlift him to a second hospital? How could they let him die alone? I pressed for details about the accident, held them close for inspection, forced myself to read news accounts, and then fell apart afterward. I could not fathom the reality of these reports. How dare they write about my father's death? Words, words, words. Who gave them those words?

Nights were the hardest. Intrusive thoughts paraded through my head. I was haunted by my father's end, the pain, his helplessness as he watched his beloved wife, immobilized by shock, unable to stop the burning. Wordless tears slipped down my face. I turned to books for comfort but found the pages seemed to contain an encrypted code.

The weekly meetings with my doctor became a refuge from the challenges of re-entering the world. Gradually, my spoken words began to line up — sharp and angry — marching in their own direction. I told him about my compulsion to grill the hospital staff, EMT, police officer, my mother and sister — anyone who was witness to the tragedy. The doctor held my angry words without judgment, as if he was storing them in a safe place. He explained that anger seeks a root. I was looking to make sense of what had happened, to assign blame. But as long as I was looking "out there," he said gently, I was distracting myself from what was going on inside my fractured brain and heart.

But where were my written words? My novel-in-progress remained untouched. Each day, I pushed myself to face the unfinished page, to listen for the characters' voices. But the words didn't come. This state felt different from the writer's block I'd experienced in the past; it was more like a muffled silence or a bad phone connection. I worried that my brain had been permanently jumbled. My writer friend advised me to treat myself with compassion. "Don't be so hard on yourself. Put your energy into healing. Then the words will come." I had imagined that writing would be part of healing. I wanted this to be so.

"I need to write the story of what happened," I told my doctor.

"It's too soon for that," he said.

But writing is how I made sense of the world, so I gave it a try. Where to begin? Did I start with the irony of having a lifelong fear of fire? Or the anxiety I've always harbored about my father dying? Perhaps I should begin with my anger at the Universe for revising the neat ending I'd imagined (believed in) — the good goodbye, or how I always pictured myself delivering an eloquent eulogy instead choking over impromptu words that I would not remember saying.

Trying to craft this story's beginning led to thinking about its violent ending. Sensory fragments assaulted my brain. An unbearable grief pressed down on me.

It was too soon to assemble this tangled story.

The doctor remained at my side as I pushed through the dark winter months. Then, one day, I woke up to the spring sunshine, and I felt my mind mending. The sharp edges of grief had smoothed, allowing me to safely trace my hand along its ever-shifting shape. By summer's end, my field of vision had widened. Inside this panoramic view, details came into focus. Images surfaced. Memories floated by.

I grasped at them, attempted to put them in order. My story stirred.

Autumn arrived with the crimson maple trees. I stepped into the season's circle of loss and renewal. At last, I felt ready to traverse my story's landscape, cross the perimeter of trauma, and move closer and closer to its center. Here, in the shadow of grief, I gathered my lost words and began again.

—Evelyn Krieger—

9

I Was Somebody's Sister

*Siblings will take different paths and life may separate them,
but they will forever be bonded by having
begun their journey in the same boat.*
~Author Unknown

"**D**o you have any siblings?" It's a question that's polite and unassuming on the outside, usually wielded by a friendly stranger somewhere between "Where are you from?" and "What do you do?" It's a question I had been asked many times before and answered many times over.

But this time, on that Uber ride home from work one night, it was different. The weight of the driver's words caused a sudden tightening in my chest and a buckling of the knees. I blinked furiously while trying to catch my breath, playing with different permutations of what my response should be.

Having a sibling was part of my identity, just like my upbringing. My personality, my occupation, my hopes and dreams. And now I needed to suddenly contend with what it meant to be someone's surviving sister.

Am I an only child? No, that would have erased my little brother's existence entirely. An only sibling? That doesn't sound right either. Why isn't there a label I can quickly and easily affix to my situation?

Seconds before, I was just another passenger engaging in small talk like so many who came before me. Now I was about to be that passenger who experienced an emotional collapse in the back seat of this guy's car. *I need to start coming with a warning label,* I thought to myself.

When grief gets suppressed in the name of work, in the face of the general public, for the sake of one's sanity, energy takes a blow. After putting on a face for nine hours, exhaustion assumes a whole new form. It's a grueling, full-body sensation — a bit like what I supposed removing a spacesuit feels like.

That night, I just didn't have it in me to play along with the storyline that everything was fine. It wasn't fine. So, I referred to my brother in the past tense.

"I had a brother. His name was Aaron. He died a few months ago."

There was a moment of silence. The thing with grief is that being uncomfortable is par for the course. I used to try to fill awkward silences with platitudes and meaningless words. After experiencing the most intense inward pain imaginable, other socialized feelings — like embarrassment or uneasiness — no longer rate.

So, I let the quietness envelop the space we were sharing. I also needed a second to internalize what my words sounded like now that they were suspended in the air.

I had a brother once.

After a few seconds, I searched for his eyes in the rearview mirror. He was staring right back at me, with eyes visibly glistening. I was bracing for pity, but what I got in return was empathy. It was a shared understanding, all in one look, that the thing we all fear the most becomes a reality for so many.

"I am so, so sorry," the driver replied with sincerity, a slight tremor in his voice. "I lost my son when he was really young. His mama died, too. I carry that with me wherever I go." He shared what led to their demise, while I shared the tragedy that was now my story. We cried and gave each other advice. ("Take care of yourself and keep a watchful eye on your parents for that first year," he told me.) We exchanged words of comfort. When he pulled up to the entrance of my place, I lunged toward the front seat and threw my arms haphazardly around his neck, my heart aching — but still the opposite of empty.

After that indelible ride home, it occurred to me that there's a ripple effect with grief. After we experience the loss, there are aftershocks. Sometimes, they come on sneakily. I not only lost my brother that one solemn June day, but I lost the history we had, the memories we were supposed to make, and my identity as his sister.

But the pain of losing my identity in the wake of a loved one's death was understood by this man. I didn't feel alone. And I didn't feel judged for the raw emotion I exhibited. So often, our grief can make those close to us feel uncomfortable. They tell us, well-intentioned as they are, to "look on the bright side" or that our loved one wouldn't want to see us "like this." This special stranger sat in my pain with me, as I sat in his for twenty whole minutes. And, for a moment, time stopped.

Often, we respond to the small talk with polite nothingness, withholding a world of pain. But what if revealing our true selves could serve as a lifeline to the person on the other end?

—Jamie Korf—

Saying Goodbye

10

The Truest Thing

*The love between a dad and his daughter
is unbreakable.*
~Author Unknown

I'm trying not to feel anything. My father-in-law is terminally ill and spends his days and nights in a mechanized lift bed. My brother-in-law wanted to purchase a house to help take care of his father, but he needed a cosigner on his loan. I refused.

My father-in-law stayed for months in a nursing facility not far from where my wife, Quyen, and I live. I visited him once while Quyen saw him on a regular basis. Two weeks ago, my brother-in-law managed to buy a house without my signature and brought his father home.

Quyen is close to her family. I'm not. They speak Vietnamese. I don't. I did not go to my brother-in-law's house after his escrow closed. Quyen did. I haven't been there to watch over her father. Quyen has.

My wife asked me to come to her brother's house today because her father is going to die soon. I do it out of obligation.

I greet Quyen's relatives in an awkward manner; I don't know what to say to them. Quyen's mother leads me to a room where my wife is sitting on a wooden stool beside her father. He is in bed, and Quyen is holding his hand. I've only seen this look on her face once before — after she suffered a miscarriage two years into our marriage.

Her mom leaves, and my wife and I are alone with a dying man. His face is pale and emaciated, and I see the outline of his skull. His eyes are dark, empty. His lungs have collapsed from years of smoking and chronic asthma. He is hooked up to an oxygen machine and breathes through a tube. His frail body is bone thin.

Quyen tells me he can only eat a few spoonfuls of baby food a day; it's all his stomach can handle. She says something to him in Vietnamese, and her father nods once. She releases his hand, picks up a remote, and inclines the bed so that her father is in a sitting position. She gets up and walks over to a tray table at the corner of the room. It holds a plastic pitcher of water, a Styrofoam cup with a bent straw protruding from it, and a Kleenex box. Quyen wheels the tray table next to her father. She pours water into the white cup, sets down the pitcher, and dips the straw into the cup. Quyen suctions liquid into the straw by covering one end with her index finger. She lowers her father's breathing tube, brings the straw to his lips, and releases drops into his mouth. This is how he drinks.

Quyen puts the straw into the cup, adjusts her father's breathing tube, and reclines his bed. She sits on the stool and says something to him, but he doesn't respond. His breaths are shallow, rapid, like the panting of a winded dog. Quyen says the hospice nurse placed the oxygen tube in his mouth because he was struggling to breathe through his nose.

He is on morphine to ease his pain. It's all they can do.

Quyen gets a tissue and dabs her father's eyes. She tears up when she tells me her father is crying, and she can barely suppress the sobs welling up within her. She puts the tissue on the tray table, turns to her father, draws closer and touches her hand to his face. Then she leans and brings her lips to his forehead, kissing him several times the way a mother would kiss a newborn.

It is the truest thing I have ever seen.

It is the love from a child to the person who gave her life. And in that moment, I am no longer looking at a withered man gasping for his last breaths. Instead, I see a father who took care of his daughter for most of her life and the now-grown woman who returns his love.

— Raymond M. Wong —

11

Packing Up a Life

My mother is a never-ending song in my heart of comfort,
happiness and being. I may sometimes forget the words
but I always remember the tune.
~Graycie Harmon

After my mum died, walking into her little apartment by myself was more than I could bear. I lay down on her bed and cried into her pillow. I pulled her blankets around me, trying to breathe in any remaining scent of her. I sat in her favorite chair and looked through old family albums. In a few short weeks, I knew I would have to let her apartment go, my last remaining connection to her.

As hard as it was to slowly sort through and pack up her things, in many ways it brought me great comfort. It was my quiet time, away from the noise of everyday family life, where I had to be strong and not cry every second in front of my little girl who had just lost her Nanny.

Sorting through Mum's things was emotional hell, but it also felt, in a strange way, like she was still there and we were spending time together reminiscing about old times. I would shut the door and be transported back in time to when she was alive, when I would drop by for visits. Some days, all I could do was sit, look around and soak it all in, trying to take a snapshot in my mind so I would never forget.

And, at times, it was like finding buried treasure. Secret envelopes revealed poetry my mum had written over the years. A lover of words, she also had clippings and Post-it notes of inspirational and humorous thoughts literally everywhere — taped in cupboards, hidden in closets. My mum and I are both writers, so although I wasn't surprised to find some of her writings and clippings, I had never seen some of them before. It was like discovering a whole other side of her that I wish I could have gotten to know better while she was still living. It is a regret far too common after loved ones are gone forever, never to return.

As I was packing up my mother's life, I was also unpacking some of it into mine. Boxes of her photos, books and other personal mementos I couldn't bear to give away ended up on my shelves and on my walls. I started wearing her jewelry, her watch. I wrapped her favorite blanket around me as I watched her favorite movies.

People said they were just things, that you couldn't keep it all. That was true. But I was determined to keep whatever I could and also ensure that some of her treasured possessions were given to friends and family. These "things" are not just "things" — they are the last remnants of my mother's life. And when I wrap myself in the soft warmth of her favorite lime-green housecoat, I can still feel her close to me.

—Aimee C. Trafton—

12

Watching Over Me

*Sometimes the most productive thing you can do is rest
and let your angels wrap you in their loving wings.
They've got you covered.*
~Anna Taylor

A t first, I didn't understand the gift: a slender ceramic figure, a woman with outstretched arms holding a star. She wore a simple blue tunic over a humble golden-brown skirt.

"She's an angel," my partner Ron said.

Inscribed on her side: "Perhaps they are not stars but merely openings where our loved ones can shine down and let us know they are happy."

I put her on our dining room table, which held an abundance of flowers, fruit, casseroles, and chocolates. Several days earlier, my forty-seven-year-old daughter Hilee had died suddenly. Friends and family had rushed in to cradle me. And now, a poet from my writers' group had sent an angel to watch over me.

Until that moment, my main concept of angels came from the gospel hymn I'd sung as a Jewish kid at a Christian summer camp: "All night, all day, angels watching over me, my Lord…." I loved the song because of its rhythmic beat but didn't really relate to the concept of angelic supervision.

Now, I was revisiting that idea. Over the next week, the flowers drooped, and we gradually, gratefully, ate everything people had brought. Soon, the angel stood alone.

Meanwhile, I was trying to track down my daughter. Because her cause of death was unknown, she'd been taken to the coroner for a toxicology report and autopsy.

Hilee hated being out in the world alone and panicked in strange places. The idea of her unattended in some cold, dark morgue haunted me.

I called the coroner's office to see if I might sit near my daughter and keep her company. The woman was kind but firm.

"It doesn't work that way," she told me. "But don't worry, she'll be released soon and sent to the funeral home."

I called the funeral home to see if I could sit with her before her cremation.

"It doesn't work that way," Dawn, the director, told me, her voice gentle. "We send her straight to the crematorium."

"Can I go there and sit with her before she's cremated?" I couldn't believe these words came out of my mouth. I desperately wanted to be near my child one last time, that desire a primal scream building inside me.

"It's against the code."

"Will they tell me when they're going to cremate her? I want to pray during that time."

"She'll probably be taken care of this evening, but they don't tell us when."

"Can I call and ask them?"

"I will call for you," Dawn said. "But they might not tell me."

I paced the house, wringing my hands. I didn't want my child to be alone during such a difficult and crucial time.

"Let's set up an altar on the table," Ron suggested. "Then we'll be ready. We can start praying any time."

We circled the angel with votive candles, sticks of sandalwood incense, and the few surviving flowers.

At 5:30 that evening, Dawn called. "She'll be going up at 6:30."

With the angel presiding, we began our prayers and reminiscences. We talked about how amazing Hilee was, a woman who rarely left her home due to mental-health issues, yet who'd managed to find love and create community. Somehow, she always charmed or pestered people into procuring her "daily bread," which in her case consisted of a large Diet Coke and something chocolate.

We celebrated Hilee. I read and reread the angel's inscription. We gazed into the celestial being's uplifted eyes, so wide and open, so ready for miracles.

As my daughter turned to ash in some far corner of our city, I thought of the funeral pyres we'd seen when we visited the holy town of Varanasi in India. We'd been on a boat on the river Ganges, close enough to the shore to feel the heat of the fires and hear the chanting of the priests, our eyes burning from the smoke.

"Where are the women?" I asked as we passed the flaming pyres and the clusters of mourners.

"Sometimes, the women wail too loudly. They usually don't go to this ceremony," our local guide told us.

I didn't wail that night as I sat with Ron and my angel in Kansas City, Missouri. Despite the unspeakable, unthinkable truth that my daughter was dead, I didn't have the strength to cry out. Instead, I wept quietly, my eyes closed against the flickering candlelight. I imagined Hilee sipping her Coke, the Route 66 Special — extra-large, no ice, half-price at Sonic during "Happy Hour." I imagined her watching me, wondering why all the fuss, ready to ask if I had chocolate stashed anywhere.

Then I looked at my angel holding her single star, reaching past the firmament into the bold, boundless beyond, her arms never tiring, her patience never thinning, her hope never dimming. And I understood: She was watching over me, watching over my beloved Hilee.

— Deborah Shouse —

The Day Basil Died

There is a comfort in rituals, and rituals provide
a framework for stability when
you are trying to find answers.
~Deborah Norville

The day Basil died, he and I were alone. My husband was away. Basil was a cat, a resplendent Abyssinian with russet fur, and a bladder and temper that were chronically inflamed. His twelve years were punctuated by episodes of aggression, mysterious fevers, and ever-changing regimens of diet and pills. Finally, the cells inside his bladder knotted into a tumor that could not be removed, and for which there were no drugs.

In spite of — perhaps even *because* of — all this, oh, how we loved each other. He napped draped across my shoulders as I sat at my desk. He would stand on the kitchen counter, wrap his arms around my neck, and press his face to mine with a purr that could be heard across the room.

The day Basil died, he could not urinate. Black blood dripped onto the floor as he walked. When I felt his belly, he cried out. I texted my husband: *B in trouble. Going to vet now.*

Weather can be eerie and violent in the Kansas prairie. I drove into a summer squall, into a bank of cloud or fog or both, with a screaming wind driving milk-white sheets of rain across the hood. It would have scared me if I wasn't already so distraught.

It's not that I hadn't done this part before: coming to the moment, knowing it was time and what had to happen. The tears, the farewell, murmuring my shattered love into his unhearing ear as he melted away from me. Before this, living then in a city house, we had to turn over "disposing of the remains" to others. They waited in the vet's freezer for the weekly pet-cemetery pickup, to be laid in a trench or incinerated with others, or we would go back a few days later to pick up a plain white box. A couple of times, we carried them there ourselves and waited in a hushed room while a gentle man in blue jeans fired up the furnace to cremate them then and there, and we went home an hour later with a still-warm urn.

This time, there was no pet-cemetery service. I was alone. It was raining. But we had seven acres of grass, trees and birdsong, and a corner by the front porch where Basil liked to lurk in the greenery and ambush grasshoppers.

I brought the crate and its motionless burden home. I went upstairs to my office and found a sturdy, lidded cardboard box that a laptop had come in. I placed the box on the dining room table and folded a soft green towel into it. I laid Basil's body in the box, arranging his paws and tail comfortably as though in sleep, although his eyes were still slightly open. I lit a candle at his head and took his photograph. I poured a glass of wine and called my husband. We wept together, my husband choking out, "I'm sorry! I'm so sorry I wasn't there!"

I sat with Basil for a long time. I cried. I stroked and kissed him. I pressed my face to his. I drank more wine as the rain pattered outside. Then I blew out the candle and went to bed. He lay in repose on the table until morning.

At dawn, I waded through wet grass to what was usually a damp spot beneath some trees, but that day was almost a pond. Among the rocks and fallen branches were some chunks of the local cream-and-rust-hued sandstone, the color of Basil's fur. The stones were mottled, freckled with lichen spores, some rippled from when they were sand at the bottom of some inland sea. I turned them over, hefted them, and chose several, juggling them in my bare arms back to the house. Out in the workshop, I found a thick piece of plywood, maybe two feet square. Coyotes live here; I wanted to at least deter their digging if I could. And in the woodpile was a perfect half-cylinder of elm, faded and split, frilled with luminous orange-yellow fungi called "witch's butter." Then I fetched the shovel.

In a sultry summer mist, I dug deeper and wider than I needed to. I scraped the sides of the hole smooth. Back inside, I kissed my cat one last time, covered his face and closed the box. I wrote all his names in thick black letters on the lid: Bingo Crepuscule, Basil, Beezer, Mr. B., Big Brown B, and just B. I carried him out.

This was only the second funeral I had attended in my life. The hardest part was to drop the first dirt on top of him. I did what people in television shows do: I sprinkled some in by hand. After that, it felt possible to spoon in the dirt with the shovel, leveling and layering it, tamping it down. Then I set the plywood square firmly on top. I spent some time arranging the stones in a way that pleased me, to display the ripples and the markings best. The brightly streaked elm log served as a headstone. And then it was done: a neat, small, rustic grave where butterflies and grasshoppers would flit, where Basil's cells, tissues and molecules would slowly return to the soil. I had chosen the place and dug the hole. I put someone I loved in it, filled it up, and set the markers with my hands. I had performed the right and necessary duties, and solace bloomed from the muscles of my sorrow.

The funereal trappings of mahogany and brass, flowers massed in crosses, silver hearses, organ dirges and black-clad processions are not for the dead. The dead do not care, and we should not pretend they do. The rites mark out the work that we do in their name.

Sitting up late, alone with the dead, I cleared space for memory because that was the only place Basil could be from then on. I did something that he never asked for, but I offered it anyway. Every bite of the shovel that morning felt deliberate and focused, with mindful attention fully paid. I walked the road with Basil all the way to the end. The simple energies of thought and labor had begun to frame the new path I would now walk without him and guide me into it.

I still go out to talk to him sometimes. The first snowfall on the grave wrung fresh tears, as I hated to think of him so cold. I do not show anyone the deathbed photo in my phone, but I do not delete it.

There is now a second neat, rustic grave next to his for another dearly loved cat, surrounded by an impasto of purple iris in the summertime. The house wrens raise their young in the elm overhead.

The day after Basil died, I learned the power of ritual.

—Julie Stielstra—

14

Joy Amidst the Sorrow

*Writing is medicine. It's an appropriate antidote
to injury. It is an appropriate companion
to any difficult change.*
~Julia Cameron, The Artist's Way

I had always been incredibly close to Grandma. I rode my bike to her house almost every day after elementary school, and I still pedaled there often in my teen years to hang out. We shared the same wacky sense of humor, laughing at the Muppets and old British comedies until our stomachs cramped. We sang Christmas songs by clucking like chickens. We spent hours reading books in companionable silence with corny, old TV murder mysteries as our background noise. When I became a published short-story author and eventually a novelist, my grandma wasn't surprised. "You were always good," she said with lofty confidence.

In short, she had been more than my grandma. She was also one of my dearest friends.

Now here I was, over 500 miles away, dreading every telephone call and text message. My grandma was dying, and I couldn't make the trip home to say goodbye. My husband couldn't get time off from work, and my car couldn't make the long drive. I checked on airline prices, and my jaw almost hit the keyboard.

The grief over losing Grandma was bad. The guilt over being away from her and my family made it even worse.

I especially wanted to be there to help my mom. She had retired as a teacher years before so that she could take on the almost full-time task of being caregiver for her mother. With Grandma now in the hospital, beyond the scope of her care, my mom sounded broken and lost on the phone.

"It's okay if you can't come," Mom said, her voice strangely raspy. "You don't need to spend thousands on a flight just to be here for a few days. This isn't how you need to remember her anyway."

"But I want to be there...." I could barely speak through my sobs.

"I know that. She knows that, too."

"What can I do? How can I help?" I asked, desperate to do something, anything, from afar.

"She won't be around much longer," Mom said, then paused to think. "Maybe you could start writing the piece about her life for her memorial...."

"Of course," I said automatically. Grandma had decided years ago that instead of a large graveside funeral, she wanted a memorial gathering at the small church where my late grandpa had been a minister. "Anything in particular I should concentrate on?"

"Just write about her life and who she really was," Mom said. Such a simple statement, such a complex task!

Several days later, Grandma passed away in the dark of night. My family's focus went to her final arrangements. My husband's work schedule was still awful. Flight costs remained exorbitant. I still couldn't make the trip back home.

So, I did the one thing I could do: I wrote.

How could I do justice to ninety-four years of vibrant life in just a few typed pages? I was intimidated by the task before me, but I also knew that Grandma had placed full faith in my ability to do it. I wouldn't let her down — if such a thing had ever been possible at all.

All through my childhood, Grandma had bought me nice pens and gorgeous journals. "Writers need to write!" she had said, time and again. "You have a gift. You have to use it." When I was about ten, she commissioned me to write and illustrate stories about a plush family of pioneer-dressed rabbits she kept on display in her house. When I was a teenager, she was nothing but nice when I came over to type up (wretched) poetry on her word processor. I think, in a way, she was living vicariously through me. Before I was even born, she had tried to write a murder-mystery detective novel and gave up on it partway. In me, she saw that same spark, and she did everything she could to encourage the flame.

After days of writing, deleting and revising, I sent the eulogy to my mom. She called me back, crying. "It's perfect," she said. "This is what Mom wanted."

Though it did ease some of my pain, I cannot say that writing that document made me feel all better. No, more than anything, I wanted to be there in the church that day. I wanted to see my aunt and cousins whom I hadn't seen in years. I wanted to cry, hug and grieve with people who shared the same loss. But life is tough sometimes. It takes away the people we love. It makes husbands work long hours and airplane flights cost too much.

And yet, life is full of delight sometimes, too. It means singing Christmas songs while clucking like chickens. It means watching the Muppets and giggling together, tears streaming down our cheeks. It means soft, wrinkled hands scented with Avon lotion pressing a book between my palms as I'm told, "This is a great book. You should read it, too, Beth."

That's the spirit I tried to weave into my words. From the messages I received afterward, I succeeded. People told me that my voice came through as I told the story of Grandma's life, of her very character. It was like I was there — as was Grandma. My mom said that as her cousin read my eulogy aloud, everyone laughed even as they sobbed.

That's what Grandma would have wanted: joy amid the sorrow. A real celebration of her life as we came together, physically present or not, to say goodbye to the woman we would all miss so very much.

— Beth Cato —

15

Finding Our Beat

We must develop and maintain the capacity to forgive.
He who is devoid of the power to forgive
is devoid of the power to love.
~Martin Luther King Jr., A Gift of Love

My father-son experience was, shall we say, complicated. There were many good times but few pictures of us together.

My parents had divorced when I was thirteen years old. Up until that point, I can remember never wanting to stay home with Dad alone. It was not because he was physically abusive. He was, in the most respectful way I can put it, a broken man. Now, I know a lot of us would say, "Me, too," but my dad wasn't as self-aware, and his brokenness created a living space that was rocky to say the least. When my mom would go to her second job at night, I would go with her to the mall and do my homework in one of the dressing rooms so that I didn't have to face his fury. I understand now that his mood swings were out of his control and heavily rooted in untreated PTSD from his time in the Vietnam War.

I can remember being nervous when the day finally came that my dad would be taking me to a WCW event. I hadn't seen him much since the divorce, and the few times I had seen him, he only talked about how my mother had hurt him even after years of him hurting her.

Growing up, I loved professional wrestling. The drama, strength and acrobatics of these men and women had me hooked each week. It was one of the few things my dad really knew about me. However, even though I probably complained to my mom that he was taking me to WCW and not WWE, I was still excited to see what the other side was doing. It was the one and only time I got to see Ric Flair wrestle. My dad and I were amazed that this man, THE MAN, Ric Flair, who was my dad's age, was still going for it. Boy, he was impressive. He was being thrown in the air, doing crazy flips, and putting his opponent into the figure-four leg lock. It was a special occasion I'll always remember.

On my dad's seventieth birthday, I went over to my brother's girlfriend's house for a small get-together. I showed up in sunglasses because my eyes were bothering me that day. My dad began to make fun of me for wearing the sunglasses. I just wanted to spend some time with family and not have any arguments, so I avoided his attacks. I asked my dad what he wanted for his big day, and he said there was no way I could get him what he really wanted. I said, "Try me," so he went on to say he wanted a pair of Beats headphones. I told him it wasn't a problem and asked when he would like to go get them. I'd never seen that man jump up so fast. He got his keys, and we headed to the closest store. We ended the night taking a picture together, both of us in our sunglasses.

I found out later from various people close to him that he loved those headphones. He took them on golf trips and to visit my brother in San Diego, and he would wear them around his place when he was in the mood for music. I was happy that I finally found something to give him that he really wanted.

Time passed, and I'd see him on Christmases. He might call or text on my birthdays, but we still weren't very close. In 2019, I found out that my dad was sick, and it didn't look good. I called as soon as I heard, but the line just kept ringing. I was traveling at the time with work and kept sending him texts and calling, but I could never get through.

I became angry. Why was this man avoiding me now? What had I done that he didn't want me there during his final moments? I knew we weren't the closest, but I had to mean something to him, didn't I? It went on like this until one of my brothers called and said my dad had been asking about me. I told my brother that I had been calling and sending text messages but never got a reply. If he didn't want to see me, why would I go down to his hospital room? Well, turns out, my dad had recently gotten a new cell number, and no one had told me. Apparently, my dad and brother shared a laugh over this. I was less than amused.

When I arrived home from my business trip, I planned on going to see him with my oldest nephew. We felt that going together would soften up my dad, his grandpa, so that it would be an easier conversation to have. It had worked in the past, but it didn't work out so well this time. My dad had recently gotten into an argument with some other family members, and my nephew and I had to hear all about it. Even though he was clearly very angry, I could tell he was sad, too. My dad's voice had become weak and raspy.

I didn't know it then, but I'd never hear his normal voice again. So, my nephew and I sat there and took all the yelling my dad was able to muster before he finally got tired and changed the subject. He told my nephew and me to come back individually next time so he could talk to us in private.

I went back the next week and sat with my dad again. This time, he was in a better mood, but he was starting to fade. Due to the chemo, his hair fell out, he was bedridden, and he started to lose his appetite. At first, he'd ask whoever was coming to bring him a Jamba Juice or Mexican sweet bread. After a few more weeks, he stopped eating, and we knew it was close to the end. I got a gig to go to Atlanta for Friday and Saturday and told my dad I'd come watch football with him that Sunday. He was a big 49ers fan, and we bet a dollar on who would win the game.

I can't remember who the 49ers played that day, but I do remember that Sunday being a turning point in what would be the end of our father-son relationship. He told me not to hold grudges like he had and not to ruin my relationships. He encouraged me to try and be the bigger person when an argument came up.

The last time I visited, I walked into his room and heard him banging on his tray. When I opened the curtain, he was gasping for air. He signaled that he needed help, so I went to get the nurse. They gave him a breathing treatment, and he seemed to calm down a little. He could barely talk at this point but tried his best to communicate with me. Mostly, we sat in silence as we had plenty of times throughout my life.

Later that night when I got home, I got a call from the hospital telling me it was close to his time, and I should gather whom I could to come to his room and be with him. By this time, my parents had miraculously made amends, and my mom came with me as well as two of my aunts and my middle brother. My dad couldn't talk anymore, but he signaled for me, pointed to the gold chain with a naval cross, and then pointed back to me. He was letting me know it was time for me to have it. We sat with him that night as his breathing slowed and his eyes went dim. Then, he was gone.

The hardest thing about my dad passing was that we had finally gotten to a point where we felt comfortable around each other and were enjoying each other's company. I spent my entire life wishing that it was easy to be around my dad, and I only got that for a few weeks.

After we said goodbye and had his funeral, I spent a lot of time reflecting on that. I wished we had started mending fences sooner and that he could have been the kind of man he had been at the end. But that wasn't meant to be. It did, however, teach me valuable life lessons that I'll never forget. A few weeks later, I went back to work. I cried by myself at the airport, after a show in my hotel, and right after I moved to Los Angeles. I mourned a relationship that should have been stronger.

Whose fault was it? It was both of ours, and time was the enemy. Unfortunately, my dad taught me a lot about what *not* to do in life. But one major thing he did teach me was that there is still time to make things right if you try and fight for peace in relationships. It may not be possible with every person in your life, but it may be with those whom you feel *should* be loved and love you back.

We bet a dollar on that 49ers game. I bet him they'd lose, but they won. I didn't get a chance to slip him a dollar before he died, but I did get to slip one to him while he lay in his casket. His funeral was a perfect sendoff — with a gun salute, a dollar bill and a mariachi band playing some of his favorite songs. I now listen to some of those songs on those Beats headphones, and I am grateful that I have a picture of us together being silly and wearing sunglasses.

— Nicholas R. —

16

The Golden Years

What we have once enjoyed deeply we can never lose.
All that we love deeply becomes a part of us.
~Helen Keller

The roller-coaster car shot away from the platform with a jolt. I gripped the handlebar holding me in place, investing hope that it would prevent my imminent demise. My two adult children sat casually nearby, highlighting my irrational fear.

Many years earlier, life had clamped me into an irreversible course that mirrored the ups and downs of that amusement-park ride. My young husband, Peter, and I saved for years to take a trip to his native Germany to visit his extended family. Our sons were young; traveling internationally with children required a lot of planning. My grasp of the German language was weak, and I knew I would need my husband to be my translator. Still, I learned key phrases like "I don't speak German," "Where is the bathroom?" and "Do you have diapers?"

Despite our preparations, nothing could have equipped us for what we faced one week into our travels. Peter's persistent cough, increasing lack of energy and a troubling immobility found us sitting at a doctor's office in southern Germany. Trying to ignore the symptoms and not disrupt our longed-for vacation, my husband and I sat in disbelief when he was told to immediately go to the hospital.

In a nightmarish blur, the next few days flew by as a dire diagnosis required us to abandon our plans, pay exorbitant travel fees and fly home to Chicago. Frightening and increasingly discouraging news followed invasive tests before we were told Peter had mesothelioma, an incurable, untreatable cancer. The best-case scenario was nine months of life.

Peter was an avid golfer, passionate about the sport. He often encouraged me to join him on the links, but I chased around two little boys for exercise, and I couldn't imagine spending four or five hours playing golf. I promised I would join him in our golden years.

Once our future had been revealed, I realized with horror that the next nine months were our golden years. I had missed the chance to share what he loved and would never have that chance again.

Sadness, grief and desperation took over, and we explored every medical option in search of a shred of hope. In the late 1980s, an autologous bone-marrow transplant was almost unheard of, but Pete was a fighter. Despite the crushing cost, he opted to try.

In isolation for weeks, removed from family, friends and golf, he endured the excruciating extraction of his own marrow and the debilitating infusion of poisonous chemotherapy. He could not leave the hospital for a round of golf, but I found a way to bring golf to him. I researched how to contact the top twenty-five golfers and I sent each of them a letter describing my valiant husband, and his love and respect for the game and his heroes.

Also enclosed was a self-addressed, stamped, get-well card with a request to sign and send it back to Peter. All the golfers returned their cards, with many enclosing personal messages and signed photographs. Peter read the cards over and over during his month of isolation, often with tears in his eyes.

The roller coaster rose and dipped with false hope, treatment, love and support until there were no further options. I continued gripping whatever could get me through the day until my hands and heart were numb.

At the amusement park, at the end of the roller-coaster ride, the car pulled to a jerky stop while my children and other joyful passengers bounced out. My hands were frozen on the handlebars, but I knew it was the end of the ride and I had to get off. Somehow, I managed to loosen and pry off my fingers one at a time, and my shaky legs landed back on the platform.

When Peter died, I'd looked at my two young sons and knew I had to pry open my broken heart and find a way to live again so I would not miss precious opportunities with them. Taking what I knew and loved in Peter—his confidence, courageous spirit, faith in God and family, hearty laugh and warm heart—became my pledge to live those qualities as his legacy. I even learned how to play golf. Grief had its grip on me, but every time I embraced one of Peter's qualities, he lived on in me, and I was able to move into a shining future—for both of us.

—Diane Helmken MacLachlan—

17

Laughter at a Funeral

As soap is to the body, so laughter is to the soul.
~Jewish Proverb

My mother died in a car crash on my father's birthday. She had a painting in her art studio that she'd finished for him and was planning to give him after dinner that night. They had plans for that day. They had plans for that month. They had plans for retirement.

The days leading up to the funeral were somber and hard. My sister, sister-in-law, and I picked out her burial dress. My brothers selected her casket. We collaborated with my dad on the hymns and scriptures for the funeral. We cried some, but mostly we were in shock.

At the funeral, we filled the front few rows. (There are eight kids in the family, and most were married with children of their own at this point.) I don't remember much about it except that the pastor, in the middle of this very serious Presbyterian funeral, stopped it all and said, "I'd like you to turn to a neighbor and share a favorite story about Trudy."

My dad, siblings, and I couldn't participate. So, we just sat there and listened to the din. First, there were sniffles and whispers. Then, we heard giggles and chuckles. Then, there were snorts and guffaws! It felt like the walls of the church itself were shaking with laughter.

I was stunned. I couldn't believe it. *You mean to tell me I'm allowed to laugh? Laughter is permitted in my grief?*

My mother was a funny woman. She would drive up to visit me

at college for a few days, and when we'd go to the grocery store, I'd fill my cart with supplies for the week. At the cash register, I'd unload my cart onto the conveyor belt, and under the cereal boxes would be an enema kit. Under the toilet paper she'd hidden a pack of women's disposable underwear. Under the bag of apples would be a box of condoms. I'd have to hand each embarrassing item to the clerk and explain I'd changed my mind on that item, all while my mother would innocently thumb through a magazine, pretending she had nothing to do with my shame.

Once, when I was still in high school, she was running late and needed to cook dinner but hadn't been to the store in a while. She decided to make spaghetti, but there was no hamburger in the fridge or freezer for the sauce. Knowing my dad liked meat sauce, she grabbed the hotdogs from the bottom drawer of the fridge, tossed them in the blender, and hit puree.

This meal was so disgusting that even she refused to eat it. However, my parents were both born during the Depression, so food in our house was never discarded. She took all the leftovers (there were a lot), put them in a freezer container, labeled it "wiener spaghetti," and froze it.

After that episode, if she was running late or was just too tired to cook, she'd wait until my dad was soon to arrive home from work. She would pull out the wiener spaghetti, put it on the counter, and leave it there to "defrost." Inevitably, he'd see it and suggest he take her out for dinner. Both were in on the joke.

Writing these stories, I already feel closer to her. I feel reconnected and lighter.

Is it okay to grieve with humor? Oh, I think it's imperative.

The day my husband died, his breathing grew more labored. Slowly, the death rattle got louder.

At 6:15 P.M., he opened his eyes, looked up, and exhaled. His breathing just… stopped.

My two teens and I just stood there in stunned silence. It felt like all the air had been sucked out of the room.

We waited. We watched. We held our breath. He was indeed gone.

The kids each told him they loved him one last time. I kissed him my final goodbye. We drove home in stillness and silence, breathing softly, saying nothing.

We walked into the house, and I finally held my children to me in the kitchen. We started to cry.

We were so afraid of the pain that would come that we were terrified of our grief. We were scared of what the future would hold for us now that he was gone. Standing in the kitchen, we wept. Wordless laments. Choking sobs. Gasping cries.

And then, unexpectedly, my daughter said something that struck us all as funny. Out of the blue, we were laughing! Choking, gasping, breathless sobs transformed into choking, gasping, breathless laughter!

I know what you must be thinking: Wasn't it too soon to be laughing with your kids when your husband just died?

Too soon? Absolutely not!

We were facing the reality of his death, and there was undeniable life in that laughter.

When we laughed, we inhaled! There was oxygen! There was BREATH!

And there was a message in that laughter. It told us all something critically important: I heard my children's laughter, and I knew they were going to be okay. They heard my laughter, and they could trust that I would be strong. That laughter indicated that we would get through this together. We were going to survive this. Even in the very worst moments, we would still be able to laugh.

Was that laughter "too soon"? No. That laughter was just in time.

— Melissa B. Mork —

18

Gone Too Soon

Sisters make the best friends in the world.
~Marilyn Monroe

"Hey, Kat!" I said cheerfully as I answered my phone. It was around 2:00 P.M. on a weekday in September. My sister's voice sounded pained, almost inaudible as she whispered, "I am in the emergency room with a terrible pain in my side." I could tell she was holding back tears as she said, "They ran some tests, and they think I have cancer." Paralyzed by her words, all I managed to say was, "Katherine, I am on the way."

Engulfed in fear, I drove to the hospital to be with my sister. On the drive to the hospital, I kept thinking, *You didn't come this far just to get this far.* After a marriage that didn't work and with many trials to follow, Katherine had flourished and made a beautiful life for herself.

Being only twenty months apart, Katherine and I grew up doing everything together. Our personalities couldn't have been more opposite, but our souls couldn't have been more alike. Katherine was fearless and full of life, while I was cautious and reserved. Katherine always did the courageous things, and I did the worrying. I told her when to be quiet, and she told me when to speak up. She was the yin to my yang, and I to hers. Katherine's gentle, kind heart was always a soft place for my secrets to be understood, kept, and protected.

When I walked in, Katherine looked up at me with tears in her eyes. She looked so fragile and childlike in her hospital gown, covered in blankets. Speechless, I hugged my sister. The white room looked harsh beneath the fluorescent lights. It was unfriendly, cold, and smelled sterile. Machines beeped, and tubes ran from her arms. My vibrant sister didn't belong here. It wasn't long before the doctor entered the room. I saw the concern in her eyes as she explained that more testing would be done, and we would have the results in a couple of days.

Two days later, on Katherine's thirty-fourth birthday, in a hospital room filled with balloons, flowers, friends, and family, we received confirmation that Katherine had stage IV colon cancer. It was advanced and inoperable. As the doctor spoke words like "extremely uncommon" and "very unfortunate," the devastation in the room was palpable. Katherine had three children who needed her, whom she loved more than anything in the whole world. How could this be? Just three days ago, Katherine seemed to be the picture of health, doing yoga and working two full-time jobs as a counselor. Now, she was a terminal cancer patient.

Katherine started chemo to slow the cancer's progress, and we desperately clung to our hope for a miracle. It was our only lifeline as we boarded this sinking ship. Chemo was a true test of Katherine's physical, emotional, and spiritual endurance, and she fought with all her might. She fought for a future with her children

As we sat in the waiting room before each doctor's appointment, Katherine closed her eyes and sat in silence. I stared at her in awe as peace emanated from her. With each appointment came a discouraging report. "What will we try next?" Katherine asked. "I have to try everything. For my kids." We were running out of options, but Katherine refused to give up.

As the cancer got worse, Katherine knew it was time to fully live each day, so we made a little bucket list. Katherine had been dreaming of going to a beach with turquoise water, so we traveled to Turks and Caicos. We rode horses through the ocean, relaxed on the beach in the day, and sat beneath the stars at night. Katherine had always been religious, but she embarked on a deeper spiritual journey that gave her much comfort and light, especially in her most difficult days. Most amazingly, Katherine wrote letters to her children to be given to them in the future. I watched her cry as she thought about all the moments she would miss: first day of high school, marriage, the birth of their first child, and so many more.

I witnessed the supernatural strength it took to find the words she would never get to speak to her children but could say through the letters. This was, perhaps, the hardest thing Katherine had done in her life, but it was worth it to her because, through the letters, she would, in a sense, be with her children.

Katherine focused on what a blessing each day was. To Katherine, her doctors, nurses, family, friends, and prayer warriors were "angels" whom she believed had been placed in her life. We all felt the power of this divine orchestration of angels who blessed Katherine as her life came to an end.

Katherine's "angels" made her cottage in the woods a place of comfort and joy. Lights were strung over the back patio of her cottage, gardens with her favorite flowers were planted, and her porch was filled with potted plants. Her "angels" made sure that the inside of her home always had burning candles and fresh flowers, two of her very favorite things. The cottage had a magical essence and looked like a scene from a fairy tale. Katherine enjoyed her time with her children here and the peace that nature provided her.

I spent many precious nights with Katherine in her final months. We often sat on her back porch, a fire blazing in her fire pit, as we visited beneath the canopy of twinkling lights. We listened to music and talked about life. Fireflies sparkled in the night, and coyotes howled from deep in the woods as we laughed about stories from our past and cried as we mourned that these would be the last of our memories together. Katherine cried as she told me she wished she could bring me with her, and I cried as I told her I wished I could keep her here to grow old with me.

Katherine's health declined quickly. Her body became weak and feeble, but she was more beautiful than ever. Katherine's strength, faith, and courage gave her a veil of supernatural peace and grace. She was truly majestic. Katherine died peacefully on May 7th, about seven months after her diagnosis, much sooner than anyone anticipated. All our hopes and prayers for a miracle weren't enough to keep my sister here — not when God had other plans.

I miss my sister terribly, and the void in my heart is indescribable. I find myself seeking peace in nature now, just as Katherine did. Through nature, I feel my sister's presence.

— Rachel Chustz —

19

White Shirt

We must embrace pain and burn
it as fuel for our journey.
~Kenji Miyazawa

The sun is high and bright, and there is not a cloud in the sky on this brisk but beautiful mid-October day. I'm standing at the ironing board contemplating my strategy for ironing this brand-new, wrinkle-filled, white dress shirt. It came folded and packaged in cardboard and plastic. I would like to take it to the cleaners to be lightly starched and pressed, but, due to time constraints, that is not an option. I will tackle this task myself.

I take my time assuring that every wrinkle is flattened out while listening to the steady whooshing sound of the smoking hot steam shooting out from the bottom of the iron and the creaking coming from the ironing board that's in need of a good oiling. I iron one sleeve and then hold it up for inspection before moving on to the next one. Unfolding the collar, I flatten it out on the board with my hands and then iron in a similar way. When the collar is done, I flip the white shirt back over to the right, front side. To me, this is the most difficult side; the evenly spaced, iridescent buttons are staring at me. I continue in slow, meticulous motions until the shirt is completed. The creaking and whooshing has stopped.

I'm standing in the middle room, the one that I shared with him, and I'm going over my mental checklist: suit, shirt, tie, briefs, T-shirt, shoes and socks. Everything is checked off. I had to buy a three-pack of T-shirts and a three-pack of briefs, even though I only needed one of each. Everything is new, even the brown suede loafers that I bought.

I take the hot white shirt off the ironing board, but before I place it on the hanger, an overwhelming urge comes over me. I carefully slip on the white shirt over my clothes. I wrap my arms around myself like when we were kids and were teasing someone about being boyfriend and girlfriend. Back then, we would make kissing noises. I hug myself tightly.

I am in the room alone but not alone in the house. It seems to be draped in a soothing warmth, and a yellow glow surrounds me. It's like being inside a warm bubble. I can hear voices coming from other parts of the house, but they are muted and seem faraway. I feel suspended between the physical world and the spiritual world. But I'm not afraid; it's not scary but welcoming and protective. At this moment, I am alone with my thoughts, untouchable, not able to be disturbed. I hold back the tears as I smell the shirt and cuddle it. This task will be the last that I will ever do for him. I sigh and shake off the sadness, determined to keep my private moments to myself.

I stop squeezing myself, check the shirt again for wrinkles and, seeing none, gently arrange the shirt on the hanger. My hug, this final hug, will follow him into eternity. My embrace will carry him to the other side, and my hug will hold him as I say my last goodbye.

Tomorrow is the funeral, and the funeral director will be by shortly to pick up his clothes. I've never had to prepare anyone for burial. When it dawned on me that I would have to gather his clothes, I had momentary paralysis. It was a jolt to my system, just like an electrical shock. I couldn't move or think! You never think about why the person in the casket at the funeral is wearing the outfit that he or she is wearing. We're born uncovered but die clothed in an outfit that someone else decides upon.

Never in a million years would I have thought, at the age of thirty, that I would be preparing the final wardrobe for my husband. Due to a car accident, I didn't get a chance to say goodbye. *No tears, no tears*, I repeat to myself.

Deep breath in, hold it… deep breath out… I have to stay focused! I better go check on my girls.

—Angela Larks—

20

Ashes to Ashes

My sister may not always be at my side,
but she is always in my heart.
~Author Unknown

I couldn't breathe. Where was she? How could this have happened? Whose fault was this? Was it mine?

First, she died, and then we couldn't find her.

The year was 1989, and my beloved only sister, Holly, had died several days earlier by her own hand. That was hard enough. She had a family. A husband who loved her. Two little boys. An older brother and sister who watched her grow up, sometimes helping her, sometimes hindering her — in the usual ups and downs of family life. Nieces and nephews — my young children — who thought she walked on water.

She was everything I was not: magical, creating fun with nothing but a cardboard box, a bottle of bubbles, and a Michael Jackson album. She had a flair for the dramatic — missing in me — that never ceased to amuse those close to her. And she loved her family hard and fierce.

And our mother and father. This could be a deal-breaker for them. They'd lost our little brother — their youngest — in a traffic accident five years before. Parents never recover from the loss of a child — a child of any age — but two within five years? Humans are wired by God to believe their children will live on after them. Anything else is... obscene.

After her wrenchingly tough funeral service, we drove to Boulder

Cave. It was a favorite hiking place in the area. Mom and Dad used to take us there for hikes when we were young and invincible.

A wide path led up to the cave. We could hike all the way through the cave from one end to the other. Sometimes, we saw bats hanging upside down from the moist ceiling. As kids, we thought that was pretty cool. We'd scattered our younger brother's ashes along the path to the cave, and it seemed a fitting place to take her.

As family and friends piled out of cars in the parking area, the turbulent emotion of the day caught up with me. I gazed at the sad faces of people my sister had touched over the course of her thirty-one years of life. I felt there wasn't anyone big enough or strong enough to deliver us from this grief.

I stood motionless next to my car, the sun peeking through the pines. I willed my mind to recall the innocence of long-ago family hikes and picnics in this place. I heard my sister's shrieks when our brothers waved a bug in our faces or threw pinecones at us. I heard Mom tell the boys to stop bugging their sisters and the laughter at her unintentional pun. Would we ever laugh like that again? I didn't think so. Nothing would ever be the same again.

Those days of laughter and sibling rivalry were the good days, I thought. Days when grief was a grown-up word, when our family shone with unbrokenness. Days of simple enjoyment in being together.

We had to make this unbelievable journey again. My loving parents would say the long goodbye to another child. My remaining brother and I were now two siblings who used to be four. And, hardest of all, my two young nephews — Holly's boys — would now navigate this world of pain I'd never known at their age. Our orderly universe had shifted again to the unrecognizable.

Someone yelled, and I returned back to the present. I collected myself, turned, and saw my parents slowly exit their car. Dad took Mom's arm as they shuffled toward me. Mom's pain-filled eyes — somehow ten years older — met mine, leaving me breathless with sorrow for her.

Where was the box?

"Dad, do you want me to get Holly out of the car for you?"

"Huh? We don't have her. Don't you?"

The absurdity of it bubbled up from somewhere deep inside me and threatened to erupt in giggles. We'd spoken as if she perched on the back seat waiting for someone to open the car door. I swallowed hard, pushing the laughter back down where it belonged.

"Dad, I don't have her," I whispered. "D'ya think someone else — "

"Go find her. I have to help your mother."

Obediently, I sped to each family who'd arrived. No one had the box of ashes we'd come to scatter. I panicked.

Now what?

I was incapable of making a plan, so I hurried back to Dad.

"Dad, no one brought the box. What do we do? We can't — "

"What? She's not here? We have to go get her."

"It's an hour back to Yakima, and the funeral home is closed now — "

"We have to go back. Come with me — we'll call the funeral-home director from Whistlin' Jack's. I have his number on a card somewhere."

Whistlin' Jack's was a mountain resort and restaurant situated back down the highway a short way from Boulder Cave. We had to go there to call because cell phones weren't yet a thing in 1989.

Dad announced to the bewildered group what had happened and what we were going to do. Amused shrugs, blank stares, a few complaints, and Dad and I were on our way.

That drive, although short, was one of the longest of my life. I couldn't think of one thing to say to Dad, the one man with whom I'd never had trouble talking. We'd shared heart-to-hearts my whole life. It'd always been easier for me to talk to him than to my mother.

But on this drive, the silence thundered. I recall that I prayed we could reach the funeral director, and he would know what to do. That somehow God would reach down from his throne and scoop all of us — particularly my parents — into his arms and help us make sense of this day. But, most of all, I prayed we'd find those ashes — the last remaining touchable part of my sister. I had to touch her once more.

Fortunately, we were able to contact the funeral director. He graciously went to the funeral home and retrieved my sister. She'd been left on a bench in the foyer. He brought the box of ashes to us, and we arrived back at the Boulder Cave parking lot an hour later to start our last hike with Holly.

And, during that drive back to Boulder Cave, the dammed-up grief dislodged for a little while and slid quietly away, like so much floating debris on a river.

Dad looked sideways at me. "She made us wait again, didn't she, Deb?"

It started with a giggle. Then Dad and I laughed and laughed because Holly had — as in the good, old days — made a grand entrance with her usual dramatic flair. I'm sure I heard her laughing, too.

Losing her ashes had, somehow, been transformed into the delightful centerpiece of this tragic day — a pause in the staggering heartbreak — that continued to carry me through the grim days ahead.

Thirty-two years later, I still hear her laughter if I pause and listen hard enough.

— Deb Gorman —

Let It Out

21

Turning Point

A good laugh is a mighty good thing,
a rather too scarce a good thing.
~Herman Melville

I had always heard that grief is a storm that hits in stages, but I didn't truly understand what that meant until I lost my mother. First, her death blindsided me with the sudden, irrevocable reality of her departure. That initial blow quickly became a piercing heartache that curdled into overwhelming sorrow. Denial came into play, too, as well as anger. Soon, the mourning process swelled into a gnawing melancholy I couldn't escape. Even cherished memories of things I'd always loved doing with Mom — playing word games, making blueberry muffins, watching old musicals — brought tears instead of smiles.

"Your mother wouldn't want you to be sad," family and friends would tell me. "You should celebrate her life, not grieve her death."

It was good advice; I had given it myself over the years to people who'd lost loved ones. And, of course, it was true. My mother had spent decades laboring to make her children happy and never had any higher priority. Yet, in the days following her death, I was utterly incapable of casting off the pain and focusing on the joy.

The closest I could come was to turn off my brain altogether. I put myself on autopilot and went numb, hiding behind a polite smile and meaningless small talk, focusing only on immediate tasks. I passed long hours sitting in my back yard, staring at the sky or arranging and rearranging paperbacks on the family room bookshelf. When thoughts of my mom would start to creep in, I'd turn my attention to something, anything else: the kids' homework, what to make for dinner, that pile of laundry beside the washing machine.

And so I slogged through the days, refusing to deal with the emotional toll of my mother's death. I felt like I was doing pretty well until a simple errand forced a course correction.

Three weeks after my mother's funeral, I was going through the motions of my Friday routine, disengaged from any other thoughts. It was grocery day, and I managed to fill my cart and make it all the way to the checkout counter in "numb mode."

"How are you today?" the cashier asked, ringing up my purchases. She was young, probably working her first real job. Her perky sunshine-orange name tag declared, "Hi! My name is Christa."

"Fine," I responded.

"How 'bout these storms we've been having? Looks like it's going to rain again this afternoon!"

Good, keep it bland. Weather chat is perfect.

"Yes," I said, making brief eye contact. "The news says maybe rain all weekend."

Christa turned her attention back to scanning the milk, bread and cereal while I took out my coupons. I thumbed through the stack to the *blip, blip, blip* of the register, maintaining my wan smile. Midway through the bundle, I came to a fifty-cents-off coupon for blueberry-muffin mix, and that was all it took to send me tumbling through time.

In a flash, I was a child back in my parents' home, waiting eagerly as the oven timer ticked down the minutes, the smell of sweet, fruity goodness heavy in the air. Next, I was transported to my own kitchen, where my kids were helping me make muffins to bring to Gramma. Then I was handing my mother a plate of her favorite baked treats, savoring the smile on her face. I'd forgotten how beautiful her smile was and how much I'd been missing it.

The first tears came then, no stopping them, cool and sudden and insistent. I let out a raspy sniffle as those memories of Mom came rushing back.

I was pulled back to the present by the feel of a gentle hand patting my shoulder.

"It's okay, ma'am," Christa said softly. "I'll still take the coupon even if it's expired."

And then something amazing—and quite unexpected—happened: I started laughing. Poor Christa cocked her head and gave me a baffled look, which made me laugh all the harder. I stood there, I don't know how long, letting the tears and the guffaws come, unconcerned with how odd I must've appeared to everyone in the supermarket.

The only thing that mattered was realizing that's exactly what Mom would want me to do: laugh. At first, I thought, *If she were here, she'd be laughing, too.* Then I understood immediately that she was there with me and always would be. My mother would forever remain in the fun times and the wonderful memories, and she'd be watching over me during difficult times and awkward moments. She'd be there for me, for the rest of my days, in the taste of a blueberry muffin.

That was my turning point. There, in the checkout line with sweet Christa and a coupon for muffin mix, I had found my way through the grief and back to my mother. There'd still be tears (still are, all these years later), but from that time on they were layered with joy, just the way she would want.

—Miriam Van Scott—

22

A Hallmark Story

When we focus on our gratitude, the tide of disappointment
goes out and the tide of love rushes in.
~Kristin Armstrong

The collapse of my marriage was brutal. "We're going our separate ways!" my husband screamed. That was how our spats usually ended.

"We used to be together. What happened to us?" I asked.

"You're gone too much," he said.

"I can't ignore my brother dying from lung cancer. Come with me. I don't enjoy driving six hours by myself."

He wore a stony expression when I hefted my satchel and walked into the garage.

"He asks for you. Why won't you visit him when he needs us most?"

I paused, hoping he would stop me. The canyon between us widened when he turned away.

"I want to be free," he said when I returned. "Lonely women all over the Internet want to hook up with a good man like me."

I stared, stunned to silence. We once were best friends with years of good memories.

"What about this lonely woman?" I said when I found my voice. "Where is our plan to travel during a carefree retirement?"

"I'm going travelling," he said.

"But not with me," I said, choking on tears.

Soon after, we negotiated the divorce settlement.

Abandoned by the person I most trusted, I left with a handful of belongings: Gidget, my aging cat, a slightly younger Honda, and enough rage to fuel a nuclear submarine.

Overwhelmed by the triple traumas of divorce, the death of my brother George, and a move across state lines, I felt as rootless as a tumbleweed.

In a new town, I stumbled through house hunting in a thick fog. Could I qualify for a mortgage on Social Security and a nurse's pension? I couldn't tolerate another humiliation or loss.

Gidget hid for days and refused food. I feared for her health.

Hoping to ease her transition, I played with her and coaxed her to eat. I took her to a veterinarian when patches of white fur sprang up within her black coat.

"She's sad and stressed from changes," said the vet. "Give her lots of patience and love."

Between crying jags, I watched Hallmark movies. Within two hours, the heroine throttled fears, overcame obstacles and successfully recharted her course. The supporting cast were friendly, compassionate people. They all cooperated and watched a gorgeous sunset or snowfall at the end.

"Who writes this tripe?" I yelled at thin air.

"You need this," said my sister. She held a notice for a divorce-support group and another for grief management.

"These women help each other cope with changes after divorce and death," she said.

"Two support groups? I don't tell my problems to strangers," I protested.

She left the ads on my kitchen cabinet.

After another sleepless night, I dialed the number and dissolved into tears when I spoke to the facilitator.

"You're welcome in both groups," she said. "Come to the next meetings."

I forced myself to walk into the first group session where women with kind eyes and boxes of Kleenex gently guided stories of crippling pain.

"You'll likely think of an excuse not to come to another meeting," a facilitator said before we closed with a Bible verse and prayer. "Don't stop. We're waiting for you."

I continued. Through the program, I learned that it isn't selfish to pray for personal needs. In the past, I'd mostly prayed for others. I began each day with a prayer of thanksgiving and request for guidance just to get out of bed.

In a divorce-support meeting, one of the leaders shared that she kept a notebook with five blessings specific to that day. "I'm surprised at how fortunate I am."

Her suggestion seemed a Pollyanna approach. I felt mortified, not fortunate. Still, it wouldn't harm me and sounded better than pounding my pillow until I slept from exhaustion.

After listing the same few items each night, I dug beyond the superficial. I had excellent health, some financial resources, and support from family and friends. Many women start over with less. Soon, I filled pages with the good things in my life. Maybe I was closer to the Hallmark story than I thought.

Counting my blessings calmed me and even soothed Gidget. Listening to her purr released a tight knot in my chest. Having her with me was a joy.

Gratitude led me to explore more Scripture. I found a treasure of comfort in the beauty of Jeremiah 29:11: The Creator is in control and has a plan. I need to trust and obey.

Changes were slow, with more pitfalls than summits. After listing blessings, I frequently added another page of laments.

"How are the lists coming?" asked the group facilitator.

"The future isn't dark and scary. I think more about solutions than problems."

"You're never alone," she said. "Come to us."

I admired these women who suffered extreme loss. With common sense and practical advice, they channeled their grief and frustration into helping others. They listened — one of the greatest gifts of all.

I exercised and squelched the temptation to exist on fast food.

Glad to volunteer, I delivered library books to shut-ins and assisted with a ministry to aid Haitians.

Still, many days closed with rough edges. Notable were the times my ex called. "I still have it," he bragged. "I'm having so much fun."

Who was this heartless person who once was the center of my world?

On those nights, I flounced on the mattress until Gidget abandoned her place on the end of the bed.

"Don't rush," said our facilitator. "Healing from emotional trauma requires time and effort just like a physical injury."

"I read countless inspirational publications and start each day with a devotional or funny story," I said.

"Laughter helps."

"I miss George," I said. "I'm fifteen years older. His death at such a young age outrages my sense of order."

"Who decides life and death?"

Her comment stopped me. Longevity is not my responsibility.

I purposely cultivated connections with other family members. I jumped at the opportunity to visit my stepson and his family in Alaska. It was my first chance to meet my eight-month-old twin grandchildren. Now that's a Hallmark moment!

Throughout this journey, I've learned to be optimistic and turn the ashes of the past into hope. I'm writing stories again. I began art lessons. I've kept in touch with friends. I'm busy planning trips with a travel group. Appreciation for the benefits I have saved my sanity when my outlook was bleakest.

Recently, I watched a couple of Hallmark movies. Each story emphasized new possibilities and fulfilled dreams. My life isn't what I expected, but the adventure continues.

— Mariah E. Julio —

23

Contingency Plans

All the art of living lies in a fine mingling
of letting go and holding on.
~Havelock Ellis

On January 31, 1993, as I was skiing in snow so bright it was a privilege to be alive, my daughter was killed in an automobile accident. She had just graduated from college and moved out west to begin what she called her "real life." On the way home from a birthday party, her boyfriend fell asleep at the wheel and rolled her Chevy Blazer. She seemed to have only bumped her head, but that was enough.

When my children were young, I played mind games. What would I do if they stepped on a nail or swallowed Clorox? What was the quickest route to the emergency room? How would I evacuate the house in case of a fire? I envisioned them critically ill and tried to summon in advance the courage I would need to nurse them back to health. My fabrications all had happy endings. I depended on them.

The unexpected happened with remarkable speed. One Sunday, my husband and I were waiting for Courtney to join us in Colorado for a few days of skiing. The next, we were saying goodbye to friends and relatives who had rushed to be with us when we brought Courtney's body back from Nevada. The intervening week had flown by in a rush of funeral plans, airplane arrivals, and phone calls to friends who had moved away. I sat on a kitchen stool directing traffic and reveled in the Courtney stories her friends were vying to relate.

"Do you remember...?" one of them would ask, and off we'd go on a string of tales.

"Do you remember when Courtney hid Glen in the basement for a week... was seasick for ten straight days on the way to Japan... was the leading scorer on her undefeated lacrosse team?"

"Susan, did you know Courtney borrowed your car to go to a Dead concert while you were asleep?"

Occasionally, there were tears, but it was impossible to stay sad for long. After all, who really believed it? Wasn't it just possible that Courtney, the ardent prankster, would fly through the kitchen door and tell us it was all a joke?

"Gotcha," she would chortle with delight.

Even the funeral was upbeat. The minister suggested we celebrate her life, and we did. We sang Grateful Dead songs and reminisced about her adventures when she went around the world. We all wore purple, her signature color, and laughed when her dog howled along with the hymns. We tried to say goodbye but couldn't. We felt suffused by her life, not her death, and dispersed on a high note. I changed into Courtney's favorite sweats, turned off the phone, and readied myself for the grief I assumed would naturally follow.

The first morning, I lay in bed and scanned my body much as I would if I'd fallen off my bike. Where did I hurt? What was injured? How could I start to heal? Remarkably I felt nothing — or, rather, I felt a numbness so complete it felt like nothing. I waited for the overwhelming sadness that I expected, the tears that wouldn't stop. I yearned for them, in fact. Instead, I found myself in a fog. My impressions of grief were secondhand. Like many American families, we were fortunate to have lost few close relatives and those at an age that was appropriate. I thought that women in mourning sobbed uncontrollably and took to their beds like they did in films. I thought something must be very wrong with me.

When the grief I expected failed to come, I got up and began to go through the motions of being alive. I bought groceries and walked the dog. I returned to Literacy Volunteers and my hospice work at the hospital. I played tennis on autopilot and defeated opponents I'd never threatened in the past. My friends praised my strength, but there seemed to be no alternative. I returned to life as I knew it not because I was strong, but because I didn't know what else to do.

The first year went by in a haze. My friends claimed that once I'd gotten through all the firsts — first birthday, first Christmas, first death anniversary — I'd be healed. Even the bereavement literature supported the idea that once you survived the first year, you were well on the way to recovery. I looked forward to January thirty-first like I would to graduation, hoping that the conventional wisdom was right and, once the year was behind me, I'd find myself back where I'd started. We planned to commemorate the anniversary by letting go of purple balloons from Courtney's favorite spot on the mountain where we'd been skiing when she died. It was a fitting memorial, but also, I hoped, a metaphor for my spirits.

Once the balloons disappeared from view, though, I didn't know what to do next and was overcome by fatigue. I claimed it was too cold to ski and slept for the remainder of the afternoon. By the time we got back home, I was in a state of hibernation, sleeping ten hours a night yet feeling too tired to leave home during the day. I cut back at Literacy Volunteers and quit hospice entirely. I left my tennis league in mid-season even though I was in contention for the lead. I went from being in a functional fog to a nonfunctional one.

One day, on a rare outing, I pulled into a convenience store for a cup of tea on my way to a meeting. Distracted, I spilled it all over the front seat and dashed back into the store for more water. When I reached my destination, my pocketbook was gone.

Oh, my God, I thought. *I must have left it on the car seat when I went back in the store. One of the people pumping gas probably took it.*

I started to shake. There were pictures in that bag, some special letters. There was a fortune from a cookie that Courtney and I had shared when I visited her at Berkeley.

"There is a true and sincere friendship between you," it read. She had agreed, the closest I ever came to a declaration of love from her. I couldn't stand to lose it. Couldn't stand to lose anything more.

I drove back to the store in a stupor. I didn't expect to find the bag, but I didn't know what else to do either. Amazingly, it was on the shelf behind the cashier.

"You left it by the coffee machine," the young woman explained. "I called to you, but you weren't paying any attention."

I tried to explain how important it was to me and offered her all the money that was in the bag. The faster I talked, the more she hoped I would just leave.

Once in the car, I frantically grabbed my wallet to see if the fortune was still there. As soon as I saw it, I started to sob, great choking, involuntary bursts that steamed up the windows. I would begin to calm down only to be reminded of some other long-forgotten memory and start to cry all over again. Eventually, I ran out of tears and crawled home.

I awoke the next morning feeling rough, raw and unprotected. I was flooded by memories: Courtney in her jolly jumper, kicking a game-winning goal, dressed in spattered clothes from her house painting job. I had thought of her before, but always on my own terms. Now, I was in the middle of a wild, chaotic, waking dream over which I had little control. I was frightened, but I also knew this was the grief I'd been searching for. Sensing it was the way out of the fog bank, I didn't try to stop it.

It has been seven years since my daughter died, five and a half since I lost my pocketbook. I'm still grieving, still growing, still feeling my way toward a meaningful life without my oldest child. I'd like to say I no longer play mind games, but old habits die hard. I know the Coast Guard number by heart in case my husband isn't back from sailing on time, and I insist my grown children check in from road trips. I make contingency plans in case of a fire. I understand my limits, though, and have learned to accept the unexpected. I still hope for happy endings, of course, but I no longer depend on them.

— Susan Evans —

24

Not So Strong

To weep is to make less the depth of grief.
~William Shakespeare

My former high-school friend texted me to let me know that her mother had transitioned. "This is a hard one for me, and I'm struggling, but I know I have to be strong," she ended the text.

Strong?

My response to her was, "Who says you have to be strong? She is your mother."

Later, I felt compelled to write to her about the misconception that we have to be strong during such a time. My letter said:

> I'm so sorry to hear of your loss. I pray for peace and increased unity for your family. I pray that you find truly compassionate and fair funeral assistance, and that your mom rests in peace.
>
> When my mother-in-law passed last month, I called my job the same day to say I needed a day off to help take care of things and be by my husband's side. The boss said he understood and to let him know if I needed more time. But I told him I wouldn't. (After all, I am a strong woman, right?)
>
> It was business as usual upon my return to my job. No card, no flowers, no words of comfort. And when I finally confided in a few co-workers that I had lost my mother-in-law, they said they hadn't heard about it. (I didn't post it on social media.) Only one

person expressed her condolences (my direct supervisor), and when she saw that I became teary-eyed, she quickly changed the subject and walked away. Well, I guess I was about to "act out of character" because everyone knows that the black woman is strong, right?

Then, a dear friend said, "Robin, if you are not feeling strong at the moment, so what? Go to that quiet corner, sit down, and cry yourself to a comfort level because, guess what? Who says you must be strong all the time? For whom? For what? Why? It is a painful time in your life. You feel it. Embrace the moment. Find that special quiet place and cry boogie-snot kind of tears if you need to. Then get a napkin, wipe your tears, and get up. Why? Because you are a strong woman, and someone else may need to lean on your strength. But have your moment without apology, without embarrassment, without explanation, without condemnation, and without feeling that you've let other women down by not being 'strong' through every circumstance or occurrence in life, especially during the loss of a mother."

My advice is cry if you must. Yes, we're strong women, but we are women. And women cry sometimes. And we feel pain from the loss of a loved one. And we feel the need to embrace that moment even if for a little while in our own quiet space. And if someone comes along and wants to comfort us, and we're comfortable with it, we should allow it. If they want to do things for us to make this time of mourning easier, accept it. And know that it does not weaken us to accept help or to cry for a moment.

I felt better after a good cry. I hope you do, too.

I mailed the letter off to her the following day.

— Robin D. Hamilton —

25

A Different Me

*Sometimes asking for help also means
you are helping yourself.*
~Renuka Pitre

M y friend steered our golf cart down the concrete path. The sun was high in the sky as she coasted to a stop at the tee box for hole number four. That's when I saw Brownie across the wide expanse of the fairway. She was lying stretched out on the green grass. Motionless.

"Oh, my God," I whispered. "Not her, too."

Her tan coat and four long legs had been a common sight for months, so I named the dog Brownie. Many of us had informed our rescue personnel, but Brownie eluded their attempts to bring her in for care. They left food. She had water.

I studied her. She didn't move. "Not today," I breathed. My companion phoned the front gate of our community. "We're aware she's there. We're on it," they advised.

"There's nothing we can do," my friend said.

I choked down a sob. When I looked back as we drove down the fairway, the dog lifted her head. "She moved. She's alive!"

My cart friend didn't realize how the day's events had impacted me. When I told her that it was five years ago on this date that my great-granddaughter had died, she was shocked I hadn't said anything before. But I couldn't. It was too painful.

I'd become quite good at masking my sadness. I didn't talk about it. I tried to keep it a secret. Every time I mentioned Hailey, I cried. She'd been only seven weeks old when she succumbed to whooping cough. The disease invaded her lungs and ravaged her tiny body. She couldn't fight it. Her parents did everything they could to save her, and the doctors did, too. In the end, we all relinquished her to heaven. But baby Hailey left a hole in my heart.

Months and years fell away as I held in my pain. Hailey's mom and I cried and cried together. Three years later, I met up with some old friends who asked how I'd been. It was an innocuous question, one that warranted an "I'm good" type of response. Instead, I poured out my heartache.

"Why didn't you tell us? Why didn't you ask for prayers? Why didn't you share?"

Through tear-blurred eyes, I sighed. "I didn't know how."

And that's how those five years gathered speed to the day when Brownie lay in the emerald grass, and I thought she was gone, too. It had started as a new day, but with the same pain. I had resolved to put that fifth anniversary date way down deep and cover it up by playing golf, getting outside into the fresh air, keeping my mind off it.

But it didn't work. Seeing Brownie was the final straw that broke open the dam.

Later that day, I called a girlfriend who lived out of state. Julie was one of a very few who knew about Hailey. She'd lost a baby, too. She was the only one I trusted to let me pour out my sorrow when I felt overwhelmed. Today, she gave it to me straight. "You need to see a doctor. I think you're depressed, and you may need medication," Julie said.

"I don't need pills," I answered, but what I feared most was the stigma.

"Talk to somebody then. A counselor."

"I'm talking to you."

Julie's voice was soft when she said, "It's been five years. Don't you think you need help?"

I curled up in bed that afternoon and thought about what she said. I did need help. I couldn't do it on my own. Days later, I sat before my doctor. She wrote out a prescription for an anti-depressant. She also gave me the name of a counselor.

The first time I set foot in that counselor's office, I couldn't stop crying. "See?" I said to her. "I can't talk about baby Hailey without sobbing. I want to be able to talk about her without crying."

"Why? What's wrong with crying? Cry if you want to. It's okay."

I cried some more and finally wiped my eyes.

"You've been through something very traumatic. Life-changing."

"I want to get back to the old me. I want to be myself again, how I was before."

She gently laid her hand on my arm. "You'll never be the same. You will always have that hole in your heart. You are changed now, and that's okay."

I eventually didn't need the pills and said goodbye to the counselor, although she said her door was always open. I wish I had done something sooner… talked to others sooner. But finally I found acceptance. And I built on it, knowing I would always be different from what I was before. I would always have some sadness, but it was who I was now.

I believe God cares about all living creatures, tiny babies, and all the rest of his family here on Earth. I'm thankful Brownie was rescued and found a good home. And I finally realized that God saw how sick our tiny baby was and did the only thing He could do: He called her home to heaven.

Hailey's mom and I still share often. I'm honored she chooses me to pour out her heart, fears, sadness, and joys. I have a new great-granddaughter who is almost eight and another one on the way.

I am blessed. I am grateful. I am thankful.

I'm a different me.

Every day is a new beginning, hole in my heart and all.

—B.J. Taylor—

My Pretend Happy Face

*Only people who are capable of loving strongly can
also suffer great sorrow, but this same necessity of
loving serves to counteract their grief and heals them.*
~Leo Tolstoy

I looked around the table, thankful to have everyone together for a happy reason this time. My eyes settled on the Birthday Boy, my seventy-four-year-old father-in-law, Larry. For most of the past two years, I'd only seen these family members at the hospital and my in-laws' home, where we were all pulling together to care for Larry. He'd suffered multiple strokes and had lost the ability to walk, speak coherently, or care for himself in any way. His care had become a never-ending task for my mother-in-law, Judy, and a part-time job for the rest of us.

But today, we were gathered at Larry's favorite restaurant to celebrate his birthday. It had only been a few weeks since his most recent stroke, which had stolen even more of his cognitive abilities. But today was his birthday — possibly his last one — and we'd all decided to make it a special day.

Besides, our family had an additional reason to celebrate, although my husband, Eric, and I had decided not to share the news with anyone yet. We'd recently found out that I was expecting. While it wasn't planned, we were very happy. I was thankful to have something to take my mind off the constant demands of caregiving.

And I knew Eric would need something joyful to focus on after his dad was gone. I could hardly wait to share the news. After nearly two years of hard times, our family needed something to look forward to.

But, less than a month later, I suffered a miscarriage. Larry died the following week. At his funeral, I stood beside my husband and greeted the hundreds of people who came to pay their respects to my father-in-law. I broke down multiple times, and everyone assumed I was grieving the death of my father-in-law.

And I was. But I was also broken over the pregnancy loss. No one but Eric even knew about that. And I couldn't tell them because they were already in enough pain, and I didn't want to add to their burden.

In the days following the funeral, Eric worried constantly about his mom. "This is such a huge change for her," he said. "The entire time Dad was sick, she had one of us kids there with her to help with his care. Now that he's gone, there's no reason for us to go over there every day. She's all alone for the first time in her life."

I rubbed Eric's back and suggested we invite his mom over for dinner more often. We organized a schedule with his siblings to ensure that someone was reaching out to her every day, with at least a text message or brief phone call.

"If you lived all alone because you were recently widowed, would a text message from one of your kids be enough to get you through the day?" Eric asked.

We'd already planned to eat dinner out that night, so I suggested we invite his mom. While I adore my mother-in-law and was concerned about her, I knew that including her in our plans meant that I would need to be extra vigilant to keep my Pretend Happy Face in place that night.

It was my new persona, designed to protect those I love from any additional pain. I hadn't cried in front of anyone since the funeral. Instead, I'd put on this mask and pretended to be okay. I had to. Eric was mourning his dad, and my children were mourning their grandpa. They needed me to be strong and hold it together.

When I felt the Happy Face slipping, I found ways to grieve in private. I cried in the shower and when no one was home. I blamed my red eyes and stuffy nose on allergies and kept my focus firmly on how my family was doing. I thought my Pretend Happy Face would assure them that I was all right, and they could count on me to support them through their grief.

But pretending to be okay had a consequence I didn't anticipate. I found myself feeling resentment. When Eric was concerned about his mom and our kids, I wondered why he didn't care how I was coping. When my kids broke down because they missed their grandpa, I held and comforted them, but I also envied that they were able to express their grief so openly. I longed for Eric to hold me while I cried for everything we'd lost.

But I couldn't put that burden on him. Not now, when he was already going through so much. So, my grief stayed all bottled up, safely hidden behind my Pretend Happy Face.

It was absolutely exhausting.

Two weeks after Larry's passing, my six-year-old, Nathan, found me sitting on the bed, sobbing and surrounded by a huge pile of laundry that needed folding. I hurried to wipe my face. "I'm reading a really sad book," I said quickly.

He eyed me suspiciously. "What's it called?"

I reached for the book on my nightstand. I hadn't read it in months, but I handed it to him anyway. He flipped through it and handed it back.

A few days later, Nathan caught me crying again. Once again, I blamed the very sad book on my nightstand.

That night at dinner, Eric asked the kids what they'd learned that day. Nathan said, "I learned that Mommy is a really slow reader. A few days ago, she was crying because of her sad book, and she was on page 42. And today, her book made her cry again, and she was still on page 42."

"You've been crying?" Eric said quietly. I nodded without looking at him.

That night after our kids were in bed, Eric and I had an honest conversation about everything I'd been feeling. "I hid my grief so I could help you and the kids with yours," I confessed. "But then I resented you for not knowing how much pain I was in."

"Even though you were purposely hiding it from me," he said.

"It's my Pretend Happy Face. It's like a mask, so I can be strong for you and the kids."

He shook his head. "The only way to get through this is to be real with each other. Pretending to be okay when you're not will just force your grief to come out in other ways." He looked at me pointedly. "Like resentment."

That night, I shared my true feelings with Eric, and he held me while I cried. I thought my pain would be an additional burden on him, but it allowed us to share the burden and, somehow, it felt lighter for both of us.

I'd thought my Pretend Happy Face was a useful coping mechanism in handling grief, but all it did was cause distance between my loved ones and me when we needed each other most. I pretended to be okay so I could be there for them, but I didn't allow them to be there for me, and that's not fair.

When I stopped pretending, our healing began.

— Diane Stark —

Freedom to Feel

Crying does not mean that a person is weak,
but it means that a person has a heart.
~Author Unknown

Just a few years ago, I received a call from my stepmother that my father had fainted from a standing position and had broken most of the bones in his face and many in his neck. I took the first plane out and rushed to the hospital where I found my father nearly unrecognizable after many facial surgeries.

Despite the swelling and scarring, he could open his eyes a little and say a few words. I could tell the surgeries, recovery and ICU bed with its alarms were all a little overwhelming for him, but none of them diminished his dry sense of humor.

"I guess you probably had other plans for today, huh?" He did his best to wink at me. I winked back, living up to my childhood pet name, "Stinkywinks." I smiled and maybe told a joke, but I was panicked inside. What would happen to my funny, wise-cracking, go-getter father to whom I looked for guidance when things got tough? I continued to smile and joke as I collapsed inside. I didn't know how to handle seeing him this way.

I spent several days with him before he finally insisted that I return home. He would be fine, he said. I should get back to my wife.

"Hey," he said as I put on my coat, "thanks for coming. I'm glad you came. I love you."

"I love you, too, Dad. I'll see you soon."

That was the last conversation we would ever have. Just days later, his heart stopped. Although the medical team worked heroically to revive him, his brain had been without oxygen for too long. I received the call that my father was brain-dead.

I returned to the hospital and found him in the ICU again, but now connected to a ventilator that was breathing for him. A neurologist told us what had happened and said he no longer had brain activity. His health-care directive said he did not want his life prolonged, and so he would be disconnected from the machines the next day in accordance with his wishes. I listened carefully and understood all she was saying. I am a hospital chaplain and have accompanied families on journeys like this. I knew what to expect.

I also had no idea how to feel. Over the years, I had learned to contain my emotions when I visited patients and families who were in deep grief. I walled myself off from the suffering I found in those hospital rooms just to survive, but years of shutting down had left me a little numb and hollow. I had grown so used to detaching from my emotions that I couldn't feel them anymore.

I called my wife that night.

"What's happening?" she asked.

"Tomorrow, they withdraw life support," I said.

I could hear a catch in her voice. "I'm so sorry. I wish I could be there with you."

"I know. It's okay. It'll be fine."

I heard her pause. "How are you feeling?" she asked.

"Kind of sad, but I guess this is how life goes sometimes," I said. I didn't want to tell her the truth — that I felt nothing.

"You know, it's okay to cry," she said. I nodded.

"I know." We were quiet for a while, and then it was time for bed. I knew the next day would be long.

The next afternoon, my stepmother and I sat with my father. I held his warm hand as the ventilator beeped and sighed. The respiratory therapists came into the room and disconnected the machine with what felt like reverence. His nurse felt for a pulse. "He's gone," she told us and laid a gentle hand on my shoulder as she left the room.

As I sat with my father, I saw images of him throughout my life. When I was eight, he clapped and hooted as I took my first wobbly bike ride without training wheels. When I was twelve, he stood quietly with me on the neighbor's porch as I apologized for breaking a window with my kickball. When I was seventeen, he stood behind me, proud hands on my shoulders, as I received my Eagle Scout badge. When I was twenty-two and graduated college, and forty-six when I graduated seminary, he was in the audience, clapping and cheering. He was there during so many important points in my life. As I held his hand, I saw them all. I didn't know what to do.

And then I remembered an afternoon decades ago when he described being with his own father when he died in a hospital bed. My father wept as he told me how he held his father's hand as he slipped away, knowing that they'd never talk again. My father had showed me how to grieve.

As I sat at his bedside, I felt a knot grow in my throat, and then felt my lip tremble. Soon, I was heaving great sobs as I realized how much I'd miss him. The memories and tears overwhelmed me as I wept for a long time, longer than I had ever cried before. I felt a little embarrassed and kept apologizing to the nurse who hovered just outside the door.

"No need to be sorry," she said.

How many times had I said that to patients and families? Now it was my turn to believe it. After a while, I did. I continued to weep, and the years-long numbness evaporated like a stifling fog. When the tears eventually subsided and I took a deep breath, I realized I was feeling something else. Love. Joy. Gratitude. My father had given me permission to feel again.

I sat with those emotions for a long while until it was time for us to go. We gathered our things and, before I left his room, I bent over his bed, caressed his gray hair, kissed him on the forehead and whispered, "I love you, Pop," just as he had done with my grandfather decades ago. I had received a gift from my father, an invitation to become whole again, and I loved him for it. I still do.

— John Kevin Allen —

Grieving My Ordinary Life

To practice any art, no matter how well or badly,
is a way to make your soul grow. So do it.
~Kurt Vonnegut

I n 2016, my organs began to shut down from being strangled by the very arteries meant to provide them with life, the flow of my blood. That September, I was hospitalized for twenty-eight days with a rare, incurable disease. Doctors prepared my husband and me for my imminent death. But I didn't die; instead, my life changed. It changed in a way that was deathlike, as the change was permanent, significant and absolute.

No one can say for certain what saved me. Maybe it was luck. Maybe it was prayer. Maybe it was medical innovation that allowed a team of forty dedicated doctors to save my life. Perhaps it was a combination of them all. I'm so grateful to be alive, and yet I cry some days. Living with a chronic illness isn't easy, not at my age. Back then, I was fifty-six years old, an age when normal aches and pains are just signs of the aging process. But mine were magnified and more painful.

If I complained, my husband and family members would downplay my angst. "At least you're still here," they'd say and smile. I knew they meant well and were happy that I was still alive, but sometimes my level of pain made me question what I was still around for.

On the evening before I was released, the hospitalist came to visit me. He talked about my condition and how I would need to watch for warning signals. I listened quietly because each breath I took caused me pain. My lungs had been permanently damaged, and the scarred tissue rubbed against the pleural lining and made breathing difficult. The hospitalist patted my hand and reminded me, "It's important that you avoid stress, DaNice. Go home," he said, "and do nothing."

I knew that being home was going to be hard for me. I was married with two grown daughters, one in college. To top it off, I was my mother's caregiver. I didn't know how to avoid stress. Then one day, I just started drawing, and somehow that led to painting.

I would get up early in the morning and paint while everyone in the house was still asleep. I found it extremely soothing to watch paint dry. At first, I painted abstracts. Just mindless dots and circles. I spent most of my time painting the canvas just one solid color. I'd let that dry and add another. Gradually, I started to use more colors. I liked to paint the various hues of a color. My favorite was blue. But here's the thing: I had never had art training, so there was no right or wrong way to do it. Therefore, painting for me was completely stress-free.

In time, it also became organic. I painted pictures that expressed my moods and used brushstrokes like a spatula. I went from abstracts to eventually drawing and painting the shapes of puzzle pieces. Lots and lots of puzzle pieces using only the primary colors of red, yellow and blue.

At that point, life was just that — puzzling. I didn't know why I had gotten sick, and I wanted to find blame where there was none. My disease isn't genetic, and doctors don't understand what causes it.

My goal was to not be readmitted into the hospital and to not succumb to the illness. It was hard to let go of my former self. Oftentimes, I'd get depressed just thinking about my earlier life. I had been physically fit and very active.

I had a career as a telecommunications technician who climbed telephone poles. I had been a truck driver for FedEx. I had played basketball from third grade and been offered college scholarships. At thirty-eight years old, I was still playing, and for Mother's Day my husband had bought me a basketball hoop. And then, just like that, POOF! It was all gone.

It was now just a footnote, an asterisk in my life. So, I painted as much to forget as I did to achieve some semblance of "doing nothing."

Every six months, I go in for a treatment that takes five hours. I can't tell you how many needles I've had or how many vials of blood have been taken. I can tell you that I shed lots of tears in the shower, and it's about self-pity nearly as much as pain.

I cry out of fear. This disease is known to flare and come back with a vengeance. My husband and I don't speak about it. I'm a mother who used to shield her daughters from a world of hurt, but I can't protect them from the pain my death might cause. Of course, death is inevitable, but I'd like for it to be twenty-five years from now. That's my plan; I want to age out.

Meanwhile, I'll paint and endure these never-ending needle jabs. I'll participate in the monitoring of labs, test results, blood markers and blood counts, as we wait for signs that the disease is waking up. For me, early detection is key, measured against the baseline and changes in components of my last, most recent bloodwork.

I'm hopeful that a cure will be found for granulomatosis with polyangiitis in my lifetime. I've learnt how to pronounce the name of the disease because I want to own it. After five years, it doesn't own me. And I'm empowered knowing that my medical history has helped hundreds of doctors save thousands of lives.

It's nice to say that I laugh more, that I no longer paint puzzle pieces, that nowadays I paint people smiling and laughing. My paintings have been included in art exhibitions at the Piano Craft Gallery in Boston. And, recently, one of my paintings was selected in a solo art exhibition for Billboard Hope 2021 installed in John Eliot Square, a historic location in Boston.

I'm embracing my new life by grieving an ordinary life in a most extraordinary way.

— DaNice D. Marshall —

Chapter
4

The New Normal

The Presence of Absence

*It's so much darker when a light goes out than it would
have been if it had never shone.*

~John Steinbeck

"Absence: A state or condition in which something expected,
wanted, or looked for is not present or does not exist"
(Merriam-Webster).

It's the quiet. Vaguely present in the first weeks after
my husband died. Then a distinct, impossible-to-ignore, unsettling
daily companion.

Quiet, once so welcome: With two infants a year apart. With
clamoring children's voices: "Can we eat soon? I'll be late for practice!"
"Will you help with my book report?" "I lost my permission slip! The
field trip's tomorrow!"

Back then, I savored the quiet that followed "G'night, sweet dreams."

Later, after a multi-tasking, no-time-to-pee day at a cacophonous,
chaotic workplace, and then the chatter and clatter of the crowded
commuter train, I appreciated my man-of-few-words spouse. On
weekends, in search of silence, I'd take walks in the woods or drives
in the country.

In my sixties, I left a high-pressure career to set up a consulting
practice. After months defining my niche, writing copy for my website,
and working with a web designer, everything was ready. But it was
December, not a good time to start a business. I planned a January
launch.

Hubby, settled into retirement, spent his days shopping for groceries, running errands, chatting with neighbors, reading, and playing with the dog. We'd regroup at dinner.

"This rotisserie chicken's good. Where's it from?"

"Costco. I like it, too."

"Figure out the web-hosting thing?"

"I'm down to two choices."

"Jenna called. She might have a meeting here next month."

"Great! Hope she stays a few days."

It was easy to work from home with a husband used to spending his days alone, an introvert by nature. I, too, enjoyed the quiet.

Then, one day in December, he died. I discovered a different kind of quiet: the silence of absence.

No "Good morning."

No "It seems cold in here. Should we turn up the heat?"

No "We're out of milk. What else do we need from the store?"

No sounds of someone in the house, puttering around the kitchen, shutting a door, rustling the newspaper. Just the ring of the phone, the ping of the microwave, the bark of the dog, and scary, nocturnal house sounds broke the silence.

Until my husband died, I hadn't realized that marriage shielded me from silence — even in our dotage when most conversations were quick exchanges:

"When's your next dental appointment?"

"My car's due for service. Will you take it in?"

Now I see that those modest placeholders — keeping the lines open for important exchanges — stood between me and solitude. My husband and I were a tiny community unto ourselves. In his absence, quiet descended.

Once a luxury, a welcome break from a house full of children chattering or an office humming with activity, quiet became a force to contend with, an absence, a void. A constant reminder of the solitude that arrived with and persisted after "death did us part." The antidote? A social life. Hmm. New to the area, I'd been immersed in work. I hadn't developed friendships or outside interests.

Losing my husband sapped my energy and clouded my ability to focus on the deluge of legal and practical matters demanding attention. I put the consulting practice on hold, but the need to escape the silence of solitude pushed me out of the house and into socially fertile situations. After many misses but some hits — a multi-year volunteer project and a friendly bridge game — my calendar and my life filled with the welcome sounds of convivial conversation and lighthearted laughter. It took years of effort.

On days when my Google calendar scolded, "You have no events scheduled today," I'd go to the grocery store, pick up a takeout meal — anything that promised a "Have a nice day" from a checkout clerk or a chance meeting with a neighbor.

From time to time, when the kids and grandkids visited, or a plane ride would bring me to them, sounds of life returned: kids giggling, hair dryers whirring, showers running. Too soon, bags would be packed, and my chest would tighten. After goodbye hugs and kisses, the silence seemed louder.

Then, ten years a widow, a pandemic dropped an invisible cloak over my life. Suddenly, a deadly, highly contagious virus invaded the air we breathe. Our best defense? Avoiding human contact. People my age? "At high risk." Suddenly, scientists blew the whistle on shopping, dining out, attending events and engaging with friends — not for a few days or weeks but indefinitely. The risks of air travel kept me and my family apart. Fear — a rational, reasonable response to this new reality — catapulted me back to the isolation I'd felt when newly bereaved. The shroud of quiet enveloped me again. Zoom and FaceTime? Like photos of food you can't smell or taste.

Huddled at home, the silence rushed back with a vengeance, broken only by electronically transmitted conversations and "meetings" with family and the people who populate my widened circle of friends. Like a solo shipwrecked sailor, I was safe and dry but stranded on a tiny islet of isolation.

At long last, when the "masks off" siren sounded, like Punxhatawny Phil I peeked out and then emerged from the darkness of solitude into the light of simple, social pleasures: lunching with friends, chatting up neighbors, enjoying home-based book-club meetings and writing workshops. And, once again, taking to the sky, melting into the arms of family, and savoring the sounds of lively households before returning to the silence at home.

— Barbara Rady Kazdan —

I Choose Joy

Joy is a decision, a really brave one, about how you are
going to respond to life.
~Wess Stafford, Too Small to Ignore

"It's a girl!" the ultrasound technician announced. My husband swallowed hard and whispered to himself, "A little girl," followed by his perfectly contented, squinty-eyed grin. My flood gates opened as they often did, even when not pregnant, and I was overtaken with joy and the grand feeling of being overwhelmingly blessed.

We already had two perfectly imperfect boys, ages five and three. Parents understand what I mean by that. It is that unconditional love that, with the knowledge of all your children's strengths, as well as weaknesses, they are as perfect as they can be.

Like most pregnant women, I had that joyful pregnancy glow. Mine, however, was derailed five weeks from my due date with my husband's unexpected stage-four colon-cancer diagnosis. The stress of that discovery sent me into early labor, and our baby girl was born three weeks early. She was beautiful and perfect!

I had never experienced such a mix of emotions: true joy from the birth of my precious baby girl and deep devastation and crippling fear from my husband's cancer diagnosis. Little did I know that my greatest life lesson would be learned through the death of my husband only four months later. I was now a single mom of two little boys and a baby girl.

That was when I learned two simple words: CHOOSE JOY. I had to make a choice and protect my heart, mind and spiritual soul daily by choosing joy! It was a conscious decision and a choice. I had to fight daily for my joy because, deep down, I was very sad.

I remember significant instances when I had to CHOOSE JOY...

When my world began to spin out of control with my husband's cancer diagnosis, I had to CHOOSE JOY.

When my husband's death left my heart broken in a million pieces and my soul numb, I had to CHOOSE JOY.

When I looked at myself in the mirror in the morning and my face was so swollen from my grieving tears all night, I had to CHOOSE JOY.

When I had to tell my five- and three-year-old boys that their daddy died and try to do so in truthful yet understandable terms and then hold them while they cried — even though, at that point, they didn't understand what death meant — I had to CHOOSE JOY.

When my five-year-old son got off the kindergarten bus months later and ran into the house crying and throwing around anything he could get his hands on in the kitchen because he was overcome with grief. He was beginning to understand what death meant and the reality that his daddy wasn't coming home. He screamed, "I want my daddy!" and then dropped his head and arms like a rag doll and just stood there sobbing. All I could do was helplessly hold him and love him. When I powerlessly watched the grief of my children and failed in shielding their precious hearts from that loss of innocence, I had to CHOOSE JOY.

Every day was and still is a decision and a choice to CHOOSE JOY! I was beat over the head with the reality that I can't control my circumstances or the trials that I will face in this world, but I can choose my attitude.

I noticed early into the grieving process that my kids fed off my reaction and attitude. I needed their lives to continue to be joyous and to lead them by my example. I often hear people say they just want to be happy, but I believe happy is a feeling, and feelings come and go. Joy is a state of being. This world is sometimes broken and painful, but my attitude does not have to be.

It is sometimes a struggle to rise above my circumstances. I sometimes have to "fake it 'til I make it" and fight for JOY by taking positive actions like writing in a gratitude journal, listening to positive music, reading uplifting and inspirational articles and books, going to bed counting my blessings, and waking up thankful for a new day. And I remind myself... CHOOSE JOY... because then I can live in peace, contentment and JOY, despite my circumstances! When I truly am living in a state of JOY, my step is lighter, my mind is at rest, my heart is at peace, and my soul is smiling. I CHOOSE JOY!

— Diane Rumbo —

31

What I've Learned

Grief is in two parts. The first is loss.
The second is the remaking of life.
~Anne Roiphe

One year ago on this day, I lost my husband. Many people reached out to me because they thought it would be a hard day. It was! But it was not any harder than the last three hundred sixty-four days. Here are some of the things I've learned over the past year:

I've learned my house is very quiet when I'm the only one here.

I've learned that a single word can trigger many a tear.

I've learned the life I knew is over, and I must start anew.

I've learned that I have no idea of what I want to do.

I've learned I feel better when I spend some time with friends.

I've learned that once grief begins, it never truly ends.

I've learned many family members and friends want me to be okay.

I've learned there are no magic words that anyone can say.

I've learned to make decisions without my other half.

I've learned that even though I'm sad, it feels good to laugh.

I've learned some folks avoid me because they don't know what to say.

I've learned I will not ask for help but appreciate it anyway.

I've learned some people stood beside me and would not let me fall.

I've learned others took off running and have been no help at all.

I've learned to like cereal for dinner and controlling the remote.

I've learned I can't remember anything unless I leave myself a note.
I've learned to feel grateful for the years of life we shared.
I've learned that when you lose a spouse, you never are prepared.
I've learned there are some mornings I feel ready to move ahead.
I've learned a few hours later I want to hibernate in bed.
I've learned I still expect to hear him coming through the door.
I've learned I miss the bickering and the making up even more.
I've learned to go places solo, like a movie, restaurant or store.
I've learned I hate the word "widow," it chills me to the core.
I've learned although we're not together, I carry our love within.
I will learn to live the best I can until we're together again.

— Gail Nehamen —

32

My Husband Died, But I'm No Widow

Some people say you are going the wrong way
when it's simply a way of your own.
~Angelina Jolie

Recently, I called my investment company to make a withdrawal. The representative, who sounded quite young, introduced himself as Matthew and reminded me that we were on a recorded line.

"Let me look up your account," I recall him saying after the preliminaries. "I see your husband passed away recently. I'm sorry for your loss."

After I murmured something noncommittal, he said he would change my marital status to "widow." Something in me balked.

"Don't change my status," I responded. "I'm not a widow."

There was a puzzled silence on the other end of the line. "I'm sorry," said Matthew. "But my records indicate your husband passed away."

"He did," I said, "but I'm not a widow."

Matthew mumbled something unintelligible. I knew he had no idea what I was talking about. To be honest, neither did I. But I didn't want a stranger on the telephone to tell me what I was. Especially that I was a widow.

"But I thought —" Matthew began.

"Don't worry about my marital status," I interrupted. "The IRS knows my husband passed away, and there are no tax implications for withdrawing money from a Roth account." The thought flashed through my mind that our recorded conversation might soon make an excellent training tape: "How to Deal with Crazy Widows."

Unlike others who have survived their spouses, I did not change my marital status on Facebook when my husband died. Whenever friends posted condolence messages, like "Our hearts go out to you during this difficult time," I quickly deleted them.

I did sign into my husband's Facebook account to "redecorate" his page. Nothing major, I just fixed it up a little. Well, maybe more than a little. Maybe I accidentally friended someone while I was in there. It seemed like a normal thing to do at the time.

Shortly afterward, my daughter sent me a text. "Dom is really freaked out," she wrote. "He said Dad tried to friend him on Facebook." I pretended it was all a big mistake, but I was glad I hadn't friended Dom's girlfriend, too. One friend request from a deceased person is a plausible mistake, but two would be hard to explain.

The truth is, I don't feel like a widow. Our vows, after all, said, "'Til death do us part." To me that means "'Til death do us *both* part" or "'Til *double-death* do us part."

I realize that my status as a widow has no relationship to how I feel about it. Probably lots of widows don't feel like it, and vice versa. When I Googled "I don't feel like a widow," I found multiple references to lonely women who were married but said they felt like widows.

Who has the final say? If you Google "Is a widow married?" this pops up from the Internal Revenue Service: "The year of death is the last year for which you can file jointly with your deceased spouse."

This decree by the IRS definitively seals the marital bond beyond death. The Bible, too, has my back: "Bring justice to the fatherless, plead the widow's cause (Isaiah 1:17 ESV)."

God, the government and Google all speak with one voice! This is a seminal moment, a moment of transcendent truth, of absolution. I am not a widow — at least not yet.

— Pamela Jane —

33

Erasers and Stars

Perhaps they are not stars, but rather openings in heaven
where the love of our lost ones pours through and
shines down upon us to let us know they are happy.
~Eskimo Proverb

Little Me stands outside at night with my mom as she points at the stars. "See that one over there? The one blinking?" she says. "That one is your sister waving hello."

Little Me, four years old, carefully removes a Kleenex from the box with one hand and reaches for a small pink eraser with the other. Blowing away any shavings, I place the well-worn eraser in the center of the tissue and carefully fold the treasure inside, making sure to leave definite creases just as I have seen my mom do when wrapping presents. Hugging the wall so as not to step on any of the hardwood floorboards that creak, I silently inch my way down the hall to the closet. There it is: her dark blue and green plaid coat with the fringe and the shiny, wooden toggle buttons. Reaching up on my tiptoes, I slide my present into the front right coat pocket as quietly as I can. I am about to tell a lie, but I want at least part of my story to be true.

The familiar clatter of Mom doing dishes echoes down the hall, and I know my timing must be perfect. The water begins to make that sucking sound, and the soap is now swirling the drain. Mom picks up the drying towel, worn so thin I can see through it. Her back is to me as she thoroughly dries each pot. Pots are always last.

Orderly, organized, dependable, scheduled, and consistent have not just been adjectives to describe my mom but were the tubes that made up her life-support system. Her internal strength was found in making perfect military bed corners, wiping away sweaty glass rings before they could stain the coffee table, and straightening the fringe on the rug. She carefully managed what she could because she had learned that sometimes life explodes, and the only way to keep from going crazy is to begin sweeping up the charred remains so it would all, at the very least, look good to the outside world.

My fingers reach up into the coat pocket, wool fibers scratching my hand for the lie I am about to speak. Slowly, I pull out the Kleenex with the prize inside. Walking up to tap her on the back of the leg, I can still remember the thin, dark blue ribbing on her pull-on polyester pants and her immaculately white tennis shoes.

My tiny hand reaches up while telling Mommy that I have a surprise for her. I explain that Shirley must have left this in her coat pocket. My mother starts to cry and asks, "This was in her pocket?" She asks in a way that questions the validity of my story. Being a child, I could not have been aware that my mom had probably gone through every pocket, every drawer, every coloring book my sister had touched looking for a piece of her, a memory, anything that could help bring Shirley back.

Little Me wants to give my mom something that will make her smile. Little Me wants to be the one who discovered an untold secret left behind and make her proud that I was the one who brought it to her. Little Me does not understand there are just some tragedies so permanent and horrible that even adults can't comprehend or make right, let alone a four-year-old.

I didn't know then that there would never be an eraser big enough to remove a kind of pain that consumes its victims yet keeps them empty; a pain that cleaves the lives of those it touches into very distinct before-and-after parts; a pain that aches so deeply and lingers so long that it will continue to cause heartache even to strangers, decades from now, who read the dates on a tombstone.

Somehow, my parents managed to give me a happy childhood despite her death. And while I remember sensing that something, somewhere deep inside, was scary and sad and broken, I was, and always would be, sheltered, protected, and cradled. Even when she couldn't be home, my mom left her red lipstick print on the toilet-paper roll or on the mirror or on little notes tucked in places easy for me to find. There she was, juggling to keep the sunshine on one child while fighting the darkness from the other.

Mommy stares at me with skeptical eyes. I recoil a bit but stick to my story. She sets down the drying towel and gives me a long hug that I can still feel. Despite my youth, I knew there was desperation in that hug even if I didn't have a label for it then.

Cancer, it turned out, didn't kill just my sister. It crept into all our lives like a snake slowly squeezing until it was hard to breathe long after the cancer itself had died with its victim. My mom would later talk about the painful, albeit innocent, comments folks would make, and the memories she said, all of them, would steamroll over her like a freight train traveling at full speed. Of course, I was four, and while I must have witnessed those moments, I never felt that crash.

Life stepped into our home, cracked a whip and demanded we all just continue. The clothes got washed, the meals were still made, Dad went back to work, and my other sister got married.

Mom, with her steel backbone and survival blinders firmly in place, made sure the heartbeat of the home kept beating. One day folded into the next until time came along and buried the memory with enough routine that we could all skim over the rough spots.

Honestly, I never really grasped how difficult it all must have been for my parents until I became one. Waking up at 3:00 A.M. and gently placing my hand on my own newborn's chest just to make sure she was still breathing, panicking when I couldn't be sure and picking her up, not caring if I woke her. I just needed to know she was okay, that some kind of cruel fate could not possibly visit the same family twice.

Staring out our sliding glass window, I would hold my sweet daughter close after a late-night feeding and marvel at how well she fit in my arms, the weight of her melting into me. I would lean back in the rocking chair and stare at the moon and stars, wondering how my parents could ever let Shirley go and, worse, how they could continue once they had.

I remember holding my chubby, little hand in the sky and waving, believing wholeheartedly that Shirley was sitting up there, reaching through a cloud and waving at Mom and me. I had no way of knowing then that the strongest woman I would meet in the world — the woman who would meticulously build a safe childhood façade of normality at the expense of exploring her own pain; the woman who would teach me coping strategies that would keep me strong in my weakest of moments — was standing next to me waving at a star.

— Patti Santucci —

Grief Grows Up

We never truly get over a loss, but we can
move forward and evolve from it.
~Elizabeth Berrien

On a quiet, snowy Sunday morning, my father had a heart attack and died. He was forty-eight. I was fifteen. And his death was the defining event of my life.

Awakened from a sound sleep to my mother screaming my dad's name — and then mine — I bolted out of bed. Shivering in a T-shirt and my dad's shoes, I ran next door to get our neighbor, a volunteer fireman. Then I sank down on our steps and covered my eyes as my father was carried past me and out of our house.

My dad died on December 28th — right in the middle of Christmas break — so his Monday morning funeral and our week-long shiva, the Jewish traditional period of mourning, was populated by my friends. Those tenth- and eleventh-graders showed up for me — and kept showing up. Crying together, embroiled in deep conversations, and eating junk food while laughing and gossiping as they tried to distract me, we became an extended family that week — and for the months and years that followed. I think we all developed a depth of feeling and perspective that made us grow up just a little bit faster, and we became more sensitive, empathetic humans as a result of our collective grieving experience.

The shock of my dad's sudden death was a trauma all its own, separate and apart from losing him. My family and I slogged through each day in a daze, one relative after another coming down with the flu. We took care of each other emotionally and physically. We sat together in disbelief as New Year's Eve came and went. We watched the outside world go on around us as if nothing had happened — while our world was frozen in pain.

When Christmas break was over, I went back to school and tried to regain some sense of normalcy. During the day I would stay busy and try not to think about my dad. At night, I pushed the thoughts away in order to sleep. I saw a therapist for a short time as my mom tried to carve out space for us to talk about and process our loss. It helped to have a designated slot to express my emotions, but nothing eased the pain. The therapist told us not to turn my dad into a saint in our minds — to remember the whole person. Even though it hurt, I tried to remember as much as I could, while I still could. I wish I'd done a better job.

Today, I don't remember much. A few isolated moments are seared into my memory: curling up next to my dad on the couch watching Fred Astaire and Ginger Rogers movies, sitting at the piano, the two of us belting out duets from Annie. It was the days before answering machines and iPhones, and I made the mistake of erasing the only cassette I had of him talking for fear that one day I'd accidentally put it on and burst into tears at the sound of his voice. Today, I'd give anything to hear that tape. I tell everyone to keep those voicemail messages as someday you may want them.

The circumstances of death can't help but affect the experience of grief. For me, in addition to the element of shock, it was the crushing feeling that life, or rather death, wasn't fair — for me, who lost my dad at fifteen, and for him, who died at forty-eight. The older I got, the younger that number became, and the more unjust it seemed. Forty-eight — barely half a life.

After I had kids, I was really able to appreciate just how unfair it was for my mom, who, at forty-six, not only lost the man she'd loved since she was eighteen but also had to completely reinvent her life and herself. She rose to the challenge magnificently. I lost her this past summer in circumstances that were diametrically opposed to those that took my dad from me. A prolonged illness, an expected goodbye, a sense of relief that outweighed the sadness. Having experienced my parents' deaths in very different ways, at very different stages in their lives — and mine — I can confirm that there is no easy way to lose a parent. But at least I really knew my mom — and she knew her kids, and their kids, and even her great-grandchildren.

Through a multitude of milestones over the years — my high-school and college graduations, my wedding, the birth of my children — and through a thousand everyday moments, my dad's absence was palpable. His sense of humor and his musicality — both traits I see so strongly in my kids — and his unconditional love. And then, as the memory of what he was like started to fade, my grief evolved and became more about missing having a father than missing my specific one.

I met my husband when I was sixteen — so early and yet too late for him to meet my dad. We began dating a year and a half after my dad died, very much in the midst of my grieving process. Our time together would turn on a dime from typical teen romance to me sobbing in his arms. The bonds of first love were intensified by my grief and his innate ability to support and comfort me as I navigated the emotions that overwhelmed me. These sudden crying jags went on for years, throughout our courtship, the early years of our marriage, and the beginnings of parenthood. After a decade and a half of dreading Father's Day, the holiday was finally imbued with some joy. I became entrenched in my nuclear family and, gradually, the sharp pain of losing my dad became more of a dull ache. Grief showed itself with less frequency and intensity.

The story callout for this book came across my desk on what would have been my dad's eighty-ninth birthday. This year marked forty years since his death. Four decades of carrying his loss — of feeling so many varied shades of grief — noticing it shift and fade, but always remain part of the fabric of who I am. My dad was supposed to go to the doctor the day after he died. He was "feeling off." How many times have I wondered, over the last forty years, if only that appointment had been on Friday instead of Monday, would he still be here?

Quiet, snowy Sunday mornings and Christmas vacation will forever be tinged with sadness for me. The fifty-five-year-old woman I've grown up to be will always carry a piece of that fifteen-year-old girl. But she's already lived a life so much longer than her dad's — filled with love, family, memories, and an appreciation for all of it, knowing how quickly it can vanish. A life she never could have imagined, where grief isn't the foreground but rather a subtle background texture in her mind and heart.

— Nancy Burrows —

Losses and Labels

Ain't no shame in holding on to grief… as long
as you make room for other things too.
~Bubbles, The Wire

My phone rang as I rushed toward the elevator, late for a meeting. "Mrs. Pennington? We need your husband to come back for another blood test. There appears to be an error in the lab results from last week."

Definitely not what I expected to hear. "Okay. I'll call your office after my meeting as soon as I can check our calendar to schedule an appointment."

"I'm sorry. Perhaps you've misunderstood. He needs to come in today."

Today? Her sense of urgency belied her measured, professional tone. The oncologist had pronounced Russ in remission three months earlier. This latest blood test was supposed to be a routine three-month check. "Error" is not what either of us wanted to hear.

The results confirmed our worst fears. His cancer had returned and metastasized with a vengeance. The doctor prescribed a new round of chemotherapy. Three months later, we learned the chemo was ineffective.

His prognosis arrived just in time for my sixtieth birthday. But that milestone became secondary to what we now faced. One friend who had walked this journey gave me some advice. "This is a holy time. Cherish each day you have together."

Every moment became precious, especially as our fortieth wedding anniversary approached. It sounds silly. After all, it's just a day. But the day became a symbol of our life together. When I wondered out loud if we would make it to number forty, Russ joked that he would try to hold on because the alternative would be for me to prop him up for an anniversary photo!

We did make it… and I didn't have to prop him. A special day commemorated at home with treasured, lifelong friends. A day of looking back and celebrating a lifetime of memories. Of sharing stories and laughter. And a day of holding tight, knowing this was not only our fortieth anniversary… It was our final anniversary.

Milestones and labels. The year I reached my sixtieth birthday. The year we celebrated forty years of marriage. And… the year I reluctantly owned a new label: widow.

The next time I completed a form that asked for marital status, I caught my breath as my pen hovered over the box marked "widow." An unwanted label, but one I reluctantly owned because it was thrust upon me.

Who knew that checking a box on a piece of paper would cause me to rethink my identity? And yet it did. Still, I had a choice. I could choose "widow" as my new identity or simply as a description of my status.

This loss has given me the opportunity to consider who I am, and I decided my identity is not the same as my status. Status is related to circumstances. Identity is who I am.

For more than forty years, I was a wife… and now I'm not.

For more than twenty years, I was an executive… and now I'm not.

For the past fifteen years, I've been a teacher and author.

And now, at the age of sixty, I'm a widow.

My status and labels have changed over the decades, often due to circumstances outside my control. But how I respond to those changes is completely within my control.

When the tears flow — and they do — I can lose myself in them, drowning in depression. Or I can allow them to wash over me, cleansing the pain and ushering in precious memories.

I can throw myself a perpetual pity party, cutting myself off from friends who care. Or we can share recollections that make us laugh so hard that tears flow — happy tears.

I can lament that a piece of my heart is gone. Or I can remember my faith... and the assurance that our spirits will be reunited someday.

It's all about the perspective I choose to embrace.

Sixty is the new fifty, or so I've been told. Still, this next decade will be filled with more uncertainty than I had originally expected. But isn't that true for all of us? Even if we think life will continue as it always has, surprises abound. Some will be joyful; others will be heartbreaking.

My phone continues to ring. "Haven't seen you in a while. What are you doing for lunch tomorrow?"

And again. "Heading to the mall. Want to window shop with me?"

And yet another. "Have an extra ticket to the concert next week. Come with me?"

Each time, my initial instinct is to say no. It's safer in the house, alone with my memories. But the outside world beckons. And in that moment, I face two choices: surround myself with life and joy or bury myself in solitude and sorrow. One will bring healing. The other will make me a prisoner of grief.

King Solomon said it best when he wrote: "For everything there is a season, and a time for every matter under heaven... a time to weep, and a time to laugh; a time to mourn, and a time to dance" (Ecclesiastes 3:1, 4 ESV).

There's a time to mourn. But I can't live there forever.

So I say "Yes," because the best way to enter this new decade of life is to say "Yes." Yes to growth. Yes to new experiences. Yes to friends and love and laughter. And yes to the cherished memories that keep my husband close until I see him again.

As I enter life after sixty, I choose to say, "Yes."

— Ava Pennington —

A New Home

When someone you love becomes a memory,
the memory becomes a treasure.
~Author Unknown

After fighting COVID-19 for almost two weeks, my brother had taken a turn for the worse on Easter Sunday evening. My mom was getting reports almost hourly on his deteriorating condition. She sent updates throughout the evening to my sisters and his children.

With every update, I prayed harder, asking God to heal my brother, but he passed away shortly after midnight. I was in a state of shock. I held my daughters as they wailed in my arms.

I stayed in bed the entire day. Unable to fully process my grief, sleep brought me temporary relief. My husband responded to the countless calls and texts sent to my phone as the news spread on social media.

After a couple of days, my youngest daughter Kassadi came into my room, lay next to me on my bed, and asked, "Why did God have to take Uncle Ty?" I was still struggling with this question. How was I supposed to explain it to a twelve-year-old?

As I worked to process the enormous loss I was experiencing, I kept reminding myself that Tyrone was in heaven, the most amazing place that he could ever be. I knew whatever he was experiencing there was a thousand times better than the life he left behind. Although I loved and missed him very much, I would never want to selfishly bring him back from the utopian paradise where he now lived. But how could I explain this in a way that my daughter would understand?

While we both lay there staring at the ceiling, I thought more about her question and decided to give my interpretation of a eulogy I had heard six years earlier when my brother-in-law had passed away unexpectedly. My husband and I were devastated as we tried to make sense of the tragedy. I remembered how the words the minister shared at his memorial service had managed to ease my pain a bit. I wanted to say it in a way that would help lessen her heartache as well.

I explained to my daughter that life on Earth is just temporary, like a pregnancy. And when someone dies on Earth, it is their birthdate in heaven. I told her that once we get to heaven, we start a new life there forever.

I shared that the day she was born, everyone was so excited and couldn't wait to meet her and welcome her into our family. I went on to tell her the same thing happened to Uncle Ty when he woke up in heaven a few days ago. Just like her doctor was the first one to hold her when she arrived, Jesus welcomed and held her uncle. Then he met God, our grandparents, and the rest of our relatives and friends who left Earth before us.

As I had the vision of that family reunion in my thoughts, I suggested that he also probably met his niece or nephew, the baby that I miscarried before she was born. That reflection brought a quiet smile to both our faces. My daughter nodded her head as she took it all in. I asked her if that helped, and she replied, "Sort of." A few minutes later, she got up and returned to her room without saying another word.

Later that evening, I went into Kassadi's room to check on her and noticed a drawing that she had taped to the ceiling over her bed. I asked her to tell me about the picture. She shared that the top half was our family crying while surrounding my brother's casket on Earth. Then, when the paper was turned upside down, the opposite side showed him in heaven, getting out of the casket and reaching to the outstretched arms of God. There were huge smiles on both of their faces, with the words, "MY SON! So glad you're home!" To see how she had interpreted my explanation into that visual image provided more comfort at that moment than I could have ever hoped for.

I read somewhere that grief is the love in our heart for a person who is no longer with us to receive it. I continue to be curious about what Tyrone's life in eternity is like. I know he is completely healed, not just physically, but from those things in his mind and heart that no one knew needed healing.

Whenever a wave of grief hits me, I respond by picturing my brother in heaven. I often wonder who he is with and what he is doing that very moment in heaven. Was he reunited with someone new that day? I picture that same huge smile on his face, and his heart filled with joy and happiness as I know there are no tears in heaven. It helps to ease the pain when I focus more on what he has gained instead of what I have lost.

Now, when a family member or friend passes away, I can't help but imagine that Tyrone is right there, waiting to welcome them to their new home. I look forward to the day when we will be reunited again.

— Tonya May Avent —

The Day I Became the Spider Killer

*You only feel powerless because your fear has given your
power to the object of your fear. Once you realize this,
you can claim it back.*

~Kamand Kojouri

ohn was a perfectionist. He built custom homes and he did it
well. One of the last homes he built was ours, a lovely home
with vaulted ceilings.

I've always liked antiques and old things — vintage, as they
are called now. This is partly why I moved to a 100-year-old home
after John's death. Once I put the kids to bed, I would spend hours
every night removing old wallpaper, patching, and painting — making
that old house my own.

I've always been afraid of bugs. Even the smallest of insects makes
me jump. During my relationship with John, any time I found a bug
of any kind in the house, I would call for him to take care of the situation. Translation: He would kill the bug and flush it down the toilet.

One time, there was a bee in the room. John tried to trap it with
a tissue, and the bee stung his finger. That only confirmed my fear
of bugs.

One night, about three months after he died, I was up late, smooth-
ing out the plaster on the walls in my bedroom. The kids were asleep,
and the house was quiet.

The New Normal | 119

I opened the closet door, and there it was: a spider. I'm terrified of spiders.

Without a thought, I ran toward the stairs to find John, my spider killer. I was halfway down the stairs when I remembered he was gone. That left just me… and that spider.

I grabbed a box of tissues and went back to that closet. Though I was shaking, I took the tissue box and killed that spider. After flushing the spider down the toilet, I sat on my floor for a while until the shaking subsided. I realized I was the only one in the house who could get rid of bugs.

That was the day I became the spider killer.

My children have grown up to believe that I am the fearless warrior who will come as soon as they call when a bug is in the house. I will trap and kill any insect, large or small. My kids think I am a force for any insect to reckon with. What they don't know is that, to this day, bugs terrify me. But someone had to become the spider killer.

— Christine Malone —

Chapter
5

Honoring and Remembering

38

Welcome Back

A great soul serves everyone all the time. A great soul
never dies. It brings us together again and again.
~Maya Angelou

The call came about 3:00 on a Wednesday afternoon. The Caller ID was from the nursing home where Mom lived. They would periodically call to check in, but for some reason I knew this call was different. This was *the* call.

Mom had been failing. It shouldn't have been a surprise, but I still wasn't ready for it. After ten years of Alzheimer's eating away at her mind, her body was ready to let go. The strongest woman that I ever knew was finally giving up the fight.

As I sat by Mom's bed watching her breathe quietly, I tried to picture the mom I had grown up with, but it wouldn't come. All I could see was the pain of the last ten years and how she had drifted away from us. First, her confidence and judgment had eroded. Later, her ability to communicate failed. Finally, her spirit was gone, too. She no longer knew us and, I suppose, no longer knew herself.

My brothers, sisters and I were at Mom's bedside for most of the next few days. In the early hours of Saturday morning, she left us. We were there to say goodbye, filled with a mixture of sadness and relief. Ending this long journey seemed best for Mom. But it was with profound sadness that we packed up her few belongings.

Later that day, we turned our attention to the memorial service.

"Perhaps a graveside service would be best," said my youngest sister. "Very few people are left who even knew Mom. We should keep it simple."

While that idea had merit, none of us was comfortable with it. Ten years earlier, we had buried our father. He had a loving and personal service, a tribute to the man he had been. Mom certainly deserved the same service of reflection and honor.

By the end of the day, we had outlined a memorial service. Our overriding objective was to honor Mom. That meant reaching back before she became sick and celebrating the person she had been. We focused on the attributes that most represented her: humor, strength, diligence and an overarching love for her family. We wanted to tell her story in her terms. As we talked, it all came rushing back.

"Do you remember the frogs?" asked Kristi. "If you want to talk about humor, let's talk about those frogs we put in her washing machine. Mom hardly batted an eye when they started jumping all over the place."

"And what about the wooden spoon?" reflected Mike. "That was tough love for sure when you messed up, and she would introduce that spoon to your behind. Mostly, it was your dignity that suffered because you knew you probably deserved it."

The stories flowed, one after the other, like a dam had given way. For years, it had been too painful to dwell on the woman whom we had lost. But now the spell of Alzheimer's was broken.

Two days later, we held her service in a small chapel at the mortuary. As our guests entered, a portrait of Mom driving a very snazzy convertible greeted them. That set the tone. There was a slideshow filled with favorite photos and great music from the 1940s. We were diligent in letting this memorial be about the woman whom everyone in attendance had loved for so many years.

We told our stories and asked for people in the audience to offer theirs. One by one, they stood and shared their memories. Escapades we had not heard about surfaced as her sister shared childhood events. Unsung acts of kindness were revealed.

Without really intending it, the mood in the chapel evolved from sadness and was replaced by a sense of peace. Mom had been a joyful and loving woman. As we spoke of her, that joy slowly overtook the room.

I found myself smiling, even laughing, as we reconstructed a life well lived. She had been a remarkable person in so many ways and, to my great delight, she had returned. Her memory would no longer be defined by an endless illness. For me, she was once again that energetic and exuberant woman driving a convertible down life's highway.

We had welcomed back the mom we had missed.

— Kathy Humenik —

39

Graying Memories

Humans, not places, make memories.
~Ama Ata Aidoo

olidays at my grandparents' house usually meant TV, puzzles, and old photos. At some point in our visit, my grandma would sit me down at the kitchen table and show me some of her favorite photos. They usually involved the same small collection — Great-Grandpa in his blacksmith shop, Great-Uncle Doug in his youth, and my mom's baby pictures.

When I was much younger, I thought these old pictures were boring. I couldn't fathom why people took time to look at these old, grainy pictures. I'd inwardly sigh when my brother and I were headed to the back yard for some fun, and Grandma would pause our romp around the house with her usual "Have I shown you the picture of Great-Grandpa?"

"Yeah, I think you showed it to me last time," I'd politely say, knowing that even though she'd shown it to me on almost every visit, I'd see it yet again.

"Well, look at it again. You wouldn't have known him because he died before you were born." She'd hold out the picture for my perusal, and I'd pause to assume my normal position next to her chair in the kitchen.

"Oh, wow, that's cool!" I mustered emotion and awe into my voice, knowing that response would assuage her. I didn't know what else to say. What do you say about a grainy, hardly distinguishable picture of someone you never knew?

"This was in his blacksmith shop…" Grandma would start her explanation. I mentally checked out, still looking at the photo and nodding my head once in a while to look like I was emotionally invested. When she'd continue with Great-Uncle Doug's photo, I'd pull up a chair at the kitchen table to wait out the explanation, wondering how much longer until my brother and I could escape to our water-gun fight.

As I grew older, I began to appreciate Grandma's photo collection. I understood why she enjoyed looking at the old photographs. They connected her with the past — with the people she'd lost. For just a brief second, they solidified the blurry memories of her lost loved ones.

Somehow, I began to feel a connection to the people in the old black-and-white photos. I wondered if black-and-white photographs had something that color photographs didn't — emotion, stark contrast, and mystery.

When we look at a color photo, we expect soft shades, vibrant tones, and apparent beauty, but black-and-white photos test our understanding of beauty; we find their gray tones attractive, but we're not sure why. While color attempts to reproduce life as it is and immortalizes the evident emotion, black-and-white tones seem to veil a deeper emotion in their shading, inviting only those with personal attachment and understanding to discern the message beneath.

I began to see the gray-toned photographs as solid, mystical, and enduring. It fascinated me how someone could look at a black-and-white photograph and still feel an emotional connection with the person in the photo.

My last visit to my grandma's house brought a new experience. I smiled when she asked once again if I'd seen Great-Grandpa's photograph. I responded, "Yes, but I'd love to see it again," and she pointed to where she'd hung the picture on the wall.

I walked over to the picture I'd seen a hundred times. But this time, I saw it differently. For some reason, it spurred some unknown emotion within me. For the first time ever, I wanted to know this man, portrayed in front of me in shades of gray. I knew about him from Grandma's stories throughout the years, but I wanted to know who he was and what he was like. I wanted to know his story.

"What was Great-Grandpa like, Grandma?" I asked over my shoulder. I continued looking at the picture for a while before I realized she hadn't answered from her seat at the kitchen table. Puzzled, I turned around to find her lost in thought.

"Grandma?"

When she looked up at me, her eyes glistening with unshed tears, my heart dropped for a second. Then I understood. All those years of showing me his picture had been for this. *This* was the reaction she'd wanted. She'd wanted me to see him for who he was. She'd wanted me to appreciate his legacy. She'd wanted someone to share the fading memories with to make them a bit more concrete and real, even if only for a moment.

With tears in my own eyes, I crossed the room and hugged my grandma, conveying to her that I felt her loss, too. I'd felt her fading memories.

After that visit, I felt I'd come to fully appreciate Grandma's photos. I finally understood why she spent so much time poring over the old photos, attempting to feel a lost connection again. She'd wanted to know them again for who they were. She'd wanted to solidify her memories.

But that was the last time.

Not three months later, Grandma was reunited with Great-Grandpa.

As I stared at the text that told me of her passing, I realized there would be no more talks at the kitchen table. She would never again ask me if I'd seen Great-Grandpa's photo. I'd never again have that connection with her over the gray-toned pictures.

Even in just the few weeks since her passing, my concrete memories of her have slightly faded, leaving me with graying memories of my own. How could I already be losing my memories of a woman who's been there all my life?

Almost a month after her passing, my mom sent me an old photo of my grandma in her first year of college. As I pored over the picture, I felt connected to her. I couldn't stop staring at her smile — the same smile I'd seen at the kitchen table. I couldn't deny the draw I'd felt to her picture and the emotion that had momentarily solidified in those gray tones.

I treasured that photo, looking at it almost every day for a while. One particular day, I felt the loss of my grandma more deeply and pulled out her picture to see her for myself once more. I showed the photo to the friend walking beside me, expecting a similar response to my own, but only got, "Oh, wow, cool picture." I was disappointed. How could someone look at that picture and not see the emotion inside? Knowing she had died, how could someone pass it off so casually?

I quickly realized that people tried to care—to seem as though they understood—and maybe they truly did, but their care only went so far. They couldn't love my grandma like I did. They couldn't feel her loss. They couldn't feel the graying memories.

—Maegann Mansfield—

40

The Last Game

There is no love on earth greater than that
of a father for his son.
~Author Unknown

My dad grew up during the Golden Age of Baseball when there were three teams in New York, and the game was part religion, part civic rite, and part community celebration. It was his ticket to an America he adored, but his parents, Greek immigrants, only dimly understood. They found the game and Dad's passionate devotion to it incomprehensible.

He played anywhere he could — in streets, corner lots and city parks — with broomsticks and rubber balls, broken wooden bats, and rocks tightly bound in electrical tape.

As an adult, the game was pure pleasure for him, unsullied by a job he didn't care for or any of the worries of grownup life. He couldn't get enough of it — on the radio or the television or reading the morning paper on the subway or a baseball book on a lazy summer afternoon. The familiar rhythms, rituals and coded language lasted him a lifetime.

He snuck me into Yankee Stadium when I was five, taking me by the hand, pushing my brother and my cousins through the turnstile and telling the irate usher, "The little guy will sit on my lap."

When I was nine, he talked his way into the Mets dugout with nothing more than a friendly smile and two little boys in tow. While I shook hands with Casey Stengel — most mythic of all baseball personalities — Dad wandered around the dugout, batting his eyes at the ball players and collecting autographs.

Years later, as a young adult, when I told him I had "big news" (my wife and I were expecting our first child), his first thought was that I had gotten him Red Sox tickets.

At ninety-two, the passing of my mother and the onset of dementia unhinged him and ravaged his mind. My wife and I took him in to live with us, and I became his primary caregiver.

Baseball books, the Mets on TV, and Little League games at the local playground became our staples. They were my go-to moves, equal parts tranquilizer, stimulator and memory aid, and they gave Dad a focus outside of the increasingly confusing and disorienting world he found spinning around him. Some days, baseball was all we had.

When Dad was ninety-six, we took him to Fenway Park, about a two-hour drive from home. It was the last game of the season, and we sat under a shaded overhang in left field, high up in foul territory near the Green Monster. I tried to talk him through the action on the field.

"The Orioles are up, Dad. There is one out. You remember the Orioles — Milt Pappas, Gus Triandos, the pitcher and catcher, both Greeks. Look, they have a man on first with a big hitter up! Two and two, what'll he do?"

I kept the patter going, but it went nowhere. Dad smiled halfheartedly and stared at the field, lost and far away.

Every few innings, Dad would sit up and catch a glimpse of the action on the field. He'd watch the shortstop chasing a pop fly, a base runner wheeling around the bases, a dusty slide at third. Dad would come to life for a brief, hopeful moment before falling back again in his chair. Mostly, he slept.

By the seventh inning, the game was a runaway. My wife zipped Dad's jacket and grasped him by the hands to help him stand for "Take Me Out to the Ballgame." Then we sat him down again, locking his wheels in place.

Although Dad walked with little more than a helping hand, we had brought a wheelchair and a blanket to the game. It seemed the prudent thing to do, given the distance of the parking, the crowd and the walk to the seats. So far, we had firmly resisted the world of walkers and wheelchairs for Dad. "Sitting in wheelchairs makes old people older" was one of our many mantras, but this one time, we made an exception.

Making conversation, my sister-in-law told us Fenway Park had a tradition of letting fans walk the field along the foul lines after the last game of the season. Little kids got to run the bases. My wife and I eyed each other. Our simple philosophy when taking care of Dad was always, "Whatever it is, let's do it."

As the ninth inning wore down, we repositioned Dad in the wheelchair, took the elevator to field level and stepped out into a crushing sea of fans. My brother looked dubious, but we plowed ahead toward the right-field corner and our entrance to the outfield.

In old ballparks, lines bunch and move slowly, people push and cut each other off, muttering under their breath and jumping ahead. My wife, being entirely too polite and diplomatic, was getting nowhere; as she let one person in, twelve would follow. I grabbed the handlebars, and my New York driving skills kicked in.

"Pick up your feet, Dad. Hold them out!" I coached him. As if we had practiced it, he extended his legs like a wedge, and the wheelchair became a battering ram cutting through the crowd.

"Excuse me, coming through!" I shouted at each cluster of fans. Even the most diehard, as well as the suburban families with gaggles of kids, parted and graciously let us pass. Although Dad wore his signature Mets cap and blanket (a vivid reminder for Boston fans of yet another hated New York team), we got a free pass. It is hard to obstruct an old man rolling by in a wheelchair, even if he does nominally represent the enemy.

We wheeled through the gate and were on the field. It was a perfect baseball afternoon, with temperatures in the mid-70s, the sun slowly dipping behind the park and the field awash in late-afternoon highlights. I drove the wheelchair to Pesky's Pole on the right-field foul line, an old Boston tradition.

Then my wife, my brother, the grandkids and I tried to draw him out — to no avail. He slumped back in his chair. The kids climbed the pole high enough to write their names — another Boston tradition — and we woke Dad to scribble what was left of his signature with a Sharpie pen. His eyes glazed and rolled and drooped again. His chin fell to his chest. I shook him and pointed out the field and the outfield fences. He stared mutely, wrapped himself more tightly in his Mets blanket and closed his eyes.

I steered on, at a loss for what to do next.

"Let's get him up," I said to my wife on the edge of the outfield grass. We used one of our many well-practiced moves, helping him up on the count of three and steadying his legs before we let him go.

Steps from first base, I put my arm around his waist and grabbed him by his belt. He held my shoulder and smiled.

"Come on, Dad," I said.

We touched first base, and he came alive.

"Kachulis hits a shot in the right centerfield gap!" I shouted with a cupping hand, knowing with Dad's hearing aids turned up full blast, my voice would sound like an old Victrola crackling along in his family's 1940s Brooklyn apartment.

"It gets past the right fielder, and it's rattling around against the wall. Kachulis is going for two! One man scores, and the outfielder can't find the ball!"

As we approached second base, Dad seemed to pick up the pace on his own, and a small crowd of adults with glove-wielding little boys and girls started to join in. Dad stomped on the base, determined and confident, and we took a wide turn.

"Kachulis is going for third! I don't believe this!" I shouted, and some of the adults laughed and clapped along. Our entourage had grown to the size of a small honor guard, picking up stragglers along the way.

"The relay is coming into the second baseman on the outfield grass; he drops the ball! Another run scores!"

Dad was wide awake now, his eyes bright and eager. I caught a glimpse of what he must have looked like at fourteen, running the bases in a sandlot game. Or at age thirty-two, around the time I was born.

"He touches third, and he's headed home!" I shouted as he glanced at the dugout. "He's going for an inside-the-park home run!"

Now we had a whole crowd of baserunners with us. My brother was out front taking pictures, and fans were milling around the foul line in front of the dugout. Like a great wave of gathering energy, they joined in, cheering, laughing and clapping.

As Dad's foot touched home plate, my brother snapped the final shot.

"He did it! Kachulis has hit an inside-the-park home run. The Dodgers win the pennant!"

I turned Dad to face the empty stands, which I am sure in his mind's eye were filled with cheering Brooklyn fans.

As we walked off the field through the backstop behind home plate, I realized I had made one mistake: I should have had him slide.

Dad lasted another baseball season before he passed away, wrapped peacefully in his Mets blanket. Somewhere, I hope, he's playing second base for the Brooklyn Dodgers' only championship team.

— Nick Kachulis —

41

Relief Not Grief

*Losing a mother is one of the deepest sorrows
a heart can know. But her goodness, her caring,
and her wisdom live on—like a legacy of love
that will always be with you.*
~Author Unknown

I never told my brother that I felt relief when our mother died. He, on the other hand, was grieving as hard as when he lost his Cocker Spaniel, Dolly.

I had nothing left to grieve, mostly because I'd been mourning the loss of her daily for the last three years. I guess I noticed the grief the day she couldn't remember how to play Solitaire. She no longer knew that the black queen belonged next to the red king. I thought it was a temporary loss. Nope. Two weeks later, she didn't knew how to hold the cards.

Not long after that, she caught a bus and went shopping. The store manager called her brother. Uncle Lloyd then called me. At work. "How come you told your mom she could catch a bus?" That's when I realized that my mother — who had never gossiped or told a fib in her life — had just told a whopper.

It was the first of many.

"Mom, is it okay if you have a bath without the nurse?"

She gave me the look. The look that in the past warned me not to embarrass her in front of the parish priest. Or the look that clearly said there's no point in getting that look on your face because you are not going on a date at age fourteen. Or the look that was a substitute for "If all your friends jump off a cliff, are you going to follow?"

So, I trusted her like I always had. Only this time, she not only couldn't remember how to get out of the bathtub, she was stuck in it. She was slippery, too. She'd poured scented oil in the water. It took four of us to get her out. By then, all of us were swearing. She gave us the look.

She adored her grandson Michael. It was mutual. He was filming her on Christmas day while her brother spun her around in her wheelchair. Tears streamed down Uncle Lloyd's face as he told us this would be their last dance. Mom looked at Michael and asked who the person was who was taking her picture.

She thought she might be in trouble when she told me about the phone call — the one where somebody asked her to help keep kids off the street and sold her 500 coffee mugs that said, "Say no to drugs." The police and the bank tried to put a stop payment on the $1,000 charges to her credit card. I was trying to figure out how to keep her from answering the phone.

So, it came to pass that I lost a little more of my mom every day. I realized that another drop of medicine would not bring Marie Blanche Bidgood back. Neither would one more prayer.

My husband and I visited her every day at the nursing home. Then, one day, it happened.

I started to cry in the elevator. An angel was on the elevator with me. As I struggled with tears, the angel touched my arm and invited me into her office. The angel's name was Diane Armitage. Words were stuck in me like porcupine quills. Her words, as she pulled them out, were like salve.

She said, "Mary, the next time you go into your mom's room, I want you to step over an imaginary string. Make that a rope. Leave yourself on the other side of it. Let the space in that room belong entirely to her." With a mischievous smile, she added, "Well, whoever your mom is on that particular day."

Some days, my mom would be ten and waiting for her father at the train station. Some days, she would be eighteen and waiting for her young soldier. Some days, she was thirty-eight and waiting for the Dodgers to win.

Most days, I waited for her to know me. And one day, out of the blue, which is where she lived, she touched my hand and then stroked my hair and nodded as she said, "You are someone who loves me."

"Yes, I am."

"You're hurting," she whispered.

"Yes, I am."

Then, she kissed my hand and said, "There, that will make it all better."

A year to the day after Mom died, I opened the box that the funeral director gave me. It was filled with "remembrance cards" from mourners.

I read about a woman who was more than my mother.

I read about what a wonderful friend she was to a young family who had escaped from a war-torn country.

I read about how she had shared her home with an unwed mother until she got on her feet again.

I discovered that she could speak four languages. The biggest surprise was that one of them was Russian, a language she learned to make a friend out of a stranger.

I read about how many times she had hosted baby showers, wedding showers, canasta card parties and potluck dinners.

I read how many times she had shared her money when it made a difference in someone else's life.

I was crying like a baby when I finished reading. That's when I really grieved.

— Mary Lee Moynan —

42

Remembering His Name

What you leave behind is not what is engraved in stone monuments,
but what is woven into the lives of others.
~Pericles

When strangers ask about my family, the typical answer is, "I have three siblings," since I have one sister and two brothers. The accurate answer is, "I had four, although one died of brain cancer before his sixteenth birthday." My intention isn't to be misleading, but if I include Gregory in the head count, I must pause several seconds and wait for the inquisitive condolences.

Who can blame them for their questions and comments? I'm equally curious about life-altering circumstances, about the trials that shape people. Yet those times I fail to mention him, I feel disloyal to my brother.

Gregory was my parents' first child. The first red flag that began the unraveling was when my mother watched him hold a hand over one eye while he pitched a ball. Asked why, he told her it was easier to throw if he didn't have to aim at two batters. Simultaneously, he started to lose his balance. My brother was five.

Until that critical moment, he'd lived a completely normal life. But normal was a word rarely applied to Gregory after that. Following surgery, the doctors had little hope for a cure because the cancer was an insidious form that pushed tendrils deep into his brain.

After Gregory convalesced from brain surgery, radiation treatments and endless needles, my mother lived beneath a looming cloud, always watching for signs of the cancer's return. Feeling a combination of hope and horror, she asked his first-grade teacher to put less emphasis on marks, considering the prognosis.

Until recently, my knowledge of Gregory involved two milestones: his surgery at age five and the end of his remission at age fifteen. All time before or between these dates is out of focus. One snapshot from the family album is engraved in my mind — a photo where Gregory gazed toward the camera with a faltering smile that matched his shaved and scarred head.

Perhaps it was the generation or the nature of any family subjected to grief, but my brother's imminent death was not openly discussed when the cancer returned. Near the end of Gregory's life, we siblings weren't fully aware of the impending loss. Instead, nourishing meals were served on schedule, piano lessons were sullenly attended, and — punctuated by the basement's thumping iron — my father's work shirts were pressed.

At almost five, I knew something sad hovered at Gregory's closed bedroom door even though I couldn't fathom the enormity. There were clues: gifts that arrived from out-of-town relatives and the television delivered to his bedroom. Maybe it was the chartered plane ride — his first and only flight. And the motorcycle he rode a few times at age fifteen. The day he was stopped by a cruising police car and brought home, my mother quietly explained to the officer that she let Gregory ride through our suburban neighborhood because it was his only chance. He wouldn't live long enough to get his license.

This extra attention from my mother, a nurse, was the brightest red flag of all. She tended to my brother's needs with her nursing expertise to ensure he stayed in his own bed, surrounded by his pride of noisy brothers and sisters. To keep everything normal for as long as possible.

Still young when he passed away, I asked my mom where Gregory was buried so I could visit his grave. At the time of his death, she said, funeral homes offered a disposal service for the ashes, which meant Gregory had no marker. As much as I dislike most cemeteries, I longed to visit one for my brother. I needed to see his name, to read the years of his life and then a significant line: "Your short span on Earth has touched our hearts," or "Return to your flock in peace, dear son." Gregory's marker might have featured the carving of a precious lamb or fat-cheeked cherub often associated with the passing of a child. His lack of final resting place left me with a sense of the unfinished. Robbed of a brother, I was also cheated of a site to recollect him and honor our brief relationship.

While helping my mother clean out her basement in preparation for the family home's sale, I discovered a scuffed metal train engine and a few pieces of track in a box of broken toys. Mom said the train once belonged to Gregory. Until that unexpected find, I had nothing to remember my brother except for an envelope of dog-eared pictures. Today, that train with its stunted track sits atop my living room bookcase and reminds me of Gregory: the time he rescued me from painful wrestling holds of another brother; the time he stroked my hand as I perched on the edge of his bed; the time I begged him to play outside with me, perplexed that he chose to stay indoors on a perfect sunny day.

My mother recently phoned to let me know that she had Gregory's name engraved on the niche where my father's ashes are interred. She has already purchased her own companion urn to eventually join the columbarium, and she wanted Gregory to be united in family memory. This gesture thrilled me, a gift she leaves to her children and grandchildren. This is also a gift to herself, a final act of closure.

Since unearthing that paint-chipped train engine and since encouraging my family to speak of my brother, I no longer avoid the mention of him. Instead, I welcome it. Now, when people ask about the number of siblings, he is always included. I don't evoke as much pity as in the past. Now, I'm ready to talk about him and encourage others to share their own memories. It's all in the delivery, and in remembering his name. Gregory. My brother.

— Shannon Kernaghan —

43

It's Yesterday Once More

*Grief is like the ocean, it comes in waves ebbing and
flowing. Sometimes the water is calm and sometimes
is overwhelming. All we can do is learn to swim.*
~Vicki Harrison

When my mom died only a few years after we'd lost Dad, the wound of my grief was raw and deep. Over the intervening decade or so, I've managed to stitch it awkwardly together, with the ragged, uneven needlework of a child. Most of the time, I am okay, at least on the outside.

I've heard grief described as waves — first, a tidal wave that knocks you over and nearly kills you. Then, that wave diminishes, lessening over time to eddy around your feet forever. But, sometimes, a rogue wave appears, out of nowhere, sparked by nothing in particular — or something very, very particular — and there you are again, drowning.

To save myself, to regain equilibrium and balance, I play a game I call "It's 1980." Best done during a walk in the woods, always done alone, the rules are simple: think of every single aspect of the year 1980, which was a very happy year for my family. I imagine those details as vividly as possible. Where did we live? Who was there? What was for dinner?

As I walk along the path through the park — a path I've walked since long before 1980 — I visualize each family member and picture what they might have been doing. Dad is in the garage, working on a car restoration. I can smell Bondo and fresh paint. Mom is in the kitchen, with another delicious supper in the slow cooker. There'll be mashed potatoes and vegetables, too, on our Corelle dishes. She's at the table with Gramma, who drove over to spend a Sunday afternoon with us. They're talking about a cousin, or an aunt, or both. I am in my senior year at the college I love, knowing a contentment deep inside, here on the cusp between student life and real life.

On and on I go, letting this daydream become my temporary reality, feeling myself sink into the scent of Gramma's powder, what Mom's wearing, the strength of the breeze blowing in the open kitchen window. I can hear my siblings in the yard. In the summer, they're swimming and splashing around in the pool. Other seasons, they're on bikes in the driveway. My older brother and his fiancée have dropped by. We talk about wedding details at dinner, and it's all very exciting.

What a wonderful time this is! Everyone I love is present and healthy. There's no hint — and I've no idea — that one day, it will all be so different. That I'll long for this day, again and again.

Luckily, I can have it.

"God gave us memory so that we might have roses in December," J.M. Barrie said. He's the man who wrote *Peter Pan* about the boy who didn't want to grow up. That's not me. I've grown up, built a life as an adult that's functional and even good, most of the time. But, now and then, I need to retreat to a special time in my life — just a very ordinary day in 1980. I think Mr. Barrie would understand.

Eventually on my walk I come to the end and need to rejoin the present. Having had my mental vacation in the past, this is easy because I've realized — as I always do — that the girl who knew such happiness and love is still here, in the woman I am today. All is not lost, has never been lost. It's true that circumstances have changed for us, and some of my dear ones are gone now. But any time I want, I can bring them back to me for a few moments. I can live with them again, as I did on that day, and on so many others.

I don't tell a lot of people about the "It's 1980" game. But I will always share the idea of it with those struggling over loss. We all must grieve in our own way, and none of us are ever the same again. With "It's 1980," I can enjoy the very best of my past, making my present better, too. Our loving memories are here to help us, and our loved ones would want us to use them, I'm sure.

We were all happy and smiling in 1980. Thanks to my memories, I can still be like that today.

— Kate Fellowes —

44

Cemetery Celebration

The sorrow we feel when we lose a loved one is the
price we pay to have had them in our lives.
~Rob Liano

Yellow, pink, purple, blue. We release our strings, and four shiny balloons take flight into a cloudless sky. "Happy birthday, Luke!" we call as we watch them fade to tiny black dots. "We miss you!"

Every spring, my husband and I, along with our twin daughters, celebrate our son's birthday at a cemetery. When Leah and Chloe were babies, they slept in the car while Jory and I dashed up to the gravesite to say a quick prayer. As toddlers, they pointed at planes and chattered at the pigeons during our time of remembrance. At three, they were old enough to participate. We spread a blanket on the grass and ate a picnic lunch. Then we sang the birthday song over chocolate cupcakes covered with candy sprinkles.

This year, it's too cold for a picnic. Clutching flowers and balloons, we drive through the cemetery's tall iron gates and follow the twists and turns of the road to a section called Babyland. From my first visit here, I have loved this place — everything about it. The ancient oak trees, the emerald grass, the nearby duck pond that sparkles on sunny days. The statue of a kind-faced Jesus holding His arms out in welcome to the children clustered around Him. The inscriptions on the grave markers, which tell me I am not alone in my loss. Our Beloved Firstborn. Until we meet again. Love weeps; faith looks up...

there we have forever what we have lost here.

There is grief in this place, but there is comfort, too.

In the back row near a chain-link fence lies the polished granite stone of my son. It reads, Our little Luke... Forever in our hearts. He never opened his eyes or took a breath, but for one quiet hour his heart beat steadily while his daddy held him swaddled in a warm blanket.

Now that our daughters are four, we explain this to them. Holding hands, we circle Luke's grave and share what we know about him. That his head was shaped like Leah's. That he was too small to survive. That his body was buried here, but the real Luke is with Jesus.

With Jesus. This is what lends peace to a birthday celebrated in a cemetery. I have so few memories of my son. I carried him for twenty-two weeks, slept while he lived, and spent a night with his body after he died. If that were the end of it, my grief, which is deep, would be bottomless.

But I believe that Luke lives, and somehow our birthday tradition — however unusual — reminds me that someday we will see him again and do all the things we missed here on Earth. His daddy will play catch with him. His sisters will run him ragged with games of tag and hide-and-seek. And I will finally do what I've ached to do for so long: cuddle him close, smell his little-boy scent, and tell him — face-to-face — how much I love him.

That day will come. Until then, every spring, we will go to the cemetery and celebrate. Happy birthday, Luke.

— Sara Matson —

45

Show Me the Love

*Cooking is all about people. Food is maybe the only
universal thing that really has the power
to bring everyone together.*
~Guy Fieri

My mother's love language was food. After all the years of meatloaf dinners and chicken-and-rice dishes, and all the second helpings, it wasn't until after her death last year that I realized this.

It should have been obvious to me. All my favorite family memories revolve around the kitchen and the dinner table, from picking walnut meat out of the shell for holiday stuffing, to the sleek, modern gray table that she piled high with food whenever we gathered around it for dinner and, afterwards, for jigsaw puzzles.

Most of the recipes that my mother handed down to us were not in writing; but we all made our meatloaf with Ritz crackers and ketchup because she did. We baked chicken over rice with Lipton onion soup mix in a tinfoil-sealed casserole because that's how she cooked it. We ate bagels, lox and cream cheese on Christmas morning because that's what she did.

When I first brought my now-husband home to meet her, I knew she would judge him by his enthusiasm for her food. "Ask for seconds," I told him. "No matter what." He did. And she always referred to him as her favorite son-in-law. It made up for the awkward goodbye hug at the door. Mom was not a hugger, and she was a miser with compliments.

I spent a lifetime trying — unsuccessfully, it felt — to make her proud of me. But, boy, she sure showered us with food.

After each of my two children was born, Mom visited, and she cooked up a storm for a week. Being in close quarters with my mom was never a recipe for success. We argued about everything. Any way that I parented my children was not her way, was the wrong way, in her opinion, and Mom was not afraid to tell me so.

But when she visited, she left my refrigerator and freezer stacked with Tupperware filled with homemade casseroles, soups and meatloaf because that's the way she loved me.

She didn't believe in breastfeeding because that wasn't the way she had fed her babies — and I often ended phone calls in tears from defending my decision to do so until my daughter's first birthday. When I had difficulty nursing my son, she accused me daily of starving him.

Later, my sister shared her own stories about catching Mom sneaking bottles into her own breast-fed-only babies' nursery, which made me laugh and cry. But, twenty-five years later, I understand it was only my mother's need to control the feed.

My mother barely tolerated our hugs even when we were adults, and so we learned to shower our own children with affection. I took that food for granted while I was busy seeking something more, but I should have seen it for what it was — her way of showing her love.

As my mom got older and less mobile, she continued to show her love by buying our favorite lunch meats, frozen blintzes, chocolate-marshmallow ice cream and everything bagels when she knew we were going to visit her. Grocery stores were her happy place, and when the big-box food stores became popular, they were her nirvana. If chocolate raisins and cashews were good, then a gallon container of either — or both — had to be better, and I had to exercise plenty of self-control in my mom's cupboards.

I had never seen her more excited than when she found herself surrounded by five different varieties of exotic frozen vegetables. When Mom no longer drove herself, I would make sure my trips to visit included a side trip to two different stores.

And I learned to reciprocate with food, too. Mom loved grilled chicken thighs, but she couldn't grill in her second-story condominium. First, I bought her an indoor grill, which she thumbed her nose at. After that, I tried to bring a large package of cooked chicken thighs fresh off our grill whenever we drove the two hours to visit her. I'd divide them into mini packages for her to use later, and soon I was filling her freezer in much the same way she'd filled mine.

In my mom's final months at the nursing home, she didn't have much of an appetite. I tried to bring her favorite foods to tempt her to eat: a stacked roast-beef sandwich from her favorite delicatessen or a take-out order of shrimp fried rice. I cut her meat into teensy pieces, and sometimes she'd even let me feed her. She didn't eat much, but that wasn't the point anymore. And when she stopped eating entirely, we knew she was ready to go.

At ninety-one, my mother had lived a full life, although I never knew for sure that she was pleased with my performance as a daughter. "Don't hug me," she'd warn me as I was leaving. "I don't need your germs." And so, the last time I saw her, I simply kissed her forehead.

She died in the middle of the COVID pandemic, so her body was quietly shipped back to her hometown in New Jersey, and my siblings and I could not travel to see her buried. Instead, we planned for a memorial for her after we could travel and get together again.

The day after my mom died, I found myself walking the aisles of the grocery store in my own town with my facemask in place. I loaded the cart with all my mom's favorite foods and with ingredients to fix her favorite family dinners. It was my way of showing that I loved her, too.

— Sue-Ellen Sanders —

46

Hummingbird

Angels are the bridge between heaven and earth.
~Megan McKenna

My friend Louise and I sat in comfortable lounge chairs on her back deck. As we enjoyed the spectacular lakeside view, we sipped iced tea, talked about our families, and luxuriated in the late August sun. A natural blonde with twinkling blue eyes, Louise chuckled softly and said it was the first summer in a very long time that she hadn't worried about using sunscreen. She had been living with ovarian cancer for ten months and had recently been told the treatment wasn't working.

I had known Louise for thirty-three years. When I first moved to Kingston, Ontario she warmly welcomed me into her circle of friends. I was blessed by her wisdom, insight and no-nonsense approach to life. Together, we shared accomplishments and endured heartache, and through it all never doubted for a minute that the other was there.

And we laughed. A lot.

During one of our last visits, Louise joked about finally losing the baby weight left over from her last pregnancy — her "baby" being thirty-eight at the time and himself a father of two. She'd gently pull her remaining strands of hair from just above her left ear up over her bald head, then let them rest near her right temple. All the while, she lamented that comb-overs received such a bad rap.

"Do I look like anyone famous?" she asked.

"Is that the look you're going for?" I replied. We giggled like schoolgirls.

Louise had no time for pity and little tolerance for people who tried to bring her down. She wanted to spend as many of her last days as possible laughing, not crying, and she relied on her friends to support her final wish. As time went by, she faced more and more challenges, and experienced the full spectrum of emotions, but she never failed to point out the positive. The beauty she encountered each day as she sat by her beloved lake. The unwavering love and support she received from family, friends, and countless healthcare providers. The pure joy she found in full-body hugs and kitchen dance parties with her grandson and granddaughters. Her indomitable spirit shone through to the very end.

My goal during our visits was to stay with her in each moment, through the laughter and the tears, even as my instinct at times was to run. As much as I loved my friend, I felt vulnerable in the uncertainty — the not knowing. Not knowing what she would want to talk about, and if I was strong enough to meet her there. Not knowing how I would find her — physically, mentally, emotionally — from one week to the next. Not knowing which visit would be our last. As the cancer progressed, I realized the least I could do for her was face my vulnerability. Bear witness to this special woman's dignity and amazing grace, and stand beside her on holy ground.

On that beautiful day in August as we sat together on her deck, we soon realized we were not alone. Sharing our visit was a hummingbird. Rather than flitting about, as hummingbirds do, worrying about where their next sip is coming from, our little hummingbird sat calm and still, high above us in a towering, old pine. Patiently observing. Biding her time. I was amazed by this behavior, having never before witnessed a hummingbird that didn't present with bird-like ADHD. She stayed and rested for a long time. Certainly longer than either of us would have imagined. We were awed by her beauty and grateful for the miracle of her visit. I told Louise I would never again see a hummingbird without thinking of her and our afternoon together.

It took me a long time to adjust to life without Louise. There's always a void when someone you love dies, especially after a lengthy illness, when each day is clouded by the stress of what-ifs and what's next. I began to look for a token that would remind me of her. Something to commemorate the journey of the previous year. The privilege of spending precious time with Louise. The balancing act. The vibrancy of her spirit. Lessons of fragility and tenderness as delicate as the little hummingbird that shared space with us during one of our last visits.

Ah. Of course. The hummingbird.

Suddenly, they were everywhere. Little messenger hummingbirds in my garden, where for years there had been none, at least none I had noticed; ornamental hummingbirds in store windows; images of hummingbirds on magazine covers and fabric. I was getting the picture. I knew the memento I was looking for, as a reminder of Louise, had to be a hummingbird.

I found earrings, but they were too brash, too commercial. I found a mug, but the illustration was too frantic, too demanding. Then, one day, a card came in the mail with a note inside from another dear friend, wondering how I was doing.

Without knowing of my search, the card she had chosen for me featured the work of a photographer whose signature photos are close-ups of individual drops of water, each capturing a reflected image within. The picture on the front of my card was a single raindrop falling from a leaf. And the tiny image reflected within? A hummingbird.

Of course.

— Florence Niven —

47

Love, Life, and Lemon Pie

*If you have one smile in you give
it to the people you love.*
~Maya Angelou

A thin sliver of creamy lemon goodness sat waiting in a frosty glass pie dish. It was the last piece of her last pie — hidden behind a large container in the back of the refrigerator.

Every holiday, my mother-in-law would bake the family's favorite dessert using lemons from her own tree in the front garden. They were always plentiful — in full golden bloom, as if she had a personal relationship with the lemon gods.

Our family gathering at their house was now a memory. We had thirty wonderful years steeped in familial tradition, but this year would be different. Christmas wouldn't be at my in-laws' home. They were aging and no longer able to host such a large dinner. The Christmas dinner baton had passed to my sister-in-law.

My mother-in-law — in a wheelchair now — couldn't stand for long stretches of time. The festivities would go on, no less magical. My sister-in-law, my nephew, and I gathered in the kitchen at my mother-in-law's request — we were honored to act as her personal elves — to help create her lemony masterpiece. All hands on deck labored for love. Last-minute gift-wrapping would have to wait.

Instead of recording her recipe for posterity, we all preferred to bask in the glow of the present. These were precious moments we'd never get back. I almost suggested that someone grab a pen and paper, but I didn't want to interrupt the flow or the festive mood. Would it not seem blasphemous to make her think in specific measurements that didn't exist — a quarter cup of this and a half cup of that?

Nat King Cole's velvety "Merry Christmas to You" murmured in the background. The kitchen was bathed in warm scents of roasted turkey and dressing while we sipped eggnog and brandy. The fireplace in the living room flickered light through iridescent fire-pit glass. Dressed to kill in the front bay window with a thousand blinking lights, the flocked Christmas tree reached just shy of the vaulted ceiling.

The glittery brown angel perched on top looked tipsy. Each grandchild's first and subsequent year ornament graced its own branch on the tree. Like people, they told their own story from northern to southern California.

The Spanish stucco house sparkled inside and out. Christmas cards adhered to the entry wall, and a round table of crystal candy dishes filled with red-and-green mini confections gave the rustic tiled foyer the appearance of Santa's doorway at the North Pole.

In the kitchen, each of us played our part. The cutting boards under the counter were for lining the four pie dishes with a crumbly graham-cracker crust pressed by hand with butter. That was my nephew's station. On the sink under the kitchen window, my sister-in-law squeezed lemons while I separated the eggs, eventually whipped with sugar for the meringue.

Condensed milk, egg yolks, and lemon juice completed the perfectly balanced filling of sweet tartness that no one else can replicate. It seemed like a simple orchestration that would be on playback in our minds when summoned to repeat the following Christmas.

Nothing is ever as it seems.

My mother-in-law was approaching the third year of survival after being diagnosed with multiple myeloma, a blood cancer that affects the bones as cancerous cells accumulate in bone marrow.

I'll never forget standing in the oncologist's office with my husband and his sister when he revealed her prognosis. My legs felt wobbly. But my mother-in-law looked up at me from the exam table and said, "It's okay."

I guess my expression didn't mask the sadness registered on my face. It was just like her to focus on someone other than herself. As we walked out of the doctor's office, I felt like a balloon — punctured with a sharp pin. Nothing but slow air deflating my chest and pressing my heart.

As soon as we got back to her home, she started adding to her already healthy regimen. Pulling out nutritional supplements and detailing what she wanted to add. Focused on living. Over the course of her illness, I never once heard her complain or ask, "Why me?" There was no cursing the universe or wailing in pity. She would continue life dignified and looking forward to the future. An avid meditator for at least forty years, she was one of the most awakened human beings I'd ever met.

Awakened to spirit, life, generosity and, most of all, hope.

Although the years seemed to pass quickly, we all tried to give her roses while she could enjoy them. Her eightieth birthday party was fit for a queen. Childhood friends, family and their extended family came to celebrate her birthday milestone. An outsider looking in would never believe she was dealing with the heavy burden of mortality. Stunning in a flowy chiffon orange ensemble, her warm gingerbread complexion emanated joy.

Following Mother's Day five years ago, angels came to bless her with heavenly wings. She welcomed their whisper with silent grace in the middle of the night. When Christmas rolled around later in the year, I got a phone call from my sister-in-law. I dreaded the question I knew was coming.

"Hey, girl, do you remember the lemon-pie recipe?"

"I remember the ingredients but not the measurements."

"Can you believe none of us wrote it down last Christmas?"

"Yes and no," I said, shaking my head. I wanted to kick myself.

Then I smiled at the irony in remembrance of my mother-in-law's sweet spirit.

When life gave her lemons, she made lemon pie.

— Toya Qualls-Barnette —

Light It Up Blue for Jake

Pay attention to your dreams — God's angels often speak directly to our hearts when we are asleep.
~Eileen Elias Freeman,
The Angels' Little Instruction Book

Three days before Christmas, I had a dream. But it didn't feel like a dream. Jacob was there. Oh, my precious Jacob. He was there on the big white bed, giggling and laughing with his brother. His father and I were there, too. It was a simple moment of foolish tickles and priceless family cuddles.

I saw Jacob's tousled, short brown hair, and I kissed his adorable dimples as he squirmed with glee. I don't know how I knew it was my Jake, but I did. The softness of his cheeks, the roundness of his toddler belly, the sound of his laughter — there was something familiar about it all. Besides, a mother always knows.

I sat there watching the two boys play together. I noticed how good his six-year-old brother was, gentle and careful. I thought to myself, *This is it, everything I've ever needed. My family is perfectly complete.* My soul was overflowing with joy.

Then the scene changed. Suddenly, I was in my OB/GYN's office with my doctor. The paper covering the exam table crinkled beneath me. There was a smile on my face as I told her I was ready for the sterilization procedure. I had my two perfect boys, and my family was complete. I had everything I ever needed. My doctor stared at me with an expression — pity maybe. No, she looked at me like I was crazy.

It wasn't the reaction I expected. I sat there, perplexed for a moment before it dawned on me.

My family wasn't complete. She knew. The doctor knew I only had one boy at home, that the other had been lost. She knew because she had sat there and cried with me as she cradled the tiny stillborn in her hands. She had been with me twenty-four hours earlier, too, when the ultrasound wand swept across my belly, and she whispered, "I'm so sorry. There's no heartbeat." It had all been a dream within a dream, and now suddenly my bubble had burst. I wanted to go back to that perfect moment with my family of four, but try as I might, I couldn't.

The scene shifted again. This time I was in my front yard. Stars sparkled overhead in a dark velvet sky. My landlord was there, and I was explaining that I wanted to decorate one of the tall pine trees. I wanted to light it up blue for Jake. I was so focused on this task, adamant that it must be done right away. I needed to celebrate his life so Jake would know that he wasn't forgotten on Christmas. And so, she helped me with kindness and patience. We climbed the ladder and wound strand after strand of blue lights around the tree until it sparkled against the moonlight.

When we had finished, she surprised me with a box of tiny crystal ornaments. The small glistening hearts reminded me of the heart pendant the nurses had presented to me. Jacob had been photographed with it. Now it was mine to treasure, something tangible that had been with him. I clutched the pendant now worn on a necklace close to my own heart. The ornaments were perfect in every way.

I felt him there again, my baby boy. It felt good to do something to protect his memory. To remind the Earth that he had existed. He was real.

Just as the last ornament was hung on the tree, I stood back to admire our work. And just like that, it was all over. The alarm blared, jolting me awake. It was time to get my living son up and ready for school. Just one more day of first grade separated us from the holiday break, and I'd been looking forward to getting more quality time with him.

I made his peanut-butter-and-jelly sandwich and fixed his breakfast waffles while he brushed his teeth. Before I knew it, he was out the door and on his way in the yellow school bus. I turned to his father then and shared my dream.

"It felt so real. Like Jake was really here," I said.

"Maybe he is," he replied.

"Yeah, but not like that. Not alive and full of life, giggling with his brother."

I wished I could get that moment back. But I had to admit, I did feel him with me. His spirit was here. I knew that.

Three weeks earlier, we had unpacked our accumulation of holiday decorations. Amongst them were stockings. I hung our three stockings in their usual place, and then I held Jacob's in my hands, wondering what was best. Last Christmas, there was hope, a future. I was just a few months pregnant then. We didn't know anything was wrong; we were expecting a healthy baby come summer.

He was on his way, and so I bought him a special stocking and filled it with a few baby things. It was my way of getting his brother used to the idea of sharing, of expanding our family, of having a sibling. Along with the stockings I got them matching teddy bears. One now resides on a dinosaur-covered bed where it is snuggled and read to every night. The other sits in a quiet space near the small mahogany urn.

If I'd known how things would turn out, I might not have purchased the second bear, but I'm glad that I did. In moments when I want to feel closer to my angel son, I hug it close. His brother does the same and sings him lullabies so he can feel our warmth and love.

Knowing he is here in spirit, I couldn't stand the thought of packing away Jacob's stocking or putting it elsewhere in our home. And so, without really knowing why, I hung it with the other three, completing our family of four.

Maybe I'll go get some blue lights and decorate a tree in his honor, just like in my dream. He isn't here for what would have been his first Christmas, but we can still celebrate him in our hearts.

— Charlotte Louise Nystrom —

Chapter
6

Moving Forward

The Phone Call That Changed My Life

To forgive is to set a prisoner free and
discover that the prisoner was you.
~Lewis B. Smedes

I t was the phone call that no one ever wants to receive. The phone call that changes your life. The words on the other end of the phone echoed. "They shot him. He is dead." Who got shot? Who is dead? Silence.

My mother-in-law said that the police had shot and killed her son. My husband.

The day had started out like any other day in Miami. Sun, heat and humidity. Homework, cleaning the house, and errands. My husband was annoyed at it all. He decided to go to his parents' house to chill. His car wasn't working, so I drove him two hours north to what we thought was a quiet and vacant house. His parents had been on vacation and weren't expected to return for a couple of weeks. Little did we know that their plans had changed.

For the two-hour drive, no one said a word. I silently prayed. When we arrived at the house, he jumped out. No kiss, no goodbye, nothing. I sighed and started the drive back home to our daughters.

As I was driving away, a sinking feeling in the pit of my stomach started to grow. Anxiously, I called the house phone to check in. No answer. Did he go for a walk to calm down, take a nap, or what?

Later, I learned what had happened. His parents had arrived home early, and my husband burst through the door. Within minutes, he and his stepfather were exchanging words — which had never happened before. My husband respected and loved his stepfather, and the feeling was mutual. But that night was different. It was like someone had pulled a switch, and everything that could go wrong did. A gun was pulled. Police were called. In-laws were safely rushed out of the house and taken to a safe place. All the while, I was driving back home.

The police didn't know my husband. The situation quickly got out of hand.

I got a phone call from a lead officer explaining to me what was going on. He asked me questions: *Does my husband drink?* No, never. *Is he taking any medications? Drugs?* No. *Whose gun is it?* Not ours, but my in-laws did have guns in their house. My answers sounded hollow. The officer told me they didn't know where he was and to get my daughters and take them to a hotel or a safe place. I chose a hotel.

I called a friend. She told me later that I said this wasn't going to end well. I don't remember saying that, but the pit in my stomach continued to grow. I looked at my daughters. What should I tell them? Dad was having an off-day and needed a time-out? Little did I think that anyone would wind up dead. Maybe in a straitjacket but certainly not dead. After all, didn't the police have training for situations like this?

Then the call came. My mother-in-law said matter-of-factly that they had shot him. He was dead. There was nothing else to say.

The following week was a whirlwind of navigating work, going into my children's school to explain the situation, making funeral arrangements, and being questioned by the police.

At the funeral, we said goodbye. I drove toward the police station and found myself pulling into the parking lot. I thought that I wanted to demand answers. Instead, I suddenly felt an overwhelming sense of forgiveness for the officers who had called that night.

As if I was floating outside my body, I walked into the station and asked to speak to a lead officer. Whisked into an interrogation room, I sat in front of an officer, grasping for the words to explain who I was and why I was there. I knew that I had to forgive these officers.

I choked out that my husband was shot the weekend before. The officer was aware of the ongoing case. All the police officers involved had been taken off duty until an investigation could be completed.

A million images flashed before my eyes. These officers didn't know my husband, the father of my children. We had had a bad day. My daughters would never see their dad again or have the honor of him walking them down the aisle at their wedding. Tears welled up, and my voice cracked. I looked at this officer and said, "Please just let the officers involved know that I forgive them. All of them."

He started to tear up and said, "It is never easy to take a life." He was deeply sorry for my loss. I believed him.

There were still more questions than answers, but I do know that by offering the gift of forgiveness, it gave me the chance to grieve without bitterness.

Choosing to forgive the officers that evening was just the first step. I had to take the steps to forgive my husband for putting himself and us in this situation. I had to forgive myself for working so much and not seeing the signs of desperation and illness in my husband. I had to give myself time to work through the stages of grief and remind myself that there is hope. We would not just survive but thrive.

— Denise R. Fuller —

Choosing Life

If you have a dog, you will most likely outlive it;
to get a dog is to open yourself to profound joy and,
prospectively, to equally profound sadness.
~Marjorie Garber

I sat on the kitchen floor in the dark. The small light above the stove cast dark shadows around the room. The clock glowed 12:04.

My phone was silent. Everyone who loved me was asleep.

So, I sat alone on the kitchen floor in the dark with bottles of pills in my hands. One other being sat in front of me.

She never took the bottles out of my hands. She never called 9-1-1. She never talked me out of it.

But my rescue dog, Haylie, saved my life that summer.

Two and a half years later, just as things in our lives were truly starting to look up, Haylie couldn't make it up the stairs to our apartment one night. I carried her warm, fifty-five-pound body up three flights of stairs to our home.

Once inside, she lost her balance, hitting her head with a thump on the door frame as she went down to the floor.

I rushed to her and got down on the floor, my legs on either side of her, my arms wrapped tightly around her, sobbing into her soft fur, my heart aching.

I knew her quality of life at fourteen years old had finally deteriorated enough that it was time to let her go.

February 9, 2021 was the last day I held her familiar little body and kissed her soft, beautiful face.

The grief that followed enveloped me like the darkness of night slowly taking over every ray of sunlight. The days began to blur together in a kind of twisted time warp that only grief can create.

The hours stood still — the memory of Haylie taking her last breath as fresh as if it had happened minutes ago — but the days somehow passed quickly. First, one day and one night without her, then two, then seven, and then one month. Two months without her. Three.

I had experienced the loss of grandparents, great-grandparents, and friends before. But nothing compared to the multi-dimensional layers of pain created by the deep grief of losing my curly-tailed, French fry–stealing daily companion who had tolerated fourteen years of dog Halloween costumes.

The Haylie-shaped void left in my life swallowed everything.

I stopped leaving my home. I had meals and groceries delivered. I had toiletries delivered. I stayed within my walls where Haylie still existed in the fur on her blankets, the dog beds in the corners, and the box of her Cheez-Its in the pantry.

The first time I left my home was to pick up a prescription.

As I was driving to the store, I looked around at the other drivers on the road and didn't understand how they could still be running errands, taking their kids to soccer practice, and getting their cars washed when Haylie was gone. It baffled me.

I parked and went into the store, where I was surrounded by people taking things off the shelves and placing them in their shopping carts, buying their peanut butter and protein bars like nothing had happened.

I stood in line for my prescription, and the echoes of small talk floated around me. The weather, the best deal on Triscuits, that new restaurant in town, whether to buy red or white wine.

I couldn't bear the meaningless, trivial mention of crackers and rain clouds. In my mind, I was screaming at them to be more considerate. I could barely breathe through the pain. Tears lived on the brim of my eyes, threatening to fall at any moment.

As my resistance to accepting Haylie's absence grew stronger, I found myself binge eating to numb the pain, drinking to take the edge off, and sleeping a dozen-plus hours a night to avoid having to spend time alone with the agonizing truth that she wasn't coming back.

I soon found myself at month six after Haylie's passing. The weeks had all passed in the same way: A handful of showers a month. Twelve-to-fourteen-hour nights of sleep. Hundreds of dollars spent on binge food. A couple of bottles of wine in the house at all times.

Not a single day had passed when I didn't cry.

I knew this because I got up every morning and thought to myself, *Maybe today's the day I won't cry.* But it never was.

September ninth drew near — the seven-month anniversary of losing Haylie. I felt more alone than ever in my grief. I knew no one wanted to hear about it any longer. I knew I was supposed to be "over it" by now. But I found myself still mourning Haylie like the day she died and horribly self-destructing as a coping method.

In therapy, I had learned that everyone's experience of grief is different because everyone's experience of love is different.

I learned that my experience with Haylie might have been deeper than most dog owners. I learned that she had become what held me up every day. She loved me when I couldn't love myself. She accepted me, even with all my faults. I learned that after staying alive for her, she became my entire world. And I learned that after changing her pink flamingo diapers and feeding her from a fork as she aged into a senior citizen that I had created a very strong maternal connection with her.

I learned that it was okay for me to be deep in grief over my dog seven months later.

But I also learned that it was not okay to self-destruct over it.

On the evening of September ninth, I lit the candles next to Haylie's ashes. I sat on my bed, clutching her blanket to my chest, and had a long conversation with her.

We talked about how I couldn't rush my grief, but I could control how I coped with it.

We talked about how making better choices that didn't outwardly show my pain didn't mean I missed or loved her any less.

We talked about how much it hurt me to see her in pain, whether from arthritis or a bee sting in the face, and that I didn't want to put her through that by watching me cause myself pain.

By the end of the conversation, I felt hopeful for the first time in a long time. Hopeful that I could make a change in the way I was living my life. Hopeful that Haylie wanted me to make better choices for myself.

I felt hopeful that even if I still couldn't do it for me, I could do it for her. Again. I could live for her.

That weekend, I cleaned up my act.

I cleared out my refrigerator and bought healthy food. I signed up for a gym membership. I poured the wine down the kitchen sink.

And I saved my own life, in honor of the one who had saved it so many times before.

— Amanda Gist —

The Shed

*The living owe it to those who no longer can
speak to tell their story for them.*

~Czesław Miłosz, The Issa Valley

This morning I realized that my grief has been an impenetrable wall behind which I have shielded myself from everything but my feeling of devastating loss. Since my husband Dan's death, nothing has soothed me. Nothing has cheered me. Nothing has relieved my anguish... until this morning.

My usual morning routine includes driving my granddaughters, Daniela and Marisa, to school. Some very revealing conversations occur during the brief five minutes from home to school, and this morning was no exception. Daniela was telling me that the only day of the week she liked was Saturday. Friday was too long, Sunday was spent dreading Monday, and the rest of the week she had to go to school. In response, I said that every day is a gift, and that Papa would have given anything to have one more week with us. She was quiet for a minute and then asked, "Gramma, where does a person's body go after they die if they're not buried?"

I said, "Well, you know Gramma has Papa's ashes, and someday they will be spread in the place Papa was happiest in his life."

Without a pause, she said in a serious voice, "The shed?" I heard myself laughing from my heart for the first time in over a year. Then, of course, I cried all the way home — happy crying. I realized that, first, a ten-year-old can be very perceptive and, second, that his shed

Moving Forward | 165

was truly Dan's happy place.

In our forty-three years together, Dan had always had a shed of some sort. The first one, in Northern Ontario, was just big enough to fit him, our son John, one of John's friends and a problematic snowmobile. One day, Dan's workmate asked him if his son was being a pest by always getting him to fix his machine. He just laughed because this kid practically lived in the shed during the winter. It made him proud that John believed in him.

The second shed will live in my heart forever. It was a bit bigger than the first and included a little lean-to that he enclosed, giving him a little more space. If that shed could talk... Oh, my! It knew the many sides of Dan. It was his refuge from a rough day at work or a "disagreement" with me. If Janis Joplin could be heard blaring, best not to go out there yet! Creedence Clearwater Revival meant he was having a good Saturday "cleaning up." Best of all, though, if Willie Nelson was playing, bring out the coffee and have a dance. Sometimes, I would look out and see him just sitting there quietly contemplating whatever he was working on. I was always overcome with love in those moments. He was usually making something to make me happy.

The most recent shed was the one he had in Yellowknife in Canada's Northwest Territories. There was a small, unused shed on the mine town site where we lived that every man on the property had their eye on. One day at work, the mine manager asked Dan if he would like the shed. Of course, you know the answer, so the shed was delivered on Sunday morning, and the mine manager came over to help wire it. Seeing the company truck in the yard, the neighbourhood men gathered to view the new arrival. Although I was dying to go out to see what was going on, I wanted to give him this moment. Over the years, whenever we talked about that shed, he laughed about that momentous day when he felt like he'd won the lottery.

When someone dies, people say, "May your memories give you comfort." I have always found the comment trite... until this morning. Daniela reminded me of the wonderful memories I have and that she and Marisa also have memories of twirling around on Papa's stool in the shed, just hanging out. She knew this was his happy place.

For the first time in this excruciating journey through grief, I see a crack in the wall and think that healing may be possible.

— Linda C. Olaveson —

52

Beauty in the Brokenness

Our brokenness has no other beauty but the beauty
that comes from the compassion that surrounds it.
~Henri J.M. Nouwen

In the English language, we have widows and widowers and orphans, but we don't have a word for a parent who has lost a child. I like the Sanskrit word *vilomah*, which describes something that is against the natural order. It is the closest thing I've found to describing the condition of a bereaved parent like me.

In the early morning hours of June 20, 2019, I received a phone call from my daughter's half-brother. His voice was calm but somber. "Mark, there's no easy way to say this." Instantly, I knew. My twenty-five-year-old daughter Makenna had died. In the time it took for him to speak those eight words, I became a *vilomah*, a person whose life would, from that moment, be permanently out of order.

My daughter's life struggle was at an end, but my journey of grief was just beginning.

A few weeks after her death, I joined a closed Facebook group dedicated to bereaved parents. In the months that followed, it proved to be a godsend. I have learned much from reading the stories of others who've lost their children and I've taken to heart the insights they have shared. It has been a safe place for me to discuss my own experience. And, in so doing, it has provided a measure of comfort to those who, in becoming new members as I once was, are thankful for a group that nobody ever wanted to join.

One morning, I visited the group page to find a new post that said, "What have you done to get your life back in order?" Immediately, my mind went to that word, *vilomah*, and I responded by saying that my life would forever be out of order. In a moment, grief became a permanent fixture in the landscape of my life, and I had accepted that. Many others shared the same sentiment.

It is important to understand that a life that has been shattered to pieces can never be put back in order. The real challenge, as I see it, is to embrace this new reality and try to find some beauty in the brokenness. But this level of awareness did not come to me early or easily.

As it turned out, a simple piece of jewelry helped show me the way.

Among my daughter's personal possessions was a heart-shaped pendant made of porcelain, dark brown in color and highly polished. But what made it unique among all others was a clearly visible and slightly jagged vein of bright gold running through its center. It was an example of *kintsugi*, a Japanese art form in which a broken piece of ceramic is repaired with lacquer and the cracks are highlighted with the application of gold dust, rendering the piece even more beautiful than before. *Kintsugi* is often viewed as a metaphor for restoration and transformation.

My daughter struggled with alcoholism. The last few years of her life were a continuous cycle of sobriety, relapse, hospitalization, rehab and recovery. I gave her the pendant when she had completed her first thirty-day rehab at the age of twenty-two. She cherished it and wore it often, sharing its message of hope and healing with others at AA meetings.

A few weeks following the Life Celebration we held at her mother's house, I asked family members if anyone had found the pendant among her belongings. I was crestfallen to learn nobody had seen it; in all likelihood, it was gone forever. But a few days later, I received a call that Makenna's half-sister had found it, and I could pick it up at any time. I was tearful with joy!

I have always had a respect for the wisdom imparted by certain Japanese arts and traditions. What is different about *kintsugi* in contrast to other types of "broken pot" metaphors is the deep philosophical and aesthetic practice that underlies the art form — especially the concept of creating beauty out of brokenness.

The process does not attempt to disguise the damage but rather to render the cracks as beautiful and strong. The precious veins of gold are there to emphasize that fault lines have a merit all their own. I now view these fault lines as my faith lines, and I have learned to see my heart as broken open rather than broken apart. As a result, I am stronger, wiser, kinder, and able to love deeper.

For me, the gold dust added to the adhesive mix has come to represent acts of gratitude and love — gratitude for the things that remain in my life and the love I continue to feel for my daughter.

Makenna's pendant now hangs above my drawing table in the studio at my house. I see it every time I pull up my chair and am reminded of something Ernest Hemingway wrote, "The world breaks everyone, and afterward many are strong at the broken places." The places where I have known brokenness and experienced healing are the places where I have empathy and compassion for others who are broken. They are the places where I have a story to tell, and I have credibility to minister to the needs of others. They are the places where I can speak hope and shine light into the darkness... and find beauty in the brokenness.

— Mark Mason —

53

Muted Joy

Your body cannot heal without play.
Your mind cannot heal without laughter.
Your soul cannot heal without joy.
~Catherine Rippenger Fenwick

My mom had a hearty laugh and gentle voice that soothed and uplifted those around her. So, when clinical depression snuffed out her sweet spirit, the world became muted for her. It was like going to an amusement park wearing earplugs. Minus the cheers and screams of delight, the air was vacant and lifeless. On April 2, 2013, the park grew dark and then went pitch-black when Mom succumbed to the fight and took her own life.

I was stunned. How was I supposed to move forward from this tragedy? How could I live when I couldn't breathe? How could I feel whole with my insides hollowed out? How could I laugh in the absence of joy? I was completely lost.

Before Mom's death, I always saw the silver lining in every situation. Sure, I had my down days like everyone else, but I was ripe with positivity. When Mom died by suicide, however, suddenly everything I ever knew, everything I ever was, everything I ever believed in, clung to, or hoped for were obliterated. As a result, happiness took a hiatus from my life.

I don't remember the first eighteen months after she died. I can't recall what I thought, did, or said, where I went, or what I wanted. I simply existed. As the months passed, my emotions weren't quite so erratic, fragile, and volatile. I no longer cried at the drop of a hat or whimpered at the mention of Mom's name. Nevertheless, I remained trapped in a sea of sorrow.

I longed to feel something beyond the dull ache of emptiness that had settled into my soul. Yet I was terrified of what I might feel if I returned to the land of the living. If I managed to carve out a small space within my heart for joy to grow, would I be able to nurture and preserve it? I felt weak, scared, and lonely.

Something was prohibiting me from accessing joy, and I suspected it was Mom's blessing. I desperately wanted to know not just that she was okay but also that she was okay with me being okay. I realize how ridiculous that sounds, but grief is nothing if not complex.

I went to bed each night praying that I might subconsciously feel her presence. I woke up each morning hoping I'd find a sign from her that let me know she was still in my corner. Instead, months passed without getting a heavenly nod from Mom.

Then I got an e-mail from the director of the Erma Bombeck Writers' Workshop I was attending in a few weeks. I'd been selected to perform a stand-up comedy routine at the workshop and to do it on April 2 — exactly three years since Mom's passing.

"Are you nervous?" one of the fellow attendees asked prior to the performance.

"A little," I said. "Mostly, I'm excited."

Still, as my slot drew near, my heart raced, and I wiped the sweat from my face. When my name was called, I inhaled deeply and stepped up to the mic, straining to catch a glimpse of the audience as I squinted in the bright spotlight.

I began my set and noticed that my formerly muted world now entertained sound. I heard bursts of laughter. I felt the reverberation of clapping. I caught wind of my husband's distinctive chuckle, and that was soothing.

Then, at the end of my performance, I uttered the following words: "My mom, who was one of my favorite people in the world, died exactly three years ago today. And I think the fact that I'm doing stand-up comedy for the first time ever today, of all days, is her way of saying to me, 'I know that you miss me and the joy we shared, but I want you to keep on laughing.'"

Professional comedienne Wendy Liebman, who emceed the show, came on stage, extended her arms for a hug, and whispered, "Was that really your first time? You're a natural!"

As I exited the stage, members of the audience stood and applauded. A few of them wiped away tears.

After the show, my friends embraced and congratulated me. They encouraged and supported me. They mothered and nurtured me. The experience left me beaming. For the first time in a long while, I had allowed pure joy to seep inside my soul.

Mom's hearty laugh and gentle voice didn't just lead me to the stage; they led me back to love, life, and heart-healing laughter.

— Christy Heitger-Ewing —

54

Lost & Found

A sister can be seen as someone who is both ourselves
and very much not ourselves — a special kind of double.
~Toni Morrison

I knew what my brother-in-law was going to say the minute I answered the phone. I had just returned from a visit to their home, several states away. I knew when I kissed my sister Monica goodbye that it was the last time I would look into her eyes. She was the second sister that I had lost to cancer.

With hundreds of miles between us, Monica and I had relied on phone calls to stay in touch. We talked about everything under the sun. I used to complain about "telephone ear" after finally hanging up. The sore ear was the result of cradling the phone receiver between my ear and shoulder while I tended to the kids and housework. I could scrub a sink while discussing heartburn remedies with her. We shared advice and holiday gift ideas. She listened with compassion when I was upset about something. "Be a duck," she would encourage me. "Let those problems roll off your back."

She always knew the answer to any question I had. "What is the name of that relative in Ireland?" "What kind of soup did Mom use in her chicken casserole?" Sometimes, she would call just to tell me a funny story. I would end the call howling in laughter. "Love you. Talk to you later."

Losing her left me lonely for her and the connection we had between us. I missed the conversation. I longed to hear her voice through the receiver. It had never mattered that we weren't face-to-face. We were heart-to-heart.

Often in the days following her death, I reached for the phone to call her. It was always startling to remember that she was gone. It made me so sad not to be able to share my day and ask about hers. Sometimes, I would just mutter my news to the empty air. It was heartbreaking to realize my best friend was gone forever.

I struggled for months. Events, even joyful ones, seemed meaningless when there was no one to talk to about them. I was reminded of Monica so often. I thought of her when I saw a beautiful garden, as she had quite a green thumb. If I heard a cardinal, it reminded me of the feeders she kept in her yard. When I sewed anything, I heard her voice reminding me not to press so hard on the pedal. "Don't race the machine!" When I baked a recipe of hers, I was taken back to her kitchen and sharing Thanksgiving dinner.

One day, I was sorting through a box of photos, and there was Monica. I smiled at those familiar eyes for a long time. I couldn't place it back in the box. I decided to frame it. I rummaged in the closet for a suitable frame and cleaned the glass until it sparkled. Setting the photo on my nightstand, I felt the satisfaction of finding a missing item.

That was the day our conversations resumed. Yes, they are one-sided, but knowing her so well I can usually guess her response. Often, I just talk to her in my mind, but in moments of excitement, I have yelled to her from across the room. We have a lot of catching up to do. I let it all out to her now. I whisper to her when the storms get a bit scary, and I reminisce with her as warm memories rise. It's helping me to heal. I feel her with me as I chat, nodding her head and understanding. I no longer feel that I have completely lost her. She's there, listening with sisterly love.

— Marianne Fosnow —

55

Grief Is Not Just for Humans

Dogs have given us their absolute all. We are the center
of their universe. We are the focus of their
love and faith and trust.
~Roger A. Caras

When I awoke, Bonnie was frantically performing CPR. I rushed to help, but it was obvious after a brief examination that help was no longer necessary. Poor Bonnie refused to give up. She pounded on his chest and licked his face, demanding that he wake up. I pulled her away and held her on my lap while I called to report his death. She wouldn't stop crying. I have never in my life heard a dog make a more pitiful sound.

She watched intently as emergency personnel made a cursory effort to revive him, but their efforts were as fruitless as hers had been. She watched in silence as they loaded him onto a gurney and rolled him out the door.

When everyone had left, she climbed into the recliner where Gary had always sat. She leaned her head against the backrest and stared out the window. I couldn't help thinking that she was waiting for them to fix him and bring him home to her. How do you tell a dog that her world has changed forever?

For three days, she refused to leave the recliner. She wouldn't eat or drink, and the always present, mischievous sparkle was no longer visible in her eyes. In desperation, I put her working harness on her and loaded her in the car. She displayed a mild interest in where we were going but didn't have the eagerness that she formerly had when she knew she was going to work.

We arrived at the funeral home and waited a few minutes while they prepared Gary for viewing. When we walked into the small room, Bonnie jerked away from me and put her front paws on the edge of the gurney. She stared intently at Gary's face for a few moments and then barked once loudly. I couldn't help thinking that she was ordering him to wake up as she did when he was experiencing nightmares caused by his PTSD. This time, it didn't work.

When we left the funeral home, we went to the veterinarian's office. After a thorough exam, he put her on anti-anxiety medication. From there, we went to her favorite restaurant, where my slice of apple pie and coffee are always served with a side of link sausage. She ate them politely when the waitress handed them to her but didn't wiggle and wag as she normally did.

When we returned home and I took off her harness, she went straight to the recliner and resumed her staring out the window. She took her pills without argument but acted like she was unaware of the world around her. She completely ignored me when I asked her to perform some of the service-dog tasks that she had previously enjoyed.

Three months went by, and I decided that it was time for both of us to rejoin the world. My freezer was nearly empty, and I needed to do some serious shopping. I put on Bonnie's harness, and we went to the supermarket as we had so many times in the past. I clipped her harness to the cart, and we began in the pet aisle where I told her she could pick out a toy. Normally, she would walk slowly up and down the aisle and finally settle on one toy that she would proudly carry through the store. Today, she didn't find one that she wanted.

We went back to the grocery section, and she did as she was directed — stopping, starting, and turning as I commanded. When I dropped my phone, she picked it up as she always had. She was still an amazingly efficient service dog, but something was missing. The devilish gleam was no longer present in her eyes, and she didn't deliberately do the exact opposite of what I asked while looking back to make sure that I noticed, like she enjoyed doing previously. We went home and put away the groceries. Bonnie dug out the rubber, squeaky frog, which was the last toy that Gary had gotten her. She took it to her chair and gently squeaked it for about fifteen minutes.

Later that evening, I was prowling the Internet, and one of the sites that I visited described a deaf Pit Bull puppy, a parvo survivor, who was in desperate need of a home. She was in an area where breed-specific legislation prohibited her presence, and she was destined to be put to sleep. A convoy was organized, and she joined our household two weeks later.

Bonnie showed interest for the first time when Fionna walked in the door. They played steadily for about two hours, and then Bonnie looked at me with an expression that clearly said, "It was a nice visit, but now it's time for the puppy to go home." Nevertheless, they soon became inseparable. What one didn't think of, the other did. I was soon forced to install child guards on my upper cabinets when Fionna taught Bonnie the fine art of counter strolling and opening the cupboards, where all the really good stuff was hidden. Fionna's favorite forbidden snack was uncooked macaroni, and she left traces of it all over the house. It was fun to step on in my bare feet.

It took over a year for Bonnie to return to the high-spirited dog that she had previously been. She regained her sense of humor but remained far more serious than before. Most people didn't notice, as her public manners had always been impeccable.

I had a glimpse of the old Bonnie one night when I went out to dinner with a group of friends who also used service dogs. Two of the dogs were youngsters that were still in training. All our dogs went under our table as they had been trained to do. We were chatting and enjoying our coffee when we noticed an unaccompanied Golden Retriever strolling through the restaurant. Since the dog was wearing a service-dog-in-training jacket, we realized he was probably a member of our party. Checking conditions under the table, we discovered that every lead except Bonnie's had been chewed neatly in two.

It might seem strange to most people, but I was actually happy that my dog had finally chosen to misbehave.

— Kathryn Hackett Bales —

56

A Time to Move On

The beginning is always today.
~Mary Shelley

I was packing boxes in the kitchen when it hit me: I knew the date and origin of every item passing through my fingers, every cup and potholder, every precious photo on the wall. The memories flooded my mind.

Nothing seemed complete; nothing felt right. The house was empty and disturbingly quiet. This was where my son had taken his first steps and my daughter had learned to read. It was where our family had celebrated our accomplishments and shared our disappointments. This place was a sanctuary where my wife Linda had tended her plants, I wrote stories, and we watched our children grow. For twenty years, it was the glue that held our little group together.

Our home was where Linda spent her final days, lying in the bedroom, dying of cancer. This day was going to require some major grieving.

I had greatly underestimated the emotional weight of clearing out our home. Gathering the fragments of one's life to begin anew is no easy task. It's an exercise in finality. Our family had undergone major changes in the past decade, some good and some bad. We had been beaten down by cancer and uprooted and scattered by high-school graduation, college and new jobs. Now the house was being sold to pay for tuition.

We were officially kicking the past to the curb.

I combed through the dusty files of my mind for more memories. There were pictures and old yearbooks, poetry, artwork, diaries and countless other treasures that remained irreplaceable. Packing it all was emotional and exhausting. What to save and what to toss? Lives were relived through school papers and a multitude of precious, kid-made items.

There were no ordinary moments in our home. They were all extraordinary.

Can anything replace a family? A month-long vacation in the Bahamas doesn't cut it. An estate in Hawaii wouldn't hold a candle. Not when compared to the hugs and laughter, the late-night impromptu dance parties, picnic dinners in the living room, and Wiffleball in the back yard. Grieving is intuitive during moments like this, yet sadly we are encouraged not to feel, not to hang onto our connection with the past. It's baggage, they say. It just weighs us down.

Family recollections are not baggage in my book. They are a child's first tooth, a first word, a first date, and a first car. I wanted to hold onto those memories for as long as possible. For me, they were evidence of a deep connection that transcended loss. We had managed to assemble a family unit under our roof. Their impact on me would be as lifelong as the presence of their love.

I never anticipated the emotional upheaval that going through old photos, books, and toys would produce. It was like watching an old newsreel of life clicking by. Every drawing and school project had a story that I cherished and felt connected with. Every scrap and trinket in our house held the power to lift my spirit and remind me that I had experienced a great gift. Soon, another family would step in behind us. Someone else's dreams would materialize here. Little hands fueled with imagination would build LEGO creations and dress Barbie in her spring ensemble.

It was a tough transition, but I now have a better grasp on new beginnings. One chapter has ended, and another has begun. My emotions have slowly shifted from sadness and moved more toward hope and expectation. My children have grown into caring, responsible adults. They are safe and spreading their light. And those precious memories we shared as a family? The baseball practices, drama classes, after-school conversations, preschool-, elementary-, and middle-school graduations, the good times and liveliness of a house filled with children? They're safe, too. I have them all tucked away in my mind.

I've discovered the emotional importance of maintaining rather than letting go of my connections to the past. I no longer feel inadequate or ill-equipped to cope with the void of not being a family man. Losing something I can't replace means having a connection outside myself — to a moment, a place, or a person — at a level that will remain with me forever.

Before leaving that day, I found a Little Mermaid sticker and some Pokémon trading cards stashed in a bathroom drawer. I placed them in my pocket and stepped out the door, ready to begin the next chapter, but somewhat reluctant to turn the page on this one. At that moment, I felt a soft hand on my shoulder and heard Linda's voice whispering, "It's okay, Tim. We need to move on."

I wiped a tear from my eye and closed the door behind me. Who knew that a mind could hold such sweet and beautiful thoughts?

— Tim Martin —

57

Second Sunrise

I hope you realize that every day is a fresh start for you.
That every sunrise is a new chapter in your life
waiting to be written.
~Juansen Dizon

I got up early the day we had to go to the hospital. My husband, Michael, drove us up the wooded highway, drawing closer and closer to the moment I'd been dreading—when I'd give birth to death. The sun had just peeked over the hills, casting a red sunrise through the smoke-filled air. A wildfire had started to the north one week earlier, on the same day we'd received the devastating news that our baby had no heartbeat. Fetal demise, they'd called it. In an instant, my hopes and dreams for our family and our child went up in flames.

I'd become a walking grave—no longer a womb but a tomb. The red light now filtering through the pines and the ash accumulating on our windshield indicated that the fire outside, like the one inside, still raged uncontained, leaving blackened desolation in its path. More than anything, I wanted to turn around and go home. But I couldn't.

That night, our son was born—too early to say hello, too late to say goodbye. We named him Josiah, which means "God has healed." His healing had already been accomplished in heaven. The winding road of my healing on Earth still lay ahead.

Three days later, I stood under the pelting water of the shower. It felt good to wash off the antiseptic smell of the hospital and lather my greasy hair. I wished I could wash out the memory of the past week too. But the eyes that gazed back at me in the mirror as I toweled off couldn't forget. They were dull, baggy, changed. The person I saw in the mirror was stripped bare, and I hardly recognized her. I looked down at the soft curve of my belly, still round, and suddenly felt alone. *He's not there anymore.* I braced my hands on the countertop and hunched over the sink, sobbing. His birth had permanently altered me. I couldn't go back to the person I had been before. My identity had changed the same way my body had.

Five days after Josiah's birth, I opened my e-mail to start a proofreading project for a publisher. I worked as a freelance editor, and I'd contracted for this project three months before. I knew only the title and author of the book. After I downloaded the manuscript and opened it, I realized that the subject of my new project was grief and bereavement. I sat back, stunned. If I'd had any doubt of God's presence and plan, it faded. In his kindness, he'd arranged work for me that would speak to my wounded heart.

I'd had enough experiences of God's provision, providence, and protection to believe that his plans were better than my own. But my heart still asked, *If this wasn't your timing to start our family, why did you let us get pregnant? Why give us Josiah only to take him? I've followed and obeyed you — why me?* Though the author's situation differed from mine — she had lost her young husband to a heart attack — chapter by chapter, she answered the questions I had been asking God, reinforcing a deep belief in his goodness despite the grief.

Even still, making peace with God didn't eliminate my grief. Grief was a strange, unpredictable journey. I never knew what would trigger it. One evening, Michael and I watched the movie *Up* with his parents. I hadn't seen it before. I settled into the crook of Michael's arm and laid my head on his shoulder, ready for an hour and a half of blessed distraction.

I only made it five minutes into the movie. In a swift succession of scenes, boy met girl, and the movie skimmed their life together. A joyful wedding day. Decorating a nursery. A doctor giving grim news in a hospital room. A girl sitting in the yard, eyes full and empty with grief. There were no words because none were necessary. In a few brief frames, it captured the emotional highs and lows that resonated so deeply with me. I fled the room. If only I could have fled the feelings.

But there was no escape — not with the medical bills that continued arriving for months to keep the grief fresh and prevent my heart from healing. They were a constant reminder of what we'd gone through and what we'd lost, and that the cost wasn't only emotional. Then there were the ads for baby products that popped up every time I logged onto social media. And there was still the unavoidable reality of the progressing pregnancies of our friends. *I can't do this. I can't ask about their pregnancy and celebrate with them like a good friend should.* But I did. I smiled and laughed and asked, pretending like it didn't rip open my heart. And then I cried all the way home.

"It's like the loss is multiplied," I told my closest friend. "I've lost my own joy, and I can't share in other people's either."

"Not now, and that's okay. But someday you will," she said. "You don't get over something like this. You just learn to move forward with it."

She was right. My heart would be forever scarred, but it began healing in the months that followed, one sunrise at a time, through countless conversations, journaling, prayer, and many more tears. Michael and I knew the danger of isolating, so we filled our calendar with visits from friends. Our loss had come late enough in the pregnancy that everyone knew about it, which was a blessing and a curse. It forced me to be vulnerable because I couldn't hide my pain, which slowly subsided.

The day finally came when I put away Josiah's box. The hospital had given us a beautiful cream memory box tied with a green ribbon. Inside, it held his receiving blanket, my hospital wrist tags, ultrasound photos, a certificate with his birth information, his ashes, and a few meaningful letters of condolence. I'd been keeping the box on top of my dresser, where I saw it every day. But on this particular afternoon, I pulled out our under-the-bed storage box and cleared a space in the corner. Putting away Josiah's box was a small step, but I felt the weight of the symbolism. This represented moving forward. It represented the experience becoming part of my past, a final relinquishment of the future that would never be.

Just over a year later, Michael and I found ourselves back in the same hospital. My heart wasn't fully healed, but hope hung in the air instead of smoke — along with a promise of new life. I delivered a healthy baby boy just before dawn. We gave him a name that meant "blessed." We were all recovering when morning broke. I lay back in the hospital bed watching Michael hold our son. He stood next to the window, bathed in the rays of morning light that streamed in. It had been a long night, but our suffering had brought us to this second sunrise — long-awaited joy after sorrow.

— Sarah Barnum —

58

How to Breathe

Yoga does not just change the way we see things,
it transforms the person who sees.
~B.K.S. Iyenga

My life has always revolved around workouts — kickboxing, swimming, urban rebounding... You name it, and I'd be there in class, sweating it out. I was game for just about any class except for yoga. To me, lying on a mat and breathing sounded boring. If I didn't feel like vomiting afterward, the class wasn't worth going to.

When, out of nowhere, my dad was diagnosed with brain cancer, I punched harder in kickboxing and jumped rope until I couldn't breathe. They were my methods of relaxation — to push myself so hard that I didn't have any energy left to feel. Though the survival rate was virtually nonexistent for his type of cancer, I became ridiculously optimistic. If even one person could survive it, why couldn't that person be my dad? I could either believe he was dying or believe he was living. It was an easy choice — death is not something to believe in. He was in remission six months later.

Two years after my dad's diagnosis, he was well enough for us to go on vacation. But as the week went on, we noticed my dad was starting to stumble. When we returned home, the doctors discovered the cancer had taken hold again, and there was nothing they could do. In a matter of days, he went from walking on his own to using a walker to being bedridden and partially paralyzed. Then he went blind and couldn't speak. At 2:00 A.M., three weeks after our vacation, my mom, sister, and I stood at my dad's bedside and begged him to breathe. Whenever there was a long pause between his labored breaths, I'd say, "Breathe, Dad." He fought to breathe for over an hour until he just couldn't do it anymore.

One of the most unsettling things was that the world kept going. People continued to work, laugh, and talk on their cell phones. I still got tired and hungry. It felt like all life should have stopped the minute my dad's did, but it stubbornly persisted. So, I resumed life, too, wildly making plans to avoid any feelings that threatened to come my way.

In the middle of this chaos, I found myself searching for something that could slow my frantic heart and remind me how to breathe again. On a whim, I did an Internet search for yoga studios in my neighborhood and found one a few blocks from my apartment. They had classes just about every hour from morning to night. So, after spending the afternoon in the park with my friend Debbie and her baby, I headed over to the studio, prepared to be bored but hoping to find some sort of peace.

The studio was having a special deal—thirty days of yoga for thirty dollars. I signed up, changed clothes and headed into the studio. Much to my surprise, the room was hot, extremely hot. Then it dawned on me—Bikram must be a fancy name for hot yoga. I was sweating before the instructor even walked in the door. I sweated it out (literally, dripping sweat) for the next hour and a half through the twenty-six-pose sequence, completely regretting the Choco Taco ice cream and Mountain Dew I'd downed in the park before class. But I loved the challenging poses, the strength and stretch needed to accomplish them, and the focus necessary to get through the class. My mind never wandered. I thought of nothing the entire class except for a tall glass of ice water. I left class feeling like I had had a great cardio workout and an hour-and-a-half respite from life.

After four more Bikram classes to finish off the thirty days, I wanted to look for a different type of yoga, one that didn't require me to wring out my clothes afterward. I decided to try vinyasa yoga, which is a flowing sequence of poses, but in a normal temperature room, which I greatly appreciated. My first class was held during my lunch break from work, and I literally ran into the studio at the start of class, kicked a mat to unroll it and threw my hair into a ponytail before jumping into mountain pose. I was in desperate need of calm.

Throughout the class, the instructor led us through difficult poses that took my entire focus to stay balanced. All my attention was on the instructor's voice walking us through each pose step-by-step while constantly reminding us to "take a deep breath in" (followed by him breathing in) "and a deep breath out" (followed by him breathing out). This was new to me. In kickboxing, they don't care if you breathe at all; you're there to fight. But my dad and I had lost the fight — the daily fight to deal with his diagnosis as well as his fight for life. I was done fighting; I was ready to breathe.

I added this class to my roster and then decided to try a Sunday evening restorative yoga class in my neighborhood. I laid down on my mat in the dimly lit room as others were doing, seemingly just relaxing before class. As soon as my head rested on the mat, I began to cry. The tears were unstoppable and a complete shock to me. I had spent most of my days rushing from work to working out to hanging out with friends — anything to keep me from remembering my dad's last days. I guess lying down on the mat in the dark was the first time I allowed myself to slow down, to stop really, and feel all the emotions that were apparently so close to the surface that they arose in the first instance of quiet.

I pulled myself together and spent the remaining hour-long class in comfortable poses, being given blankets and eye pillows, and moving from one comfy position to another. Previously, I had considered a class particularly successful if I was so exhausted that I wanted to crawl out of the room afterward. But after this restorative yoga class, I found there were other ways to define it. This class offered me what I had been searching for since my dad's passing — a rare time when the world stopped and I could breathe.

My new love for yoga has not replaced my addiction to kickboxing and other adrenaline-pumping classes. I learned that life is a combination of fight and calm, power and peace. The other day, in kickboxing class,

I was bent over trying to catch my breath when the instructor said, "You have to train your heart to keep going." He meant physically — to power through even if you're not working at your highest intensity, to keep moving to make your heart stronger — but it fits emotionally as well. You have to train your heart not to give up — to continue to fight and live and try, even after life fails you, and you want to stop. Even if it's not at your fullest capacity, you take the time to catch your breath and then go on.

— Kerri Davidson —

Chapter
7

It Takes a Village

59

The Pink Shoe

Give a girl the right shoes and
she can conquer the world.
~Marilyn Monroe

S he clutched the shoe to her chest and looked up at me with a mixed expression of sadness and laughter. It was a bright pink Kate Spade pump. It wasn't elegant or fancy. It was the type of shoe you would wear into a business meeting to make one solid, jaw-dropping remark as you pointed to an item on a spreadsheet that no one else had caught but you. As you turned to march back out of the room, all the people would be talking about your confidence and bold choice of footwear. It was the type of shoe you wore to an evening wedding — sure to be a hit on the dance floor and yet practical enough to wear the whole night.

No words needed to be exchanged. The pleading in her eyes was enough. She wanted, no *needed*, to take those shoes home with her. I glanced around the full garage at the boxes stacked to the ceiling. We had to find the other shoe.

I glanced at my watch. Even though I had been here for two days, the time change still threw me off. It was only a couple of hours' difference, but by late evening I struggled to keep my eyes open. My body was exhausted from a day full of cleaning and sorting through so many belongings. Just last week, I would never have imagined that I would be doing this now. Just last week, she was planning a birthday party for her daughter, and I was deep in designing floral arrangements for my sister-in-law's wedding.

It all changed in an instant. I was walking out of a bookstore when I got her text message. One simple phrase changed everything: "Hey, they just called and said that my dad died." I audibly gasped, and my hands shook as I called her. She couldn't possibly bear another loss only two months after losing her mom.

"You okay?" I asked. "What can I do to help?" It was decided that I would accompany her back to her hometown to go through her parents' things and clean out their house. A plan began to form, and within days I found myself with a cleared schedule, packed bag, and inner strength that I didn't know I had.

I set the shoe on a table in the house and informed the team that this shoe was a top priority. "We must find the other one!" I called out. And, like a general going into battle, I reminded the team of our mission for the day. Pile after pile, box after box, we searched. We had piles for everything: paint cans, chemicals, beauty products, tools, clothes, books, furniture, Christmas decorations, picture frames, records and DVDs, more Christmas decorations, a pile to be donated, a pile going to the local dump, a pile to go to various family members and friends, and more.

My friend sat in a chair like a tired queen as her loyal subjects brought her box after box of items to sort through and decide their fate. For some, it was a quick and painless, "Off with their heads!" Those items would be heaped onto the pile headed for the dump. For others, it was a photo tucked in a book or a handwritten card from a holiday of years past, or a favorite sweater that still smelled of her mom's perfume that would bring things to a screeching halt. Each box and pile brought waves of grief and emotion as events were recalled and relived.

It was a collection of moments that were equal parts pain and joy. Sometimes, we laughed and danced, singing out karaoke at top volume. Other times, we stood in a moment of silence and simply held space for each other.

At times, the pink shoe was nearly forgotten. Once in a while, someone would reach deep into a bag or box and claim that they had it. The moment would fade as they pulled out a brown shoe, or a black shoe, or something that felt like a shoe but wasn't a shoe at all. No one dared ask why she wanted it or if it had special meaning. No one dared ask if it was even in her size or to her taste. There are some questions that never need to be asked. Questions of the heart to which one need not know the answer. All we knew was that if this shoe brought her an ounce of peace, a smidgeon of hope, or even a moment closer to her mom, then that was good enough for us.

Our cleaning went on for days. Each morning, we swore that the boxes must be multiplying in the night. And with each day, our fatigue grew. Our bodies and hearts were heavy. No one even remembered the shoe anymore. More pressing things came to our attention, such as wills, deeds, contracts, certificates, and other legal documents. As the house cleared, it was becoming obvious that my friend's time in this space and with her parents' things was drawing to a close. No more memories would be made there.

We trudged out to the garage one final time. There was one final pile to sort through. Fueled by sandwiches and brownies that were generously dropped off, we pushed ahead. My friend shared feelings of fear and apprehension about the future. She wrestled with questions about how would she move forward. And as she wiped away tears with her grimy, gloved fingers, she saw it. There, amidst the trash in the corner of the garage, was the other pink shoe. She choked back a laugh as she held it close. This moment when her mom felt so close, when she knew everything would somehow be okay, when what was lost was now found.

As we left for the day, the garage now fully cleaned and sorted, she walked ahead of me down the driveway wearing her dad's old jacket and her mom's pink shoes. The image will forever be imprinted in my brain. Sometimes grief looks like laughter. Sometimes it looks like pain. Sometimes it looks like holding space while the moment passes. And sometimes it looks, quite literally, like walking in someone else's shoes.

— Natasha Lidberg —

60

Paisley

There are few things in life more heartwarming
than to be welcomed by a cat.
~Isabel Abdai

During the chaos of family and funeral plans, my bedroom became an oasis for the two of us. A place where we could be alone with our thoughts. A place to escape, to be together, to remember, to cry and, hopefully, to feel.

About two weeks post-funeral, my daughter and I were enjoying the comforts of our refuge. We were snuggling together on the bed amid tears and tissues, reminiscing and embracing the art of distraction known as the Internet.

At the time, Craigslist was a place to buy and sell things you thought you once needed but, for many reasons, discovered you could live without. While scrolling through the farm category, my daughter paused, glanced at me, and said, "Mom, I've always wanted a house cat, but Dad always insisted he was allergic even though he wasn't. Do you think I can have one now?"

What do you do for an eleven-year-old girl who just lost her father? Say "yes" to any remotely good idea that pops into her head. I became overwhelmed by the parental instinct to coddle and care for my little one, to bring her some sense of happiness in a time of great sorrow. I wrapped my arm around her shoulders, pulled her close, and replied, "Why, yes! Of course, we'll get you a cat."

I clicked on the pet category. "Let's look and see what kitties are up for rehoming."

We scrolled through the postings, formulating our list of must-haves for this new family member. Being that we already owned two small dogs, a dog-friendly cat was a must. For consistency, we decided to stick with the same gender: female. I retained some sense of sanity, convincing her that a mature cat versus a kitten would be a better fit as she would most likely be spayed and, more importantly, her personality and tendencies were known.

Thankfully, she agreed. Perfect.

We began to scan the posts for a female, dog-friendly adult cat. We were no more than a handful of posts in when our girl, ticking all the required boxes, came into view. A classy jet-black cat with charming bright yellow eyes jumped off the screen straight into our hearts.

Two days later, we heard from her current owner. She was still available and located just a few miles down the road from our home. We planned a visit for the following evening.

When we pulled up to the house, the front door was open, and a small dog romped in the yard. The foyer was filled with boxes. "Must be rehoming due to a move," I said to my daughter and her best friend as they bounded toward the door.

After crossing the threshold, we met Pat, a lovely woman who appeared to be happily preparing the home for change. After the customary introductions between humans, we met our girl, Paisley. Initially, she'd been a barn cat living on a farm. When circumstances changed, she became a mostly indoor cat.

The girls quickly began to interact with Paisley, and she graciously tolerated their attention. I followed Pat into the kitchen.

Once we reached the kitchen island, well out of earshot of the girls, Pat turned to face me. She gazed straight into my eyes and said, "My husband died in a car accident seven years ago."

I struggled to breathe.

She went on to tell me about a series of life events that had led her to this moment. She'd reconnected with a high school friend back home and was moving to South Dakota to begin a life with him. While I tried not to show it, I was completely blown away. How did a simple exchange become a crystal-clear view into the looking glass of my life?

In understanding the reason for Paisley's rehoming, I had a decision in front of me. I could keep this interaction as light as possible or embrace the fateful moment that life had afforded me. I chose the latter.

"I didn't think I would be telling you this," I uttered in complete amazement. "My husband died in a motorcycle accident three weeks ago."

It felt as if a veil lifted and we were instantly connected. Pat and I began to share the details of our experiences. We talked for over an hour. She enlightened me on the paths yet to come and spoke of a support group that was helpful to her and her daughter. I made note of it.

Regarding Paisley, Pat was explicit. She'd been a great comfort to her during a time of tragedy, and now it appeared her role must continue.

"Paisley belongs with your family now," Pat declared. "Your daughter will need her. They will need each other."

My heart knew this as well. I looked over at the girls, giving them a thumbs-up glance. They quickly tucked our new kitty into the pet carrier and headed for the car. It was time to escort Paisley home.

— Beth Bullard —

61

Mirror Image

Sometimes, when we feel most alone in the universe,
God sends us a "twin" — a mirror image — to buffer
and assuage our sense of differentness and isolation.
~Yitta Halberstram & Judith Leventhal, Small Miracles

I t was a balmy Friday night in June. Dinner had run late. If I finished the stack of greasy dishes in front of me, I'd never make it to the Compassionate Friends meeting I was planning to attend.

"Why go?" I argued with myself. I'd been faithfully attending monthly meetings for a year now, trying to find a way out of the fog that had descended when my twenty-two-year-old daughter was killed in an automobile accident. The sessions had been useful. I'd learned the ground rules of grief: how to deflect well-meaning suggestions to get on with my life, what to say when people ask how many children I have, the value of new rituals to defuse the holidays. I'd been encouraged to respect my feelings and honor my daughter's memory even if it made other people uncomfortable. I'd been able to tell my story to an empathetic audience.

Still, I felt like an outsider in the group. Despite our shared experience and the group's generosity, I'd met no one I felt I could call in a bad moment or see outside the group.

"It's a beautiful night," I reasoned. "Why not just walk the dog?"

My conscience wouldn't let me off the hook, though. As had happened often since my daughter died, my inner compass overrode my will. "One more time," it nagged. "Just go to one more meeting."

I was learning to trust its guidance.

By the time I arrived, the group was already seated. A woman I hadn't seen before was in the middle of describing the accident that had killed her twenty-two-year-old son. He'd given the keys to his SUV to his best friend and was in the passenger seat without a seat belt. He had just graduated from college and was struggling with the question of what to do with the rest of his life. Other than the location of the accident and the fact that her child was male, our stories were identical. Later in the evening, she described her son Tyler as somewhat larger than life, with all the pluses and minuses that come with that gift. I had to pinch myself. She could have been describing my daughter, Courtney. I asked her if we could meet for tea.

When I arrived at her house, I was greeted by a mammoth, exuberant black mutt.

"That's Bear," she explained. "Tyler's dog."

Up to this point, I could have dismissed our similarities as random chance: noteworthy, perhaps, interesting conversation, but nothing truly out of the ordinary. Bear, though, suggested that we were beyond the realm of sheer coincidence. Courtney had left us with her dog, Harley, a mammoth, exuberant yellow mutt.

"You won't believe this," I said, the first of many times I was to use that preface during the afternoon.

Over endless cups of lapsang souchong, we discussed everything from how the death of our children had changed our lives to the stress-related rheumatoid arthritis we had both developed. It would be an oversimplification to say that we agreed on everything, but the areas of commonality were striking. We discovered we both liked to hike and thought Italy was the center of the universe. We discussed books we had loved and quoted favorite passages. As the afternoon was winding down, we both confessed to being closet writers.

"I've written some poetry since Tyler died," Dedee disclosed. "I'm about to take a course based on *The Artist's Way* that's meant to unlock the muse. Would you like to join me?"

During the eight-week program, we shared bits of our work-in-progress. I read some of the poems she had written about Tyler late at night when she couldn't sleep. I gave her a draft of the book I was writing about my experiences the first year following Courtney's death. We discovered we were both acolytes of Natalie Goldberg and began meeting to practice her technique of timed writing drills. As we gained confidence, we asked other aspiring writers to join our group. We walked our dogs along the local river and traveled upstate to hike in the hills.

I've helped Dedee plant pansies on Tyler's grave to honor the day of his death. She's been by my side to release purple balloons for Courtney's birthday. We've drunk buckets of tea. When I feel low, Dedee usually feels up and vice versa, a delicate and beneficial teetertotter. If life is a journey, our progress feels like a joint effort.

Was our meeting predestined? Before Courtney's death, I would have scoffed at the idea. Now, I'm struck by the synchronicity.

Given our common interests, Dedee and I would have been friends under any circumstances. Given our shared experience, we're soul mates. Courtney's death shattered my faith in a just and caring universe. Meeting Dedee has restored some of that faith.

The mission statement of The Compassionate Friends is "We Need Not Walk Alone." Initially, I doubted it. I've become a believer.

— Susan Evans —

What Remains

Just being there for someone can sometimes bring hope
when all seems hopeless.
~Dave G. Llewelyn

Our soldier son-in-law died young, having just turned twenty-eight. It's been eleven years since that awful day. My head knows the facts, but my heart just can't grasp them.

He has a bench in the cemetery at West Point. It's an exact copy of the virtue benches along Trophy Point. His bench reads "Perseverance." Whatever he tried in life— love, friends, sports, academics, or duty—he persevered. His personal motto was "No excuses. Play like a champion." We as a family have adopted it as our own. We persevere.

Grief can divide people from one another, but it can also unite them. After an Army career, my husband was a professor at the U.S. Naval War College in Newport, Rhode Island for fifteen years. We put a bench with our soldier's dates on a plaque there. Over the years, we have discovered what we call "what remains."

At regular intervals, someone leaves two cans of our soldier's favorite beer. One is empty, but one is open yet full—a salute to a ghostly companion. Who is this person? I don't know, nor do I want to. What remains is that one specific person knows—and that is enough.

On our bench or on his gravestone (the bench), another person left a bouquet of flowers—not just any flowers but my daughter's favorite. One time, we found a river rock, painted with his name.

We have found a well-thumbed copy of his favorite book. Left under his bench was an engraved stone. There has been a picture of a dog, similar to his much-loved pooch, Copper. Yellow ribbons frequently appear. Two sparklers were there, one burned, one not.

An old man, whose acquaintance we never made, regularly paused at the bench near our house. He stood there in silence and then continued his walk. Had the gentleman wanted to meet us, he could have. What remains are his vigilance and respect.

At our soldier's bench at West Point, we once found some crisp bacon and a pack of cupcakes — his favorite brand — one eaten, one not. This is what remains. Someone left a Chicago Cubs baseball hat — his team. Poems, letters, pictures of families, growing kids, small flags from various places, Jack-o-lanterns, and candy are left. Military challenge coins and coins of various denominations are left. Military folks can attest that these have a variety of meanings. What remains!

These offerings are special to us and the memory of our soldier.

Similar mementoes can be found in cemeteries and monuments everywhere — not just for our soldier but for the deceased from loved ones everywhere.

All these are unique to those who know the ones who have gone ahead. They are placed by those who are still here. Respect, memories, and love are what remain.

We all persevere.

— Anne Oliver —

A Shared Grief

I think miracles exist in part as gifts and in part
as clues that there is something beyond
the flat world we see.
~Peggy Noonan

Working at my desk on that chilly, early April day, I could hear the fire trucks flying by outside the nearby window, sirens blaring. I paused to say a quick prayer for whomever was in need of their assistance and hoped that everything would be alright.

Later in the day, friends told us of their young Amish neighbors whose home had burned that morning. They had not been able to save their two small boys. My heart ached for them. What kind of torment must those parents be going through? The following day, as I discussed the tragedy with my daughter, she expressed similar thoughts. Having just given birth to her own little girl three months before, it was hard for her to imagine bearing that kind of loss.

Our small community did what we could to express our concern over their loss. When some of us arranged to take dishes of food to them, I remember thinking how silly I felt bringing my feeble culinary attempts to some of the best cooks in the county. Yet they accepted our offerings so graciously.

As April blossomed into the beautiful month of May, I had no idea that my own life was about to be turned upside down. Once again, morning sirens would be heard shrieking through town, only this time it was because my daughter, a preschool teacher, had collapsed at work from an undetected heart condition.

Sitting among our family and friends gathered at the funeral home for the visitation prior to Ashley's funeral, I was silently asking God why He hadn't seen fit to give us the miracle that we had all prayed so hard for. It seemed horribly unfair that my four-month-old granddaughter was suddenly without a mother. I was completely taken by surprise when a young couple in Amish attire came up to my husband and me. They were the parents who had so recently lost their children in that tragic fire. Now, they were offering condolences.

When I looked into that sweet young woman's eyes, I could see so much expressed there: empathy, concern, compassion. Mostly, I saw a shared sorrow. As she sat holding my cooing grandbaby, smiling at her antics, I was struck by how badly her arms must ache from their emptiness since losing her own babies. I wondered if, at that moment, my own daughter was also enjoying the antics of two special little boys.

As they were preparing to leave, not even thinking, I did what comes naturally to me. I wrapped her in my arms, this young mom so close in age to my Ashley. And I started to feel, ever so slightly, the beginnings of what would be a long journey of restoration, and the realization that maybe sometimes we get so wrapped up in the big miracles that we fail to recognize the more subtle ones. Like the gift of an unlikely friend, a shared grief, and a healing hug.

—Julie Cole—

Angel on a Park Bench

Hope is like the sun, which, as we journey toward it,
casts the shadow of our burden behind us.
~Samuel Smiles

A week after my husband Mike passed away, I was on the Santa Monica boardwalk making a slow trudge toward the pier. In my stupor, I literally watched my feet as I took one step and then another, my body feeling as if it belonged to someone else.

In the first few days after his death, I hadn't been able to get farther than a block or two without gasping for breath. Yet, for the first time on this bright spring morning, there was an odd satisfaction that I had come as far as I had.

As I neared the pier, I noticed a homeless man in a bright blue poncho sitting on a bench, dozing. He had a large cardboard sign next to him:

Rescue me

Help $ or Hugs

I walked past him and then stopped, turning around to look again. Maybe it was the words "rescue me" that called. I turned around and went back to sit next to him on the bench.

"Hello," I whispered, as I watched him shake himself awake. "I don't have any money." Pause. "Would you like a hug?"

He was alert now, looking at me. I imagine he was rather surprised at this odd woman sitting down next to him, offering him a hug. He was an older gentleman with dark skin, graying hair, and one eye that looked off in a slightly different direction from the other. Next to him were a couple of plastic bags filled with clothes and that sign. He looked around before nodding, and I reached over and awkwardly gave him a hug.

Then he asked that most casual of questions, "How are you today?"

Boom! I couldn't pretend otherwise. "Not so good," I answered. "Not so good."

My lips quivered, and the tears started flowing as I shared how my husband had just passed away. He took my hand, whispering words of consolation. He told me that Mike was in a better place now, that God had called him home. I cried even harder.

Together, we rocked back and forth on that bench. At one point, he asked me to please stop crying. He was worried the police would come by and think he was hurting me.

Eventually, the tears stopped, and we sat together on that bench with my small, delicate hand in his larger calloused one. I told him a little bit about Mike and our marriage, our adventures and travels. It was a relief to be able to share some of the sweet times in my marriage since all that had consumed me for days had been the great aching loss.

My new friend's name was Merle, and he delighted in the fact that all three of our names began with an "M." He told me about his brothers and how they'd all been born on holidays: Fourth of July, Christmas Day, New Year's Eve. He shared how someone had stolen his bike, his pack, and his identification. It was tough out there.

Merle was a religious man. He believed in God. He told me that Mike was right there, watching out for me. Even as the tears welled, I laughed when he joked that Mike might not take it kindly that he was hugging me so much, this stranger on a bench.

I could feel the shift in our connection as the time came to say goodbye. I eased my hand out of his strong, warm ones and moved just a little farther away on the bench.

"Thank you," I said, from the depths of my heart.

"Thank you," he answered, from the love in his.

At any other time, I couldn't imagine myself acting this way, getting so close, sharing so vulnerably, with a stranger. My old prejudices and fears were strongly ingrained. But, on this day, during this time of great need, that wall came down.

There is indeed much goodness in the world. In that time together, we were not strangers — he a homeless man, me a recent widow. We were two souls in need of comfort who found each other on a park bench.

His beautiful eyes sparkled as he took my hands one last time. "Blessings," he said, before he kissed them and let me go.

There are truly angels everywhere.

— Marianne Simon —

65

A Silent Partner

The greatest gift in life is the gift of friendship,
and I have received it. And the greatest
healing therapy is friendship and love.
~Hubert H. Humphrey

Alice bounded up the front steps with a fistful of wildflowers and a big smile. "These are for you, my darlin'!"

I reached out toward the bouquet without even getting up or greeting the giver. Alice didn't let go of the flowers until she'd wrapped her arms around me in a short hug and placed a small kiss on my cheek. Then, she seated herself on the chair beside me and sat in silence.

Alice had become a new friend and mentor with an unmatched perkiness and a solid faith practice. Contrary to her true personality, she was willing to sit in silence with me on my front porch.

I had just lost my dad — a big, burly man, the capable and successful leader of our family, and a welder by trade. He'd eaten a lot of ice cream that summer trying to alleviate his continual stomachache. The pain became intolerable on the fourth day of August, enough that he sought assistance at the local emergency room. All sorts of tests and consults led to him being admitted and eventually diagnosed with pancreatic cancer. He declined aggressive treatment methods, never left the hospital, and passed on before the end of the month.

Shock and despair jolted all of us — the family, our friends, his co-workers, our small church, and the surrounding community where he'd lived his entire life.

I would go to my front porch to sit and stare. No tears; no thoughts. I just sat alone, empty and staring. Night after night, I sat there past dark, oblivious to traffic, time, and the responsibilities around me — failing to grieve properly, at least as I understood the expectations.

Alice showing up with flowers made her one of many in a constant parade of folks bringing casseroles, hams, cakes, cards, and other offers to help. But I didn't need casseroles, hams, cakes, cards, or their offers. I needed to sit alone and stare. So, their visits felt intrusive and almost self-serving. Their showing up forced me to smile and act a part. Thank goodness, Alice proved different.

After that initial greeting and embrace, Alice sat in the chair beside me on the porch without another word. I needed to sit and stare; she believed I didn't need to do that alone. So, Alice sat in silence with me even though she'd never been prone to being quiet. After a while — who knows how long — she got up, gave me a slight hug, and left without a word. The next day, she returned for the same. And the next.

Her gesture of showing up was invaluable in my healing. She knew baking dishes filled with macaroni and cheese, idle chitchat, or another planter would never fix my brokenness. So, instead, she showed up time after time with the gift of her presence.

Eventually, her faithfulness melted my stoicism. When I was ready to process it all — to share my thoughts and feelings — Alice was there, and she was ready.

Those porch-sitting days of numbness happened over thirty years ago. I cannot recall a lot of details from that time, but I definitely remember Alice's faithfulness to me. I still appreciate how she met my needs so selflessly and allowed me to grieve my way, but not alone.

— Cynthia Mendenhall —

66

Gary and the Bear

*It is astonishing, really, how many thoroughly mature,
well-adjusted grown-ups harbor a teddy bear
which is perhaps why they are thoroughly
mature and well-adjusted.*

~Joseph Lempa

What kind of people would keep a massive, stuffed polar bear in an antique barber chair smack dab in the middle of their picture window? That's what I thought when I sized up the houses around the place I was hoping to purchase. I was afraid the neighbors with the bear would be a bunch of wild partiers, which was not something I desired to live next to at this stage of my life.

Fortunately, I was wrong in my assessment. The day after I moved into my new home, I ran into Gladys, a neighbor I already knew as we had worked together more than a decade earlier. I explained my concerns about the folks next door, and she replied that the bear belonged to a newly divorced retiree who was a very kind soul. "His name is Gary. You'll love him," Gladys said, not realizing how prescient her statement would become.

I met Gary the next day. A tall, slender man with stunning blue eyes and a magnetic smile, he shook my hand and welcomed me to the neighborhood. For some reason, I was left remembering every moment of that first meeting.

Over the next few months, I came to realize that my attractive neighbor was quiet, trustworthy and more than a little eccentric. For example, Gary's bear took on different wardrobes as the seasons changed. The bear held a large, heart-shaped candy box covered in red fabric for Valentine's Day. It wore oversized, plastic sunglasses throughout the summer, a tall stars-and-stripes top hat for Memorial Day and the Fourth of July, and a black velvet witch's hat for Halloween.

But Christmastime was really the bear's time to shine, as Gary went all out decorating the bear and its den. Just after Thanksgiving, the bear would don a red velvet Santa hat with a fuzzy white pompom on the top. Then, the four live ficus trees that rested in their pots behind the bear were covered with strings of sparkling green Christmas lights. A white spotlight placed to the left of the stuffed animal's feet focused the attention of passersby on the transformed Santa Bear. Looking out my own picture window next door, I would frequently see cars zip past Gary's house in the evening, only to have their drivers hit the brakes and then back up to take another look at the delightfully unique indoor polar-bear display.

For three years, Gary and I spoke occasionally but mostly just waved at one another from our driveways as we were always coming and going. I was busy with my full-time job and caregiving duties for my elderly father, who lived on the other side of the state, while trying to maintain a semblance of a relationship with the man I had been dating for several years.

One summer evening, I lamented to Gary and another neighbor that I had just been unceremoniously dumped. Gary shocked me when he immediately asked, "Would you like to go out for a drink tomorrow?" I said yes, although all sorts of alarm bells went off in my head about how unwise it might be to date a neighbor.

Fortunately, the connection I felt the first time Gary and I met quickly blossomed into a grand love affair. We wanted to marry, but our tax advisors cautioned us to wait until I was also retired. Given that advice, we didn't rush to move in together. My house simply became the West Wing as Gary's house became the East Wing of our diminutive "compound."

However, our fairy-tale relationship screeched to an abrupt end soon after our nine-year anniversary. On that cloudy November day, Gary died unexpectedly. My world shattered, and I was left in an utter daze, hardly eating or sleeping. Not only was I submerged in grief, but I was suddenly the executor of Gary's estate and had two houses to take care of.

I also had to deal with friends, family members and neighbors who kept asking, "What's going to happen to the bear?"

"The bear?" I wanted to scream. "What about *me*?"

But I understood what many of them were wondering. Christmas was just over a month away. Leaving the bear sitting alone in the dark over the holidays would just add to the sadness that now permeated Gary's empty house and my own heart.

So, days after Gary's funeral and Thanksgiving, I set about decorating the bear's lair. I struggled to recall exactly how Gary looped the green lights through the tops of the ficus trees and set up the spotlight to shine on the regal Santa Bear in his barber chair. I sobbed as I decorated, but my efforts were later rewarded with compliments from the neighbors. "I'm so glad you hung all the lights and dressed the bear. I think that would make Gary happy," my neighbor Linda commented.

Once the end-of-year festivities were over, I spent a snowy January day gloomily pulling down the Christmas lights and packing away the Santa hat. I took a deep breath, dreading that the next month's holiday would be Valentine's Day, one of the worst days of the year for the newly widowed.

About a week before February 14, my doorbell rang. It was Linda, holding a large white envelope.

"We all wanted to give you this," she said. Inside the envelope was a vibrant, multicolored valentine card signed by many of my neighbors. I realized immediately that this king-size valentine was meant for more than just me on my first Valentine's Day without Gary. "This will look perfect with the bear!" I exclaimed.

"Yes, that's why I brought it over early," Linda responded.

I quickly grabbed my coat and headed over to Gary's place. Rummaging around in the basement, I found the fabric-covered candy box that Gary always placed in the crook of the bear's right arm for

Valentine's Day. With my heart feeling lighter than it had in months, I carefully placed against the bear's left arm a very special valentine, one that reflected community, caring and a bit of neighborly whimsy.

Six years later, with my house sold, I now live in Gary's place with his enormous, stuffed polar bear still occupying its space in front of the picture window. And I still have that jumbo valentine as a reminder of how crushing tragedies can inspire unexpected acts of sweetness and light from people who really care.

— Tammy Parker —

67

Finding the Unfindable

*If you're not okay, you might as well not pretend you
are, especially since life has a way of holding us down
until we utter that magic word: help!
That's when angels rush to your side.*
~Glennon Doyle Melton

Sometimes, grief involves a funeral. But, other times, we grieve things that are still right there in front of us, reminding us that our lives will never be what we'd once hoped they would be.

On October 2, 2020, amidst a global pandemic, I took my twelve-year-old daughter to the hospital for an MRI. She'd been suffering from nausea, vomiting, cyclical headaches, and bizarre afternoon fevers for over two years. Doctors from half a dozen specialties assured us that bloodwork and intestinal biopsies had ruled out everything scary. So, we weren't alarmed when a family friend — also a pediatric neurologist — scheduled Cassidy for an MRI to rule out migraines.

I waited for twenty-five minutes, expecting Cassidy to come back through the swinging doors soon. Minutes ticked by. Thirty. Thirty-five. Forty.

Forty-five minutes later, an aide approached me with a clipboard. "The radiologist would like you to sign here to approve contrast."

Although I don't practice medicine due to my own complicated medical history, I'd been through medical school. Alarm bells went off.

"I promised her no contrast today," I said. "May I speak with the radiologist?"

The aide's eyes were kind. Too kind.

"Sure," she said. "Follow me." My phone dinged. It was a text from my husband.

Is she done yet?

No, I replied. My fingers shook. *They want to do contrast.*

When we reached the room, the aide turned to me. "Oh, it looks like the radiologist isn't here right now. Why don't you go in with your daughter? You can leave your purse here."

Go in with my daughter? They never let anyone into an MRI except the patient, I thought. But denial pushed fear back down my throat, and I set down my purse.

My phone dinged. Greg again.

Why?

I had no time to answer as they were already ushering me into the room. With smiling lips, I explained to Cassidy that they needed contrast to see things a little better. I talked her through her tears, held her hand as a needle found her vein, and sat beside her in a chair as they restarted *Pitch Perfect*. Only Cassidy could hear the audio through headphones, but we could both see the movie on a screen against the wall. Cassidy watched through an angled mirror above her head. I sandwiched myself between the machine, where I could make eye contact with Cassidy's reflection, and the screen. Familiar scenes unfolded silently. But, most of the time, when I glanced at Cassidy, she wasn't watching the movie.

She was watching me. I smiled and blew kisses.

Over the next forty-five minutes or so, we repeated this ritual. Cassidy, looking to me for silent reassurance. Me, smiling and nodding while my heart pounded against my ribs. Instinctively, I knew something was wrong. I knew my husband was blowing up my phone, though I couldn't hear it. But I didn't focus on these things.

I focused only on her.

Finally, the aide returned. Wordless, she motioned for me to come. I forced myself to stand, casually, slowly, and then winked at Cassidy.

Just outside the door stood our family friend. My heart sank. His eyes were sad; his posture, professional.

"Hi… I didn't know you'd be here…" I said.

"Hi, Shannon. Let's go talk."

I followed him down an empty hall that felt five miles long. "You're scaring me," I said. "I feel like you're gonna give me bad news."

He stopped at a door, motioning for me to go inside. "Well," he said, "it's not good."

For years, I've suggested that people record meetings with doctors when discussing diagnoses. "When you're hit with bad news," I'd say, "you won't remember anything." Now, I understand why so few people actually do this. I barely remember anything from those first several minutes. I know he told me my daughter had an inoperable brain tumor. I know he told me she'd need to be admitted immediately for tests, and she'd need brain surgery as soon as possible to biopsy this monster in the middle of her head. I know he told me she'd need chemo. But all I remember is being on my knees, sobbing, pleading, begging him to tell me he was wrong.

How does one grieve something like this? The sudden loss of your child's life as they knew it to be only five minutes earlier? How does one move past such an unexpected blow?

And, oh my God, how was I going to tell my husband? Or our son? Or… my baby girl?

So many emotions twisted and tangled inside me, all of them painful. My heart fractured, and my lungs filled with cement. I wanted to scream, to run away, to break the computer. *I'll offer up myself instead,* I thought. *Go through this in her place. Welcome a tumor of any grade, any magnitude, if only she can be spared.*

For several moments, I drowned in agony. I knew I needed to find strength — if not for me, then for my husband, my son…

My baby girl with cancer.

But how? How does one find the unfindable?

Those who have studied psychology know that grief comes in stages, but many only associate these stages with death. And yet, we grieve so much more than death. We grieve lost relationships. Innocence lost to abuse. Withering financial conditions. I've grieved all these things, and more.

But this… this was different. This was my *child*. I'd buried both my parents and suffered seven years of illness and a coma, but nothing ever hurt like this.

My daughter took the news as well as any twelve-year-old could, I think. She asked if she could scream (then did), asked if she could throw her shoe at the wall (then did), and then said, "NOW can I have a dog?" On the way to have her admitted, someone stuffed a teddy bear with a cancer symbol in her arms. I must've mumbled "My phone is almost dead" because a wonderful, teary-eyed nurse gave me her charger.

"I'll give it back soon," I said.

"No. Keep it," she said.

Then I did something I've not always been good at: I accepted her help.

Then, I accepted an offer to bring Cassidy a smoothie. I accepted stew. I accepted mail, presents for the children, and books. So many wonderful books.

Eventually, our burden became easier to bear because we were not carrying our grief alone. And in this comfort, something magical happened. My daughter found purpose. She began a YouTube channel called "Candid with Cassidy" to help other children with cancer. She thought that if she documented her experiences, cancer would feel less frightening for someone else. She began accepting donations, which she now uses to buy gifts for pediatric oncology patients and their families. Because of confidentiality, she doesn't get to see their smiles. But for her, knowing there *are* smiles is enough.

Nothing about grief is simple. But some truths, I think, are universal.

When our world is at its darkest, sometimes it's best to let someone else turn on the light. Then, when our eyes have adjusted, we can turn it on for others.

— Shannon Stocker —

Words of Wisdom

68

Gift Horse

*Friendship improves happiness, and abates misery, by
doubling our joys, and dividing our grief.*
~Marcus Tullius Cicero

"Lost" was the only word I could use to describe my condition after my wife Anne died. I wasn't attending to the simplest of tasks: shopping for groceries, paying bills, or keeping in touch with family, friends, and neighbors. It wasn't that I didn't know how to do these things or was avoiding them. I just couldn't get it together and organize myself well enough to take over the activities that my wife had done so well.

Four months after Anne died, something unexpected happened that would have a profound effect on my life and help me begin to recover from my grief. It started with a note I got on Facebook Messenger.

"Hello, Wayne! I'm new to Facebook and I was going through old pictures the other day — bittersweet memories! Doing a lot of that lately. Bob, my husband of fifty-three years, died on our anniversary a year and a half ago. At any rate, thought I'd try a few names from long-ago pictures, and up you popped!! Wanted to say hello. Hope your life has been happy, and you achieved most of what you wished for. Have a great day!"

The message was from Marianne, who I remembered fondly from my college days but hadn't had any contact with for fifty-eight years. When I was a senior and she a junior, we dated pretty exclusively for a semester. After I graduated and moved to California, we quickly lost touch.

I discovered that she had also lived in California, married there, and raised three daughters. Three of my children were born in California as well, but I am currently living in Ohio, and she is back in Tucson where the two of us first met at the University of Arizona.

This is part of the message I sent in return:

"What a pleasant surprise, Marianne. Thank you for getting in touch. I want to say first that I am truly sorry for the loss of your husband. Trust me, I understand completely what the loss of a lifelong companion means. My wife died this past October. We would have been married fifty-six years the end of December. I am just in the beginning stages of learning how to deal with the loss and accompanying grief."

Marianne was quick to take the lead and offer me the benefit of her more-lengthy experience with grief:

"Advice: Don't let anyone give you a time frame to grieve. Don't hide your feelings ever. Cry if you feel like it. Be prepared for sadness coming over you just out of the blue. You can't hurry grief. It takes its good old time. Reach out to people. I had a hard time with that. I think that first year I slept and cried. I must have read a book every week. I'm Barnes & Noble's best friend! Anyway, send me texts or e-mails all you want. And scream and yell and rant at God and, of course, pray!"

That's the way our relationship began. Texting became our primary method of communicating. We quickly found out about each other's children and grandchildren (nine each). Over time, we shared stories about our respective careers (hers as a teacher, mine as a writer and film/video producer). But interspersed through all the catching up with our lives was our unspoken commitment to support each other on our grief journeys. Although Marianne was a year ahead of me in dealing with her loss, I quickly learned that neither of us was on a timetable. We both had our difficult days. Fortunately, we provided each other a shoulder to cry on or a welcome distraction when needed.

After being in touch for a couple of months, Marianne asked me a question that gave me pause. "What do your kids think about our texting?"

"I haven't said anything about it."

"Why not? Do you think we're doing something wrong? My girls think it's neat."

I had to think about Marianne's question. Why hadn't I told my children? I was close to them and shared many of my feelings, but I had kept this activity from them. I finally worked it out in a text to Marianne.

"No, I don't think we're doing anything wrong. It's just that I know my kids are grieving too, and I don't want them to think that while they're missing their mother, their father is on the Internet trolling for women. There. I said it."

"Is that what you think is going on here?"

"No, but I don't want them to think that."

"I don't know your kids, Wayne, but from what you've told me, they're bright and sensitive. I think they would understand."

We left it at that. It wasn't Marianne's decision to make; it was mine. And when I did share this important development in my life with my children, they seemed to be fine with it. They said they only wanted me to be happy, and being less lonely was part of it.

Our texting relationship—interspersed with an occasional phone call—has gone on for over three years now. We've even gotten to the point of texting good-night to each other—although with a three-hour time difference, Marianne's evening is just beginning when mine is ending. Neither of us sleeps well, and our days don't seem complete without this final wish for a restful sleep for each other.

I'm not sure what made Marianne think of me that day so many months ago, but we're both glad she did. We have developed a wonderful friendship built on mutual support of each other as we continue to navigate the journeys of our separate grief. Neither of us feels as alone. We both have supportive families, but it's different when you have someone your own age to talk to, someone who has also lost a life mate.

Although we had dated earlier in our lives, what we have now is not a romantic relationship, the rekindling of an old love affair. It didn't start out that way, and it hasn't evolved in that direction. Neither of us is trying to replace the other's lost mate. We both know I can't be

Bob for her, and she can't be Anne for me. We are totally devoted to the loving memories of our lengthy marriages and the children they produced. We recognize that those lives together with our respective partners were the very definition of love. So, what is this relationship? One that is providing friendship, support and an uplifting of spirits through our worst days? Isn't that a kind of love, too?

Marianne had talked once about her mother having a lot of old-time sayings. "Don't look a gift horse in the mouth" was one of them. We have come to realize that's what our relationship is: a gift horse. We don't have the need to define it further. It's a beautiful gift, one we will accept without further question for as long as it lasts, and each day we will continue to cherish it.

— Wayne Rapp —

69

Just Take My Hand

Anything is possible when you have
the right people there to support you.
~Misty Copeland

My nine-year-old, Ellie, jumped onto our family-room couch, held her wild curls back from her face, and yelled, "The floor is hot lava!" Her eleven- and thirteen-year-old brothers, Cameron and Finn, scrambled up next to her and then lunged for the coffee table. Cameron's lanky body betrayed him, and his foot brushed the rug.

Finn was quick to call him out. "Bro, you didn't make it."

Cameron slid onto the "lava," making dramatic, sizzling noises.

"Mommy, you have to play," said Ellie. "Quick. Stand on the couch, or you'll die!"

"I can't," I sighed. "Remember?" Balancing on a wobbly cushion was out of the question. A few months earlier, surgery to remove a brain tumor had severed my balance nerve and saddled me with a severe case of facial palsy. I left the hospital reliant upon a walker. Only recently had I rehabbed my way back to walking a few miles each day.

She groaned. "You never play with us anymore."

"Yeah," Finn whined. "The game's no fun without you."

I sank onto the couch near them. "Let's think of something else to play."

I'd gone from being a strong, hands-on mother to a shadow of my former self.

Ellie put her head on my lap and reached up to feel my palsied face. I tried not to pull back as she massaged the skin that drooped off my jawbone. Then, as if she were molding clay, she tried to push my cheek up into a smile. I grasped her hands in mine and made a decision.

"We're gonna go for a hike," I said. I wanted to show them that I was stronger than they thought.

"You can't hike!" Finn said. His mouth gaped, revealing bright blue braces. "Won't you, like, fall down?"

"I am *not* broken," I said, standing up tall. "Get your water bottles ready."

"Is anyone else coming?" Finn asked.

I glared at him. "I don't need any help." I sounded more confident than I felt.

The snap of crisp autumn air greeted us as we stepped out of the car on a ridge overlooking a valley. I leaned my head back and breathed in deeply for the first time in months. We set off down a trail lined with oak trees and coastal redwoods, my hiking poles in hand.

I stopped next to the crimson branches of a madrone tree and called the kids over. "Check out the peeling curlicues on this bark."

"You gotta feel how cold the branches are, Mommy," Ellie said. "Remember? You told us last year that it's also called a 'refrigerator tree.'"

"You remembered!" My heart flooded with happiness. For a moment, I felt normal again. We were out hiking together just like we used to. "C'mon, my little ducklings!"

Ellie walked ahead, stuffing rocks and acorns in her pockets. Her pants were practically sliding off her hips under the weight of her treasures. I followed in her steps, settling into the meditative rhythm of the soft thuds of my hiking poles against the earth.

The trail soon became much steeper, and my fingers tightened around my poles. To calm my growing nervousness about the terrain, I focused on inhaling the warm-soup smell of the bay leaves blanketing the trail. Then, suddenly, I lost my footing and stumbled, causing small bits of gravel to shoot out from under my feet. I glanced up to see if the kids had noticed, but they were busy climbing the stump of an old-growth redwood.

About fifty minutes into the hike, we reached an unmarked intersection of trails. Six big brown eyes looked up at me expectantly. I pulled my long hair up into a bun, pretending to act occupied while I improvised.

"We'll stop here for a snack!" I said as if I'd planned it all along. I handed them pumpkin bread from my daypack.

I slumped against a tree trunk. My shoulders bowed as the fatigue that had haunted me since my surgery began tugging on every part of my body. Were we lost? Since the surgery, I'd felt nothing but lost trying to adjust to my body's new limitations. I crumpled up my useless trail map, threw on my daypack again, and walked a few steps down the fingers of each trail. Finally, I picked the one that looked the most likely to head uphill back to our car.

"Okay, let's go!" I sang, trying to sound easy-breezy.

Up, up, and up we went. Ellie purged the weight from her pockets, leaving a haphazard path of acorns behind her. I finally found trail markers showing we were close to the parking lot and near a vast boulder outcropping called Summit Rock. A sense of adventure churned within me, giving me another welcome glimpse of my pre-surgery self.

"We have to get to the top," I said. I elbowed Finn playfully.

I followed their giggles down the path as they ran off ahead.

Ellie scrambled on top of a boulder around the base of Summit Rock. "Now the ground is lava!"

Cameron reached out a hand to me. "I'll help pull you up!"

"I'm good," I said, setting aside my hiking poles.

"Are you sure?" Finn asked, eyeing me with wisdom beyond his years.

"I can rely on my hands, too. I'll be fine." I wedged my hands into rock crevices for support as we made our way up the sloping side of the massive boulders.

At the top, I snapped a selfie of us, not minding for once that my face was lopsided. We stretched our arms out in the breeze and took in the view. We seemed to be on top of the world.

My joy began to evaporate as I contemplated the way down. Finn made it to the bottom first, his teen legs already solid. My legs, on the other hand, were becoming Jell-O. I'd hoped that my athletic and adventurous past would have counted for something. Instead, vertigo, which I'd last felt in the hospital, began spinning the edges of my vision, causing jitters to spread outward from my core. Even my fingers were shaking. Halfway down, I froze and pinned my cheek against the cold rock. I hoped my kids weren't watching. I heard someone scrambling toward me. *Please let it be a stranger,* I thought.

"Do you want help?"

The voice was Finn's.

"No, I can do it," I said through gritted teeth.

"Why don't you let me help you?" Finn put his hand around my ankle and lowered it to the next foothold.

I wanted to shake off his grip, but the strength of it stirred something in me. I realized I could either continue brushing off help or, instead of trying to prove my strength, I could borrow a little power from my children.

"Just take my hand," he whispered.

And so, I did.

— Katy Ryan —

70

How to Survive the Death of a Spouse

It takes strength to make your way through grief,
to grab hold of life and let it pull you forward.
~Patti Davis

After fifty-six years of marriage, my husband died of lung cancer three years ago. I've had to learn new skills to fill the large shoes he left behind. Not all those skills were ones I delighted in, but I'm learning out of necessity. As I look back over these past years, I've learned a few important lessons:

1. *Grieve, but don't stay there.* You have been left here for a reason. Discover what your new purpose is. I recently reconnected with an old friend who became a widow six years ago. She wastes her days in bed, sleeping all the time.

2. *Make a new bucket list.* Do things you never did before. Take a trip. It doesn't have to be far. It may be to a place you've never visited in your own community. Take a friend along. Make new memories.

3. *Try a new skill.* Learn to knit or bake bread. Take a painting class. Go back to college. Many colleges allow people fifty-five and older to audit classes. You don't get any credit for the class, but you learn things you didn't know before.

4. *Record your thoughts in a journal or write a memoir.* Try your hand at creating a poem. It doesn't have to rhyme. Just let the feelings you're holding inside flow down your arm and into your pen or computer

keyboard. You'd be surprised what you can pour out on paper in ten minutes. Writing is healing — even if no one ever reads your words. When you put your cares on paper, they tend to shrink to the size of the page.

5. *Give yourself to others.* Make a list of your special talents. Do you know how to budget well? Do you have a knack for organizing? Can you be a reading coach for a local elementary school? Perhaps you can write notes to other people who are hurting. Your words can help ease their pain. There are individuals out there who need your expertise and comfort. You might be the answer to someone's prayer.

6. *Redecorate your house.* If that's too big a bite, rearrange the furniture. Put different pictures on the wall. Hang some new curtains. Make your home reflect your personality. Did your spouse have a favorite chair that was long past its prime? Donate it or take it to the curb and buy a new one.

7. *Plant a flower or vegetable garden.* Digging in the dirt definitely has healing properties. Surprise a friend with a bouquet of flowers you've grown. Share some vegetables with a neighbor. Perhaps you'll develop a new friendship in the process.

8. *Organize a group of other widows or widowers and learn from them.* Plan day trips together. Form a dinner club that meets at a different house each month. Eating alone is lonely. Put together a book club or form some other group to enjoy a common special interest.

9. *Take all your photos and label who the people are in each one before putting them in an album to give to your children or grandchildren.* If you're not into the old photo books, scan the pictures and put them on a thumb drive for each child and grandchild. Even if they aren't especially interested in those mementos now, they may appreciate your efforts as they grow older.

10. *Find the silver linings in your new status.* This may sound silly but look for tasks you don't have to do anymore. Think about it. You only have to make one side of the bed each morning. Your laundry load is lighter. You can eat supper when you feel like it. If you want to enjoy guacamole with chips for supper at 4:00 in the afternoon, no one will question it.

11. *When you need someone to do a task you don't feel you can do, pray.* The most amazing things happen. Perhaps you'll see an ad in your e-mail for a gutter cleaner who plans to be in your neighborhood. A tree trimmer might knock on your door who does a beautiful job at a great price. A friend might tell you of a very reasonable concrete contractor to pour a new garage floor or patio. Help is available if you ask.

12. *Remember special birthdays and anniversaries.* Instead of turning them into pity parties, look back briefly but also look ahead to what is to come.

Being single after all these years is not the path that I would have chosen for myself, but it is the path I am on whether I was ready or not. I am doing my best to make the most of it.

— Sally Jadlow —

71

The Mirror of Death

Now we see things imperfectly, like puzzling reflections
in a mirror, but then we will see everything
with perfect clarity.
~1 Corinthians 13:12

Although it is inevitable, losing a loved one is never easy. Suddenly, a part of your life is gone, and there is a gaping hole that was once filled with love. I, like everyone else, have had to cope with this emptiness, but it took the death of my dear friend Sarah, a Border Collie who was my faithful companion for almost sixteen years, to come upon a discovery that changed my life.

Sarah was an abused puppy we rescued when we lived in England. When we went looking for a dog, I was keen on another one that was in the foster home we visited, but instead I was chosen by Sarah. Her abuser had been a man, and she feared most men. But, for some reason, she saw something in me that was different. She boldly approached me, wagging her tail. Despite my protests, it was a battle I could not win. She was the dog for me, and that was it.

When we got home, we found that Sarah could not be left alone. She was completely terrified. We guessed that she had been left alone in her former life, did something wrong as puppies often do, and was beaten when the master returned. Not being a dog psychologist and living in a dog-friendly country, the easiest solution was to take her to work. Most of the time, she hid quietly under my desk. The only hint of a dog in the office was a tail wagging when somebody walked by, especially my colleague Ann, who doted on Sarah and often took her for walks in the park at noon.

In time, Sarah proved to be a wonderful friend. She led an interesting life. When we moved back to Canada, the option of leaving her in England, although there were a few offers to take her, was never considered. We had shared too many walks and talks to be separated. Anyway, she had chosen me.

After years of devotion on both our parts, the time came when cancer took over, and we had to put her down. In the cool shade of our front lawn, we stared into each other's eyes, trying to prolong the moment. Then it was over. She was gone.

Days of grief followed. Friends tried to say the right words. Hugs were given generously. Everything helped, but they couldn't fill the void. I tried pep talks to convince myself that it was all for the best, and so on and so on.

I missed my dog.

One noon, a few days after her death, I was walking on the streets of Tavistock. I paused to look into a florist's window, and I saw my reflection. What followed, though, were the thoughts that turned my tears of sorrow into joy.

Like the reflection in a mirror or glass, death is the reflection of life. The greater the love, the greater the grief. There are people who die every day for whom I feel no grief. However, my dear Sarah's death created a deep and profound sorrow because our love for each other had been deep and profound, too. The sorrow was a mere reflection of the joy we had shared. What a precious thought. It allowed me to cope with my emotions. Every time I experienced the pain, I remembered that it was a mere reflection of our love and a reminder that it still existed. Although she was no longer with me, Sarah's love was.

Then came the question that changed the tears into sobs of joy: Would I take away any of the precious moments we had shared to lessen the sorrow I was experiencing now? The answer was an emphatic NO! As much as I mourned the loss of a great friend, there was no way I would have taken anything away from our experience together. The result was that I embraced the emotions. Embracing them meant that

I could deal with them effectively, since I wasn't trying to avoid them or push them away. And to think, one brief reflection caused me to reflect on my sorrow and surround it with light.

—John Stevens—

72

Bittersweet

We cannot cure the world of sorrows,
but we can choose to live in joy.
~Joseph Campbell

I had been saying goodbye to my mom for ten years. That was how long she had breast cancer. At first, there was the fear that she would die, leaving so much unsaid and undone. But as she survived surgery, radiation therapy, and reconstruction, hope replaced some of that fear. Life took on a new normal.

But cancer is an unrelenting foe. It was a journey of ups and downs, from despair to hope again and again, until there were no more protocols or chemotherapy infusions — only painkillers and attempts to keep her comfortable until the inevitable. At sixty-six, my mom was dying, and there was nothing that anyone could do.

Toward the end, the cancer ravaged my mother's body until she had no quality of life, only pain. I stopped praying for God to heal her but rather to take her. I learned that dying is the ultimate healing.

I know now there is a term for this process: anticipatory grief. It is the normal mourning that occurs when a patient or family is expecting a death. Anticipatory grief has many of the same symptoms as those experienced after a death has occurred. It can be short or protracted. Either way, it is painful.

I grieved for ten years, thinking about what she was going through and what was yet to come. The experience taught me so much. I learned how to become a caregiver. I learned I couldn't do it all, couldn't control it all, and that one does not care for their loved ones alone. Asking for help and allowing others to be a part of the process are gifts to all those who partake.

My mother taught me how to live with what could be changed and what could not be changed. She showed me how to fight her foe with knowledge, humor and faith. And when the time came, she showed me how to die with grace, dignity, humor and wisdom.

In those years, we laughed while buying wigs (thirteen of them, to be precise) and while simultaneously pushing a wheelchair and a flatbed cart at Costco. On the good days, we "played," and on the bad days we popped popcorn and watched old movies. Oh, we cried, too. And, at times, we fussed at each other — as most mothers and daughters do. But those moments, too, had their purpose.

One day, I will die and leave those I love. One day, those I love will die as well. Experiencing my share of medical mayhem has taught me that I must prepare for the inevitable. I don't want it to envelop me to the point where I cannot enjoy life and make memories that will last not only in this life, but hopefully into the next.

So, while it is hard not to anticipate the grief, I want to practice what I call "anticipatory joy" — the joy at what might be just around the corner. I want to look forward to making memories with my family, neighbors and friends. I want to savor the joy in the early morning hours as I sip a cup of French vanilla coffee on my patio overlooking the nature preserve while listening to birds sing and watching my dog chase squirrels as they forage for nuts.

I want to anticipate the joy of the day when all the pain and hurt of this world will be over, and my loved ones will no longer suffer. I truly believe that I will see them again. We will be whole, healed, and without pain and scars. Oh, and how we will dance with joy! The only remnants of this life will be the grace and wisdom that have come from living life as best as we could, loving and helping one another and sharing life together.

In those ten years watching my mother die, I learned that we cannot totally avoid grief in this life. But we can seek out and remind ourselves to anticipate the joy, no matter how bad things are. There is always a bit of joy somewhere amidst the pain.

— Loretta D. Schoen —

73

When the Fairytale Ending No Longer Exists

When one person is missing
the whole world seems empty.
~Pat Schweibert

I stood in the middle of the gathering I'd neither expected nor wanted to host. From 5:00–9:00 P.M., the Mackey Mortuary visitation line refused to end. Truth be told, I didn't want it to. I needed the comforting presence of family and friends.

In the casket to the right of me lay the body of the girl who, for fourteen years, I'd raised, adored, and loved.

One after another, people paused and then passed by. From Miracle Hill Ministries, where my husband worked. From the places where I had taught. From the local church. From my daughter's schools and extracurricular activities: orchestra, Awana, Upward and rec-league sports. The end of the line even ushered in her entire Southside High School marching band.

Beautiful faces met my gaze with unspoken questions and tears. With tenderness, "I'm sorry" was said again and again. A blend of perfume and cologne scents lingered on my clothes as I cherished the warmth of held hands and hugs. And tears streamed down my cheeks when a friend whispered the words I'd begun to doubt: "You were a good mom."

But the unexpected occurred. My daughter's beloved eighth-grade science teacher, whom Jenna had confided in and considered a friend, stood in front of my husband and me with his wife.

"John's e-mail is in the school directory," Kathy said. "When things settle down in a couple of months and people stop coming around, contact us. We've also lost a child."

I tucked away those words, journeyed through the weeks, and took too long to call. Seven months later, however, I finally dialed my phone.

John and Kathy issued an instant invitation to hang out at their house. While their twenty-two-year-old son delighted and distracted my young kids with Mario Kart, we talked about Jenna. About her after-school conversations and the familiar teen struggles she'd shared. About the happy memories we had of her and how it seemed so wrong that she was gone.

The hours sped by. My husband, Komron, joined us after work. Then John and Kathy ordered pizza, and John asked the question few dared: "How are the two of you doing?"

We reiterated what our counselor had said — that the death of a child takes its marital toll. She'd cautioned us against blaming one another as we chased the elusive "Why?" She'd warned us that we'd grieve in different ways, at different times, and often feel alone. She'd encouraged us to share the deep grief with other trusted friends because it was too much for a spouse alone to bear.

John listened and nodded his head. Then he told the story of losing his firstborn son, nine-month-old Jonathan, twenty years ago. Fresh tears fell as he recounted giving his namesake a ride in the baby trailer attached to his bike when a drunk driver struck.

"The grief changes shape," John said. "You'll never get over it, but you'll get through it. And, while I may not be a happier person, I believe I'm a better person because of it. For one thing, I treasure my students more because I know how precious life is."

The words resonated. He understood.

Then he smiled and looked at his wife. "Also, I stayed married because there's no one who would know our son the way Kathy did. There would never be anyone else who had walked through that with me."

This time, I was the student, sitting at the feet of the teacher Jenna adored. I pulled a tiny black notebook from my purse and wrote down the perfect words spoken at just the right time. It was what I needed to hear then. It's what I remind myself of now.

Without my daughter, parts of my identity, purpose, and future are gone. My feelings of helplessness arise from having been unable to protect her. Anger, guilt, sorrow, and despair sometimes cause emotional distance and conflict in my marriage.

Nevertheless, Komron has chosen to stay. So have I, even though a daughter's death shattered all hope for a fairytale life. Our story will never have the happily-ever-after ending we'd like.

Is it easy? No. But we need each other, and too much has already been lost. Like John said, there will never be anyone else. However messy marriage gets after a child's death, with the grace God provides, this, at least, can be one vow — one covenant — kept.

— Beth Saadati —

74

Missing Aunt Mae

Because you have seen me, you have believed. Blessed
are those who have not seen, and have believed.
~John 20:29

When I was a teenager, my sister and I got an incredible gift: a trip to Florida. It was our first plane ride, first time away from home and parents, and first time meeting our grandmother's sister, Aunt Mae. Mom told us we would recognize her even though we'd never met, and I didn't understand how that was possible. But she was right.

Aunt Mae was another version of Nana but not quite the loving personality Nana was. It took a few days for us to get comfortable around each other, but when we did, the fun never stopped. Aunt Mae was a feistier version of Nana and more independent. She had three grandsons nearly the same age we were, and we were constantly on the go for the entire trip.

It was after we got home when my relationship with Aunt Mae took off. We wrote to each other and occasionally spoke on the phone. When I graduated high school, I went to college in Florida, and we became even closer. Over the years, we kept in touch with pictures, cards and letters. When I got married in New York, she was unable to travel but she called me and we spoke for a long time.

Two years later, after sharing many letters, cards and pictures, I got a call from my mother. Aunt Mae had gone in for a routine stress test, collapsed and had immediate surgery. Due to the urgency, decisions were made that caused severe complications. As I stood praying in my back yard with my kids, I kept telling my aunt, "Don't you leave without saying goodbye."

I learned later that she lived for three days after the operation. My cousin, her daughter, told me that my aunt had asked throughout those three days that they read to her all the letters I had written over the years. I was heartbroken. And because I was nine months pregnant, I was unable to attend the funeral, compounding my grief.

And I was aggrieved. It held me like a mental vise for a long time. I could not get around my loss. We shared a connection that is rare, a way of thinking and view of living life. My aunt was strong, independent, and fierce with honesty. She spoke from a hard life, no sugarcoating. And I missed that. I missed her! She was also my last connection to my grandmother, Nana. Losing Nana was tough, and I still grieved. Losing Aunt Mae was the true end of all my extended family. They had been a family of eleven children, and now, in rapid succession, they were all gone.

I carried this loss silently, but it was always there. I'd hoped for some sign, a signal of sorts originally, something I'd recognize and know Aunt Mae was okay. But nothing. Months went by. Then a year. Two.

Then, one night, I dreamed of my grandmother. Nana looked as she always looked to me in childhood. As I embraced her, I marveled at how glorious it was to feel this way again after such a long time. We were alone in a dimly lit room. We sat together in an oversized chair, and I was happy and smiling. Beyond us, through a doorway, people were dancing in another room. My sister breezed by us with a smile, went into that room, and began twirling with everyone. I did not want to leave my grandmother, so I stayed with her, but she didn't seem the same. She wasn't smiling. In fact, she looked annoyed, maybe even perturbed. I was still smiling at her with my arm around her, but she moved back, eyeing me, and said pointedly, "Why isn't it enough for you that she's with the Lord?"

And it was like I'd been hit broadside to the head. I woke up.

As I sat there going over what Nana had told me, I realized she was right. Being solely focused on my loss, I had been unable to understand her point. And then I realized, incredibly, that the weight of grief I'd been carrying all this time was gone. I felt a lightness within me and was amazed at the difference.

That dream was decades ago, but it's as clear to me today as it was then. And the comfort and hope that were given to me are still there.

— C. Manzo Nicoletta —

75

Plain Ol' Ted

We do not create our destiny; we participate in its unfolding.
Synchronicity works as a catalyst toward
the working out of that destiny.
~David Richo, *The Power of Coincidence*

A few years ago, I took daily walks along the winding paths of a cemetery near my Florida home. The peaceful setting helped me feel closer to my dad and grandmother who had passed the previous spring — thirty-three heartbreaking days apart. Both were buried in Indiana — far away from me.

And it hurt. Deeply.

There was seldom anyone at the cemetery. An assortment of squirrels, bunnies and birds. It was usually just me and my grief.

Except on Friday afternoons.

A well-dressed, elderly gentleman would be there, sitting on a lawn chair facing a headstone, reading aloud from a book. A red rose and a Styrofoam cup with a straw were propped against the marker — presumably gifts for the deceased.

The first few Fridays, I waved as I passed. He waved back but returned to reading.

Aloud.

In a cemetery.

Eventually, curiosity got the better of me, so I introduced myself.

"How do you do, Michelle? I'm Ted Henderson," he said as we shook hands.

"Who are you visiting, Ted?"

"I'm spending time with my wife, Margie." He smiled. "Every Friday, rain or shine."

"Why Fridays?" I asked.

"For Margie and me, Friday evenings were date nights. We'd go to supper, see a movie, play cards with the neighbors, that kind of thing. It gave us a few hours away from the kids. Later, when Margie got sick and went to a nursing home, we still had date night. It was something normal to look forward to. I'd bring her a red rose and a chocolate shake from Winky's. Then I'd read to her — the newspaper, books or a chapter from the Bible. Forty-nine years and 2,548 Friday night dates. Just because I can't see her anymore isn't a reason to cancel date night. Maybe she can see and hear me. That's why I read to her."

"And bring her a red rose and a chocolate shake," I added.

"That's right."

How beautiful.

"May I join you?" I asked.

He looked pleased.

"Sure. I'd like that."

I sat on the grass.

"Would you tell me more about her?"

"My Margie was the prettiest girl I ever saw — big blue eyes, cheeks the color of peaches, long, curly hair red as a fire truck, spunky and funny as two kittens fighting over a ball of yarn. I fell in love with her on the spot. She was crazy about me, too, although I never understood why. I'm just plain ol' Ted."

He chuckled.

"She passed on eleven years ago. Folks at church keep trying to fix me up with widows. I tell them no thanks. There's only one lady for me."

"Margie must have been very special."

"Everyone loved Margie. She visited sick folks, knitted blankets for babies, gave away most of our homegrown vegetables to the needy, and taught Sunday school. Little ones were crazy about her."

"Do you and Margie have kids?" I asked.

Ted gazed off in the distance.

"We had twin boys: Theodore Jr. and Andrew. Teddy played high-school football. Andy was our scholar, quiet and smart. Both were as handsome as movie stars, but they couldn't have been more different. It's funny how that works. After college, they enlisted in the Army. We lost them in the Vietnam War. They died seven months apart. Children aren't supposed to go first."

His eyes filled.

"Please forgive me for stirring up painful memories," I said.

He smiled through tears.

"You didn't. I've had a blessed life. And I learned long ago that there's a reason for everything. Like meeting you. You asked me to tell you about my family. Hardly anyone brings them up anymore, and I get lonely for them."

"Ted, how did you find peace after all you've suffered?" I asked.

"When Margie died, I was a mess and moped around for months. Then one day, I imagined what she'd say if she saw me sitting around in my PJs at noon, my hair like shredded wheat, needing a shower. She'd holler, 'Ted, quit bawling and get busy!' So, I did. It was tough. There were many days when grief got the better of me. But I pushed through the pain and got on with it. Of course, I make an exception on Fridays."

The sun was setting.

He glanced at his watch.

"Look at the time! Margie always said I talked too much."

We laughed.

He studied my face.

"Next Friday, if you're here, let's talk about you. There's a world of hurt in those green eyes."

A few stray tears trickled down my cheeks.

He patted my shoulder.

In the days that followed, I thought about Ted and his simple acceptance of the hand he'd been dealt. He believed I was led to him so he could talk about his family. Maybe I was led to Ted for the same reason: so I could talk about mine.

However, the following Friday, he wasn't there. Or the Friday after that.

A few days later, his obituary appeared in the newspaper.

My heart sank.

A dear man who understood the depth of my pain was gone.

Although I was a stranger, I went to Ted's memorial service.

What a surprise it was. Instead of a somber gathering, it was a noisy party. A celebration of life with laughing, chatting guests, Big Band music, and a catered buffet.

A young woman approached me, and we shook hands.

"Hello. I'm Sharon, Ted's granddaughter."

"I'm Michelle Mills."

Her eyes lit up.

"You're the lady that Grandpa met at Grandma's grave!"

Astonished, I nodded.

"He told us how you met. That he was feeling blue, and a new friend appeared."

"I felt the same way," I said. "I wish we'd had more time to know one another."

"You would have loved him. He was so kind; he'd give you the shirt off his back. In World War II, the plane he was piloting was shot down, and everyone on board was taken prisoner. The men were practically starving, yet Grandpa shared his little bit of food with the others. Said they needed it more than he did. He was skin and bones when he came home. Later, Grandpa and Grandma took Mom and me in after Daddy died in Vietnam. Grandpa practically raised me."

"A hero in every way," I murmured.

The memory board was filled with photos of Ted in uniform, Margie with the twins, graduations, weddings and birthdays. Ted's awards and medals, including a Purple Heart, were on display. His was a full life.

"After the war, Grandpa became an engineer and eventually worked for NASA. He went from airplanes to rockets."

Plain ol' Ted was anything but plain.

On the drive home, I remembered his words.

"It was tough. There were many days when grief got the better of me. But I pushed through the pain and got on with it."

Over time, as my heart healed, a parade of broken hearts found me. Like I found Ted.

It was humbling to share what I learned with those whose grief was fresh. Friends new and current who desperately needed hope, as I once did.

As Ted would say, "Everything happens for a reason."

— Michelle Close Mills —

76

The Hug

There are memories that time does not erase... Forever does not make loss forgettable, only bearable.
~Cassandra Clare, City of Heavenly Fire

Twenty years ago, my daughter's seventh grade class was learning about the Holocaust. A fellow student relayed that her grandfather had lived through those years, so their teacher invited him to speak to the class. I was lucky enough to volunteer that day.

The nervous eighty-eight-year-old gentleman arrived in his best suit and explained to the class of anxious twelve-year-olds about his childhood in war-torn Germany. He shared that this was the first time he'd spoken about that life.

He said he loved sports, and his loving family had lived a life similar to those of the children seated before him prior to the war. He and his family had done nothing wrong but were sent to the camps because they were Jews. He never saw any members of his family after that. He was alone, a preteen.

His words faltered as he described what was left of him after the war. He explained that he staggered out of the death camp stunned and starved. A compassionate stranger found him collapsed on the side of the road and took him home. She helped him relocate to the United States to be with distant relatives he'd never met.

After displaying the deep grief hidden in his buried memories, he stood quietly to the side of the classroom. The shell-shocked children were frozen in their chairs, changed forever by this story about a boy the same age as they were.

I walked over to the man and held out my arms. He blankly looked up and, without a word, stumbled into the safety of my embrace. He clung to me, exhausted, motionless.

I waited until he was able to catch his breath. Then, he slowly walked off hand in hand with his granddaughter.

—Mary Ellen Angelscribe—

Finding New Purpose

77

Before & After

It's when we start working together
that the real healing takes place.
~David Hume

I t was a hot Georgia Sunday, and I was late for church. We were meeting friends for lunch afterward, and I was in my closet obsessing over shoes.

Shoes.

I think back about that now and cringe at how ridiculous it sounds. Before that lunch was over, I would get the phone call that would forever divide my life into "before" and "after."

That Sunday, I lost my son, daughter-in-law and two-year-old grandson.

My world came apart at the seams.

Before and after. Before: I obsessed over shoes. After: I didn't know or care if I even had shoes. Nothing that came before prepared me for what was to come after.

I had read of the Kübler-Ross five stages of grief, but there seemed to be no stage that described "this." I did not remember "numb" being on that list. I was numb. I couldn't distinguish words. Food tasted like paper. I couldn't focus. I couldn't understand or think or even make simple decisions. I couldn't cry. I had never imagined pain so deep and intense that, although I was screaming on the inside, I could not cry. I felt like the walking dead, and I remember thinking that "numb" seemed awful, weird and unnerving. However, when numb wore off, I certainly realized its benefits. I cried; I prayed; I retreated to the bottom of my closet. I screamed; I raged; I threw things until I collapsed in exhaustion.

I was sure there was no way I could live through it, but against my better judgment, I just kept waking up. So, if I wasn't going to die, I'd have to find a way to live. I could not imagine that anything could help, but I searched for anything that might. I signed up for GriefShare, a thirteen-week program sponsored by a church. It was a group-therapy class that went through a workbook and videos of what to expect, what helps, and what doesn't. I started a blog to help me process. I got in touch with Stephen Ministries, had a peer counselor assigned to me, and poured my heart out to her for a year. I read absolutely everything I could get my hands on, praying that I'd find some magic answer in someone else's story.

Everything helped a little, but nothing helped for long.

One day, my boss called me in her office and asked if I could do a favor for her. She went to church with a young couple who had lost their twenty-one-year-old son, and they were struggling to survive it. She knew that only another mother could know that loss, and she asked if I thought I could talk with this couple.

"I know it is a lot to ask of you, but they have no one to talk to they feel can understand their loss. If you don't think it is something you can do right now, I'll understand. Just give it some thought, will you?"

"Bev, I truly cannot imagine how I can be of any help to anyone. But if just listening and letting them talk can help them in any way, how can I say no?"

The couple was my daughter's age, so, other than the tremendous loss of a child, we had very little in common. But my husband and I met with them, and what was to be a one-time, one-hour meeting at Chick-fil-A turned into six months of three-hour visits every other week. Talking with them about their loss, sympathizing, empathizing, letting them speak their son's name and tell us about his talents and interests not only helped them but, somehow, miraculously, helped us, too. Feeling their pain made me feel something for someone else again. I realized what my boss had obviously known — that talking with someone who knew the loss of a child might also help me. Though I could not imagine that I had anything worthwhile to offer them, it turns out I did.

I could suggest GriefShare and tell them about what I had learned there. I could pass on the benefits of journaling to help them process the pain. I could let them know which books helped and which to skip and share some of what I had learned from just living in it.

I could tell them to talk about their son even when it made other people uncomfortable. I could tell them that the five stages of grief were inadequate. There were so many more, and those five did not come like a one-and-done checklist. I could tell them that there was no timeline for getting better; grief does not follow a neat, organized schedule. It comes, it goes, it comes back at the most inopportune times — and that's normal. I could tell them that when other people say, "You should be better by now," what they mean is, "I want you to get over this and be yourself again." I could tell them there was no right way to do grief, and it lasts as long as it takes. And, to some degree, it takes forever.

Shortly after my regular visits with that couple ended, my banker lost her thirty-year-old son, and she called. This time around, I didn't wonder if I could say anything helpful. I let her talk. I asked about her son. I told her about mine.

Then, a lady at my sister's church lost her daughter, and my sister asked if she could call me.

I never planned it; it just kind of happened.

I have now been an informal grief friend to many others who have had a great loss, including my best friend of sixty years when she lost her son to cancer. I have driven 200 miles one way to sit with another close friend's daughter in a hospice as we both said goodbye to her mom. And when my neighbor was dying of cancer, I read to her, helped her write letters to her family and gave her a manicure.

Today, after almost seven years, I no longer wonder how I will go forward. For my own selfish reasons, I make myself and my experience available to those in need. It isn't world-changing stuff. I volunteer as a companion for patients in hospice and as respite care for their family. I collect clothes, shoes, coats and blankets for a local homeless ministry. I take meals to those I know who are sick or recovering from surgery. I do it because I need to. It helps others, but mostly it helps me. It gives me something constructive to focus on. It reminds me that I am not alone in my suffering, and it makes me grateful for what I still have. I've learned that giving to those in need has truly lit my path out of the darkness.

—Andrea Peebles—

78

The Memory Garden

Where flowers bloom so does hope.
~Lady Bird Johnson

With my weekly weeding complete, I stood up and dusted the dirt from my hands. Then I took a step back and surveyed the square of earth at the corner of my house. That little patch of flowers had really shaped up nicely, with its array of shapes, scents, textures and colors. How different that small plot looked now, I mused. How different everything was now.

The time prior to planting that garden still seemed surreal. During the almost two-year period I put my life on hold to care for my ailing, aged dad in his home, I lost my only sibling to cancer as well as two dear friends — one way too young to suicide and a close business associate — and two beloved pets. When Dad passed away, it was game over. In the weeks following his memorial service, I was so emotionally raw that I couldn't sleep or eat. Thoughts of cleaning out his home set my entire body to shaking. The smallest noise made me jump. I could barely get through the day, never mind navigate the complications of executing an estate.

Somehow, though, I summoned the fortitude to plod through, although it was difficult beyond words. While I hoped time would heal my wounds, I still found myself months later in the vise of indescribable grief. Day after day, I asked myself not when but *if* I would ever feel happy again. In my emotional condition, I would have been grateful to just not feel miserable all the time.

One day, as I walked through the front door into my home's sunporch, I once again bumped into the two boxes of photos and assorted mementos I had saved from Dad's home. I hadn't had the heart or energy to sort through them. So, I finally moved them into my storage attic until better days. Those boxes had blocked a small table on which I had placed a dish garden sent to me by a friend after Dad's passing. The beautiful, Delft-style planter had held hyacinths, tulips and a regal white lily. Now all that remained were a few dried leaves.

My friend's gesture had truly touched me. Called to a long-term work assignment halfway around the globe, this dear person had somehow learned of Dad's passing and was kind enough to extend her sympathy in this way. I couldn't part with her gift. So, though spring was almost over and the heat of summer threatened, I took the planter outside. Armed with a hand trowel, I sifted through its dirt until I located the bulbs. A quick scan of the yard revealed only one place available for planting — a dusty patch at the house's corner. Could anything grow there? The odd spot barely got sun. It appeared so dismal that I felt this piece of earth stood like a metaphor for the place I found myself in now: dark, forlorn and hopeless.

Yet, something deep inside me made me work the soil that day, dig those bulbs into the ground, and create the beginnings of what I named my "memory garden." Day by day, I watered it and checked for signs of growth. And something inside me began to stir. While I wouldn't say the process brought back my joy straight away, it did rekindle a sense of purpose. It gave me the motivation to get out of bed early each morning, lace up my sneakers and walk out the back door to check my patch. And it gave me back the belief that, in the wake of so much tragedy, it was possible that something good could still happen.

Something good *did* happen. A few weeks later, in that sad, dusty, shadowy part of my garden, those bulbs pushed through the dirt and flowered. And in the sad, dusty, shadowy part of myself, a little joy returned. In fact, enough joy returned to further motivate me to expand my memory garden to include flowers for the other loved ones I had lost. For my mother, who had passed several years earlier, I planted lily-of-the-valley flowers, which she had carried on her wedding day. For my brother, I planted an iris in his favorite color: blue. For the friend who took his own life, I planted a yellow rose.

That little space became my sanctuary. I went to that corner often — winter, spring, summer or fall — whether the flowers were in bloom above ground or whether nature was working her magic in the dormant soil beneath the ground. I remembered the folks I loved. I remembered their smiles and laughter, their kindness and the love they showed to me while they walked the Earth. And I remembered that even in the darkest, driest, most seemingly hopeless of places, joy can still return. And, when it does, beautiful things can bloom once more.

— Monica A. Andermann —

79

Shocked into Silence

Part of the healing process is sharing
with other people who care.
~Jerry Cantrell

I'm not sure I comprehended the term "shocked into silence" until my friend Cori died. I was speechless.

She had revealed her health issues, but she was getting the best care and was making concessions — albeit minor — with her vigorous sports life. She played a mean game of golf, as well as tennis, all over the world.

Cori was a tall, slim, gracious woman. Her striking blond looks complemented her impeccable dress, and she was as beautiful inside as she was outside. She shared her warmth and wisdom with her family and friends, and we loved her for it. She died at age seventy-two.

We'd bonded almost forty years earlier in a women's volunteer group and moved onto many community activities together. We co-hosted, co-edited, co-analyzed, co-sponsored, co-presidented and, at the bridge table, co-conspired. We formed a writing group, dinner group, and book group. We traveled together.

I felt a hole in my heart when my first good friend died. I envisioned her around the corner, wondered if we should drive together to an event, and wanted to talk things over with her. I was frightened that the pattern was beginning to evolve where I would lose friends. I had built those friendships for a lifetime and expected to keep them.

But I couldn't.

What caught me by surprise was the loneliness I felt when Cori passed. I appreciated friends who called or e-mailed with condolences because that gave me validation to grieve, but grief is personal and relentless. I needed to reach the core of that loneliness, to share more deeply.

Then I got a call from Cori's husband. It helped me to share with someone who was at the core of his pain. I will always be grateful to him for reaching beyond his own grief and allowing me in.

After his call, I was able to kick my immobilized self into gear. I called people to inform them of Cori's death. Talking with our friends helped my loss some, but it was still more than I could handle. That's when I decided to write about my memories of Cori. Writing helped package our friendship into an attractive box that I could revisit when I needed to process her death in layers.

I used some of what I had written when Cori's husband asked me to give a speech at the memorial. I was honored to participate in this remembrance.

My writing led me to suggest to our friends that they might want to write, too. I gathered their thoughts, rounded up pictures and put them into a book for the family. I knew they would receive many more cards and condolences, so I left blank pages in the book. It was a gift both to Cori's family and to myself because I could do something concrete to honor her.

Other people came up with healing ideas, too. One of our writing group members suggested that we share our written remembrances of Cori with each other, and it was immensely therapeutic.

Cori's family was incredible in suggestions for recovery. They started a meal train where friends signed up to have Cori's husband over for dinner. The meals spread over several months, and the sign-up sheet filled quickly. They also asked friends for recipes accompanied by pictures. Cori had authored a successful cookbook, and her family wanted to print a sequel. Many recipes poured in — her own recipes she had shared with us or simply recipes we enjoyed when gathering with her. The sequel will be a moving tribute to Cori.

Their best idea was what they called "Cori's Keepsake Closet."

They invited close friends to the home to choose something from Cori's closet that would be a fond remembrance. We went, we hugged, we laughed, and we savored some of Cori's favorite recipes. Cori's husband joined us.

Cori and her husband shared a generosity of spirit, and that generosity is helping their friends recover. Grief takes a long time to process. It runs its own course, and I will always be grateful to Cori's family for inviting us into their hearts.

— Marcia McGreevy Lewis —

A Source of Comfort

When our heart is open everything
we do becomes love.
~Mimi Novic

When my son died after a long and terrible illness, I said kaddish for him. That's the daily Jewish memorial prayer recited in honor of a loved one in the presence of a minyan — ten or more adult Jews assembled in one place. I made it my business to get up every morning, dress, and drive to my synagogue for services, sometimes as early as 6:30 A.M.

The routine grounded me and helped put structure back into my disordered life. It helped me believe I was still in control of something when all manner of control had been taken from me. When the eleven-month mourning period was over, I felt adrift, aimless and without purpose. The comfort that honoring my son and my tradition had brought was now over.

I threw myself into my closets and drawers with a vengeance. I cleaned my apartment as though my life depended on it. I read. I talked to friends. I became an Amazon shopping addict. Of course, I needed more socks and an air fryer! An arsenal of potions to plump up my lips. A device to slim my thighs.

There had to be something more than mindless reflex buying. Something constructive and positive I could put into my life. Couldn't I help someone? Do something for someone, instead of filling my time and my cupboards with things I didn't need?

Call it happenstance. Call it fate. Call it meant-to-be. But soon after that thought occurred to me, I read an article about Queens Community House, an agency that offered programs and services to citizens in need. They were looking for phone friends — people willing to commit to an hour every week for six months to call an elderly shut-in.

I wondered who the agency would pair me with. Would we hit it off? Would I find things to talk about? An hour a week with someone I didn't even know? Would calling become a chore, a decision I would regret and do out of obligation instead of wholehearted intent?

Stop overthinking! I told myself. *Get off your bum — and Amazon — and fill out the application. Give them the references they want. Be useful for a change!*

Months passed. Had my application, references and the results of interviews gone astray? In a way, I hoped they had. Still having second thoughts about the commitment, I was almost relieved. And then they called. They had found a match for me. I couldn't opt out now.

They paired me with Sara. In her nineties, Sara has a pulmonary problem and sometimes finds it difficult to breathe. But not to talk. In the few months I've known her, she's told me about her family, her regrets, and how lonely she often feels. "I talk to the walls," she has told me more than once.

When I filled her in about some of my interests, she said I was probably too busy for her. I didn't have to call every week. But I do have to call. To experience that delighted "Hi!" that puts a high note into my day.

"I enjoy talking to you. I like to help people."

"A-ha!" she said. "I knew you had to get something out of this."

Sara may have a lung ailment, but there's nothing ailing her brain.

For some reason, I'm my kindest, most attentive self with Sara. She has taught me to listen rather than fill a pause with the sound of my own chatter. Normally all mouth, I've become all ears, waiting for the right words to come to her.

To contribute to my community, to feel good about myself, a sense of obligation to give — these are all wrapped up in my volunteering. Yet, I sometimes wonder why this one-on-one with Sara has given me so much.

Can a ninety-something stranger take the place of a sixty-year-old son? Not in a million years. But stepping outside my own life into Sara's has somehow filled part of that space my son once occupied. Those conversations we had, the bond we formed before he passed. How essential to his wellbeing I had become. Maybe Sara is putting some of that back.

My faith and heritage led the way to comfort not only me but, it turned out, a stranger as well.

— Rita Plush —

81

The Only Way to Find It

A kind gesture can reach a wound
that only compassion can heal.
~Steve Maraboli

One gloomy December day, I got a phone call from my mom. "Grandma had a heart attack. She is unconscious, and the ambulance is on the way," she said.

I rushed back to Grandma's house. She and I had gotten in a huge argument about an hour earlier. She had laid down for a nap and I had left for some shopping therapy.

Though very loving, Grandma had a fiery temper, which I inherited from her. After the argument, I apologized and tried to hug and make up, but she refused. I don't know why this happened.

As I walked into the ER, where she lay lifeless, I felt as if I had broken her heart in that unfortunate exchange of words that morning.

After her death, I felt guilty for a long time. Most of all, though, I was lost in the huge void her loss left. I had grown very close to Grandma DuBose after becoming one of her primary caregivers in the last few years. I worked for the family newspaper business, but most of the time I was on Grandma Duty. Between me, my mom and Aunt Faye, Grandma was able to live out her life at home where she wanted to be. She needed a lot of care and attention, though, and it wasn't easy.

I was needed at midnight to help Grandma in the bathroom, in the mornings to put on her shoes and socks, and at nighttime to help her put on pajamas. I was needed every time she got really upset because nobody could cheer up Grandma like her granddaughter.

What she needed most, though, was the gift of our time. So, for over two years, my mission in life was to make sure Grandma had some fun, no matter how frail or sick she was. Grandma was alone a lot during the day, but I went over at night as often as I could. And on the nights when she called for help, I usually stayed over. We played thousands of rounds of cards and had many long, late-night talks, which brought her much joy. What I didn't realize is how much joy it brought me to be that light or how close we had truly become

I was also a young wife and mother. But after the baby was asleep, I would kiss my husband goodbye and go to Grandma's house. As I walked in and sat by her on the couch, she'd reach over and rub my back gently. "I've been waiting for you," she'd say, and we'd go to the kitchen for some midnight cards and conversation. As I tucked her in at night, she would often say, "You're my daughter, not my grand-daughter. You are my best friend."

I may have been her caretaker, and she may have had a little dementia, but she never forgot how to dote on me or spoil me just like she always had.

When we lost her, I didn't know what to do with myself. There were no more frantic calls for help at midnight, 6:00 A.M., or ever. There was no one sitting there on the couch waiting to play a hand of cards. I went from being on-call twenty-four hours a day to feeling like I wasn't needed at all. I cried myself to sleep many times, thinking about the stupid argument we had right before her heart attack.

One night, I was sitting around the campfire with my dad, who was playing guitar. He saw the hurt in my eyes, and he set down his guitar and said, "You know, the only way to find true joy is by helping others — by bringing joy to someone else."

That made more sense to me than anything I had ever heard. It was exactly what I needed. I missed *helping*.

But what meaningful thing could I do to help others? I thought about Grandma and the stories she had told me about growing up "an orphan." I also thought about her love for celebrating Christmas together as a family, and how she made it magical for everyone around her. She always went overboard on the magical part because she knew what it was like to be alone and not have a magical Christmas.

As we sat at her kitchen table talking, Grandma would often say, "I can't believe how my life ended up. I started out my life all alone, and now we have four kids, fourteen grandchildren, eleven great-grandchildren, and two great-great-grandchildren."

She marveled at that, and those words echoed in my head, especially now.

About a week after that conversation around the campfire, I had the perfect idea. My mom and I decided to host a gift drive for local foster children. Now, we do it every year in Grandma's honor, and we place a note with Grandma's story inside each gift bag. It is our sincerest hope that these kids realize that while they may be alone today, they may be surrounded by the love of a giant family someday, too.

Taking the opportunity to help others in Grandma's honor has healed my heart like nothing else could. I was deeply grieving the loss of Grandma because we loved each other so much, and now I share that love with children who are walking in the same shoes she once did.

— Kayleen Kitty Holder —

82

Am I Still His Mother?

Because I feel that, in the Heavens above,
the angels, whispering to one another,
can find, among their burning terms of love,
none so devotional as that of "Mother."
~Edgar Allen Poe

When my fourteen-year-old son, Andy, was killed by a drunk driver on the street in front of our house, I reacted like any mother with a broken heart. I sobbed every day. I woke every morning praying it had been a nightmare and expecting him to come into my room to tell me he was leaving for school as he always did. But he didn't, and he never would again.

Leaving for school. That was only one of the ordinary, everyday things that I took for granted while he was here, in my home, at my dinner table, watching television with the rest of the family, or playing football in the yard with his friends. He was now missing from all these simple activities. Just gone.

He was somewhere else, I prayed, a place where he was happy and at peace. Somewhere that, even if he could, he would not want to leave. He would not come home. He would never need the things he needed from me again. He didn't need me to take care of him. It was too late.

Was I still his mother? I wondered.

I no longer took him to school when he missed the school bus. I didn't take him to the store with me to cash in the empty bottles while

I shopped. I couldn't shop with him for school clothes, or bake him a birthday cake, or wash his dirty, stinky sports uniforms. I would never go to another lacrosse game to cheer him on, see him in his football uniform, or watch him go off to high school, drive a car, or go to a dance. Those things were only the beginning of a long list of lost duties that a mother cherishes. I would never again be required to do what a mother does for her child.

So, was I still his mother?

After that, when people asked how many children I had, I said two instead of three. When we took a family photo, there was a blank space where he was missing. When we traveled on our annual vacation to the Adirondack Mountains, there was no one to keep track of how many deer we saw or to kayak around the point where we camped. Without him, sometimes it was just his father and me because our older children were working at their summer jobs. There was no boy there with us, no Andy, no son.

Was I still his mother?

Eventually, I was asked to volunteer for our local Mothers Against Drunk Driving chapter. I wanted to stop this awful crime that has taken the lives of so many victims who were the sons, daughters, fathers, mothers, and loved ones of those left behind. I found the volunteer work fulfilling and threw myself into it. We organized displays at local malls and civic centers. We invited speakers such as judges and lawmakers to talk about our state's need to crack down on drunk-driving offenses. Eventually, our work began to show results. The man who killed Andy was only convicted of a misdemeanor, even though his level of blood alcohol was three times today's legal limit. In part, because of MADD's work, his offense would be classified as a felony under today's laws.

I was asked to speak regularly to a large group of DWI offenders who had been arrested in our county each month. I told them my story, about Andy, about the agony of losing the boy who had been my baby, and the loss of my sense of security and faith. Sometimes, I could see I got through to some, and I was optimistic they would not offend again. It was gratifying, but it didn't bring him back.

I spoke at schools to young audiences, hoping at least some of what I was saying would be remembered and influence their future choices. I spoke wherever I was asked because I wanted to tell Andy's story. I wanted to make the point that drunk-driving crashes were not *accidents*; they were *choices* that caused tragedies.

I attended tree plantings in Andy's memory. I watched as his name was lettered on a park bench on the ball diamond where he played Little League. My husband and I planted a memorial garden that can be seen from the street as a remembrance of the boy who lost his life there. I wrote columns in the local newspapers addressing the awful consequences of drunk driving. I did everything I could to try to make a difference.

I was contacted by Andy's kidney recipient, a young woman who got her life back because of his gift. I decided to donate his organs when he died because I knew that's what he would have wanted. She became a good friend, and we talked about Andy often and fondly, even though she had never met him.

Again, I asked myself the recurring, agonizing question: Am I still his mother?

There are so many "motherly" things I cannot do, and the agony of my heartbreak will never leave me. I had a mother's love for the baby boy to whom I gave birth but nowhere to put it, so I channeled it into activities that would ensure he was remembered.

The question remained: Am I still his mother?

It's true I can no longer buy his school clothes, wash his clothes, or teach him to drive. I will miss him and hold him in my heart until my own death, and my life will never be the same. But I have learned there are things that I can still do for Andy. I can act in his memory. I can tell his story to DWI offenders and young men and women who will one day make their own choices about driving drunk. Most of all, I can keep him alive in my own memories of the blessing his life was. Only a mother could do that.

So, am I still his mother?

Yes, I am.

— Luanne Tovey —

83

An Unexpected Day of Feasting

*Remember that the happiest people are not those
getting more, but those giving more.*
~H. Jackson Brown, Jr.

The man and woman in front of me were irritated. "You mean we drove all the way down here for nothing?" they asked in exasperation.

It was my first Thanksgiving as a widow and my first Thanksgiving not surrounded by family (unless you count my grand-dog). I was in the volunteer check-in line for the annual holiday dinner hosted by The Salvation Army. Apparently, there was a glitch in the computer system, and the couple who thought they were registered as volunteers weren't. They were told that the positions were already filled, but if they came back at noon, maybe they could help with clean-up. The Volunteer Coordinator was apologetic as the annoyed couple turned away.

When it was my turn, I admitted I was one of the registered-but-not-registered volunteers because I also didn't receive online confirmation. But I'm good at clean-up, I told her, and my husband died of cancer, and I'm visiting from Oregon, and I'm all alone, and I used to put on events at the cancer center where I was on staff, and I understand computer glitches in registration systems, and I'm sorry she has to face rude people like the couple who just left...

And then I came up for air, fully expecting to be told to come back in three hours.

"Would you like to serve coffee to the people in line?" asked the coordinator.

"Seriously?" I responded in disbelief. "You would let me do that?"

"Yeah, because you were nice."

And that's how I got to serve coffee and bottled water to a line of people that eventually snaked across the large parking lot, around the corner, and down the sidewalk as guests arrived long before the doors were scheduled to open for the turkey dinner.

The organization is incredible. Volunteers are given name tags along with their assignments. There were greeters and seaters. Beverage pourers. Servers and pumpkin-pie embellishers. The cooks had arrived at 4:00 A.M., and the clean-up crew would be there deep into the afternoon.

Tables had been decorated and set up in the main dining hall, the entryway, on the back porch, and in a covered patio area where there were craft projects for children as they waited for the holiday feast. When folks got up to leave after eating their fill, the tables were cleaned and new guests sat down. On the way out, everyone was encouraged to shop for Christmas gifts in an improvised toy-and-book store. For free. This Salvation Army team really knew how to throw a dinner party.

At the end of the day, I was exhausted. But it was a crazy-good kind of exhaustion. I was humbled by the hundreds of people who were attended to that day. Those with homes in poor neighborhoods and the homeless. Those with minimum-wage jobs and the jobless. Those who hadn't bathed in a while and entire families with sparkling children. American-born and immigrants. The addicted, the discarded, the mentally unstable. Most of them in a hard spot, but all of them beautiful people.

And I — alone in town with no family, having lost my husband and financial cushion against retirement — was given an unexpected gift of grace. I was compelled to look away from my own lack to the larger needs and sufferings of these people. It was a startling gift to be the smiling, friendly coffee server and water distributor on this warm and sunny Thanksgiving Day in a land called Arizona.

Earlier that morning, my daughter had texted from New Jersey: "I hope you have an unexpectedly fun day today." Thanksgiving that year will go down as one of the most unexpectedly fun days ever.

I found a healthy way of managing my loss, sorrow and loneliness. Although I didn't eat the food or drink the beverages, it was an unanticipated day of feasting. On this first Thanksgiving in which I was not surrounded by family, I was surrounded by family.

— Marlys Johnson Lawry —

84

The House

Every time your heart is broken, a doorway
cracks open to a world full of new beginnings,
new opportunities.
~Patti Roberts

Wallowing in sadness is a terrible place to live. That's where I found myself residing after the untimely death of my beloved mother, who also happened to be my best friend. For the first time in my life, I had to exist in a world without her.

My mom had admirable strength and an unrelenting passion for everything she did, along with a wicked sense of humor and spot-on intelligence. Those qualities remained intact, even as the disease took away her hope, little by little, day by day. She was the glue that kept the whole family involved in each other's busy lives. She'd say — not in a gossipy way but in an informatively considerate way — "Your cousin found her lost dog" or "Your sister finally got that promotion!" She kept us connected and involved. Mom wanted to share the good stuff, while also being everyone's closest confidante.

Without our matriarch, I realized keeping our family together fell on my weary shoulders, though her loss had robbed me of my strength. My husband and adult children rallied around me, yet nothing seemed to help. I barely noticed the efforts of well-meaning friends.

I got into my bed and decided not to leave it. For weeks on end, I slept.

Then, one morning, my two stubborn friends decided to coax me out of my dark house by insisting I join them for a "quick" bike ride. I resisted vehemently, but I knew they would not leave until I agreed, so I slowly got dressed.

Admittedly, it felt nice having the sunshine hit my face and the fresh air tickle my skin. For the first time in weeks, I was outdoors.

We rode through all the familiar neighborhoods that morning, not talking about the "elephant in the room." No mom, no cancer, no grief.

Eventually, we biked down one quiet, little street that was new to me. It led to the bay and was lined with an eclectic mix of older, small, cottage-style homes and tall, majestic palm trees.

And that's when I saw the "For Sale" sign hanging from a post in front of an adorable, weathered porch.

It was as if she was sitting there waiting just for me. "She" was the most adorable 1920s cottage, equipped with a front porch swing, wind chimes and swaying fruit trees with the bay breeze wistfully helping me forget the dark house I'd just left. It was love at first sight.

My bike came to a screeching halt as I speed-dialed the Realtor.

"I'll take it," I heard myself say out loud. The Realtor didn't even question me, and I didn't question myself. My friends looked at each other in utter shock.

I instinctively knew that I needed that cottage, and that she needed me somehow, as well.

Just like me, there she sat in a state of disrepair and neglect, desperately needing love and care.

Miraculously, I came up with enough money to purchase the little house. I'll never know how it all came together in a matter of mere weeks.

My husband, my dad, my two daughters, and I soon found ourselves immersed in repairing and rehabbing this special house as a family. Nights, weekends and the time we would have otherwise spent wallowing in grief were spent spackling, scrubbing and painting.

But, sometimes, in the quiet of the evenings, I would sit on her front porch swing alone, once again in darkness, weeping and missing my mom.

I questioned how my mom could be taken so young when this 1920s cottage still sat, after having survived hurricanes, termites, floods, and utter neglect.

But time marched onward, and the house remained.

The focus we poured into restoring my cottage slowly healed our broken hearts. It kept our hands and heads busy, and our days had a new purpose.

Very subtly, I noticed my grief had lifted just a bit. As gentle as the swaying trees and the bay's breeze, my grief became replaced with excitement and purpose.

By the time we finished, my cottage's exterior was the pride of the neighborhood.

I painted her shutters a beautiful, nautical navy blue and added hanging ferns to her porch. Neighbors and passersby would stop just to comment on her transformation.

I chuckled to myself. Just as I applied lipstick for the first time in months, my cottage also became a painted lady. She was finally ready to invite people inside.

That fall, my cottage and I hosted countless small gatherings with family and friends alike. We would sit under the huge, forty-year-old mango tree in the yard and eat, enjoying the breeze, laughing and playing cornhole. Our extended family also reconnected under that tree, frequently telling stories about my mom and her many antics.

As Thanksgiving approached, we knew it was probably time to sell her. I needed to let go of that precious cottage and allow my grief to go with her.

After a few short days on the market, a darling young couple loved the cottage as much as I did. It was hard, but I knew giving her up was as much a cure for my broken heart as it was in acquiring her. If I kept her, she would be a constant reminder of the grief I felt the first day I saw her. Neither of us was the same; we had both morphed into healthier, improved versions of ourselves. It was a hard goodbye.

It took a year before I could bear to bike past her again. When I did, there she was. The majestic queen palms swished quietly and gently in the breeze as the front-porch swing moved in rhythm, and the wind chimes melodically sang along. Other than the nautical blue shutters and the big, beautiful ferns, her exterior was unchanged. She appeared to be the same old house that she always was. But I knew the truth: She was better than before on the inside, and so was I.

— Kim Johnson —

85

Dancing Back to Life

Every day brings a chance for you to draw in a breath,
kick off your shoes, and dance.
~Oprah Winfrey

"I'll be fine," I told my children after Jim's funeral. We had just buried my forty-three-year-old son's ashes in the back yard and said our goodbyes to him. I had never lost a child before, and I was devastated.

Jim had come to live with me three years earlier when he became bedridden after twenty years of declining health. He had everything to live for after college, but instead faced a series of serious health problems and later became crippled. The doctors hadn't correctly diagnosed his condition, so he struggled for years. When a thorough study was finally completed, they found that his body — and later his mind — had gradually deteriorated from multiple sclerosis. Somehow, he had managed to live on his own for years. But when that became impossible, he came to live with me.

At first, it was a big adjustment to have Jim back at home after my recent retirement, but we gradually found our new routine, and I loved having him with me. We didn't talk about his illness, but I prayed for a cure every day, researched medical journals, and never gave up. It was a sad day when he had to be transported to a nursing facility for increased care. Jim spent two weeks in hospice and then quietly passed away, surrounded by our family.

The reality and enormity of the loss of my beloved son immediately set in when I returned home to see Jim's empty bed. A few days later, the siblings returned to their homes, and I made a rash decision to sell my house, hoping to escape the memories. However, they followed me. My daughter Julie arranged my move to an apartment near my former home, and days and weeks slipped by as I grieved there alone. The children called to see how I was, and I always answered, "Fine." But I wasn't fine. A deep depression kept me in bed most days and nights, and I didn't even unpack from my move. I was just existing. No one knew how sick I was until I ventured out one day, hoping it would be my last.

I just wanted to end the pain. My confusion and hopelessness caused me to step off the curb at a busy intersection, heading into traffic. Suddenly, when I did, something stopped me, and I became frozen. I know now it was God protecting me, compelling me to step back. I did, and it was like waking up from a bad dream. At that moment, I knew I needed help.

Without hesitation, I called my daughter Diana who worked nearby, and she came immediately to take me to her doctor. Before the day ended, I had seen a therapist, was prescribed medication, and scheduled future appointments. Slowly, as I began to heal and grow stronger, I knew I needed to do something to reconnect with people and start my new life.

That's what sent me to a nearby senior center one afternoon — to look for a group to join. The art class had paintings that looked like masterpieces on the wall, and the members were working hard. Not for me. I couldn't draw. Watching the sewing group intimidated me as well. They were making blouses, and I didn't even know how to shorten a hem. Next, I observed the bridge group; they were so somber and serious. I was just looking for fun and friendship. Could I fit in anywhere?

Then, just as I was about to leave, a group of friendly-looking women walked over, and one of them asked, "Can you tap dance?"

I almost laughed out loud. "I'm sorry, but I don't have any dancing skills."

"That's okay," one of the women responded. "It doesn't matter.

It's fun."

One by one, members of the group introduced themselves, assuring me they would help. After chatting with them and feeling so welcome, I decided to join their group, The Spotliters, which performed at luncheons for The Women's Club and local events. Practice was three times a week, and they gave me a CD of the music, along with written directions to follow at home. I felt so much better having something to do and making some new friends, too.

At the time, I had no idea how this decision to join The Spotliters would impact that difficult loss and also have a ripple effect on the rest of my life. This new focus helped me through the grieving process. In many ways, I danced my way back to life. What started as joining one group expanded to others, and for the past twenty years I have been leading my own volunteer entertainment group that brings joy to retirement communities all over town.

But the best part is that, in the process, I became known as "Dancing Grammie." At ninety-two, I'm still tapping away—and I know Jim is cheering me on from heaven.

— Queen Lori —

Love That Doesn't Die

86

My January Gardenia

*Mother, you left us beautiful memories, your love
is still our guide, although we cannot see you,
you're always at our side.*
~Author Unknown

My mother died on April 27 after a short illness. I was wracked with grief and guilt because I missed being with her at the time of her death by fifteen minutes.

While she was still conscious, I'd promised her that my siblings and I would take care of Dad. I'd also promised I'd be at her bedside when she passed. It turns out that I could not be in two places at one time. My dad was only six weeks post-op from having open-heart surgery, and he had been at her bedside for hours. He was exhausted and needed to go home. One of my sisters and I were tasked with getting Dad home and to bed. My other two sisters stayed all night at the hospital with Mom. They were with her when she took her final breaths.

As the only nurse in the family, I couldn't forget the promise I had made to Mom to be at her side when she died. Looking back, I believe my grief lasted longer because of my feelings of guilt.

Nine months later, my husband was outside working in the yard on a cold, sunny January day. The doorbell rang. I answered the front door to find George standing there. "Get your fleece on and come outside. Your mother is here."

I stood there in shock. What did he mean? He beckoned. I grabbed my fleece and threw it on as I followed him off the porch and down the front steps. We walked around the corner to one of my gardenia bushes at the sunny corner of the garage. There, in the middle of the glossy green leaves was a perfect gardenia in full bloom. This was nothing short of a miracle because all six of my gardenias bloom only once a year — in May. I raced to the back of the house to look at the other three plants growing there. Not a hint of a bloom, just like the ones in the front — except for the single, perfect white flower.

"My mother *is* here," I gasped. "She loved gardenias. She carried gardenias on her wedding day. This is a message from Mom."

George put his arm around my shoulders. "I think she's trying to tell you something. What do you think it is?" he asked gently.

"That I should stop feeling so guilty?" I said as my lip quivered.

He nodded. "You did everything you could for both your parents. It's time to let it go."

I knew he was right. There was no doubt in my mind. I stood staring at the beautiful blossom in the brilliant January sunshine. I took pictures of it to remind me of the day. Finally, I walked back into the house.

I felt as if a burden had been lifted from my heart. The gardenia blossom was a gift from Mom to me, a reminder to forgive myself and a demonstration that her love for me will never die.

— Nancy Emmick Panko —

87

Special Delivery

Love recognizes no barriers. It jumps hurdles,
leaps fences, penetrates walls to arrive
at its destination full of hope.
~Maya Angelou

I was in the grocery store's greeting-card aisle looking for a thank-you card for my neighbor. Janice had been so helpful during the Christmas holidays. She had taken me shopping, baked, and helped me in any way she could. With her support, I had gotten through those days that were supposed to be so jolly and fun.

It had been my first Christmas without Clyde. We had celebrated our forty-ninth wedding anniversary while he was ill. There were many beautiful memories. One was Clyde's cards to me on special occasions. Sometimes, he gave me one "just because." Oh, how I missed those beautiful or funny cards. He always separated his name between the *y* and *d*. It made me sad to know I would never get another card signed *Cly de.*

I had gotten through his fight with leukemia and his funeral, but I was still grieving my loss months later. Now, standing in the middle of the aisle, I was surrounded by hundreds of cards.

The ones that really got me were those that said, "To my wife," "On our anniversary," and "Happy birthday, darling." I felt a tear roll down my cheek.

I was sixteen and Clyde was twenty when we married. Neither of our families spoke about their feelings, so we had much to learn about expressing sentiments. Greeting cards were a great way to communicate with each other. Clyde got cards for all the special holidays like Valentine's Day, Easter, and Mother's Day. He remembered my birthday and our anniversary. Sometimes, he gave me cards for no reason other than to say, "I love you." It brightened my day when I awoke in the morning to find a card on my pillow or on the coffeemaker.

A few weeks later, my friend Carolyn and I spent a day shopping at the flea markets and resale stores. She had recently lost her husband too, so this was a good way for each of us to forget our troubles for a while.

We spent the entire morning shopping. We didn't need anything, but we did find a few treasures. Excited and hungry, we went to lunch. At the restaurant, we had a delicious meal while talking about our bargains.

After lunch, rested and ready for more shopping, we were off again to see what we would find. As the day wore on, coming out of each store, we promised ourselves "just one more and then we'll go home."

Just before closing time, we went into a Goodwill Store. I headed for the bookshelves. Carolyn went in another direction. We had just come into the store when the voice on the loudspeaker blared out, "The store is closing for the day. Bring your purchases to the front." I had just picked up a book titled *Someone Cares* by Helen Steiner Rice. Having to rush to the checkout, I made a quick decision to purchase it.

Later at home, I picked up my new book. A bunch of cards fell into my lap from inside the book. Surprised, I began to read them. I couldn't find a name on the cards, and there were no envelopes. Most of the cards seemed to be for a mother, but there were also some that appeared to be from friends. I enjoyed reading all of them.

The last one said, "To My Wife on Mother's Day." The picture on the card was of two squirrels. The male squirrel said things like: "Sometimes, I feel like dressing up, and sometimes I don't." There were several other things that the male liked sometimes but not at other times. It ended with the boy squirrel telling the girl squirrel, "But I always love you."

The words and pictures on the card were similar to those on

cards Clyde had given me in the past. Looking down at the lower part of the card, I was shocked to see the signature. It read *Cly de* with a space in the middle between the *y* and *d* just like my husband always signed his name. At that moment, I knew Clyde's love would always be with me. There wouldn't be cards on my pillow or near the coffeemaker, but "Cly de" had found a way to send me one more card when I needed it most.

—Joyce R. Kebodeaux—

Friday the 13th

Deeply, I know this, that love triumphs over death.
My father continues to be loved,
and therefore he remains by my side.
~Jennifer Williamson

My father said it was just a superstition, but I'd always had terrible things happen on Friday the 13th. None were as bad as Friday, March 13, 1998, when my beloved father was electrocuted and killed in a tragic accident.

When I went through his belongings, the number thirteen kept popping up. He had thirteen of practically everything.

While driving his car, I stopped at the gas station. As my depressed mind wandered, I glanced up when the pump clicked off to see I had just put $13 in gas on pump #13.

Attempting to break the awful curse, the next time I needed gas in his car, I waited in a long line for a pump number that was a single digit. I also ensured that $13 wouldn't fit into his tank because it was already three-quarters full.

Back in the day, customers were trusted to pump the gas first and then go into the store to pay for their fuel. The dollar amount on the pump was $6.87, so I was confident I was in the clear.

I placed a twenty-dollar bill on the counter. When the cashier gave me $13.13 in change, I lost my mind. I threw the change into the air, screamed, and stormed out of the store in a fit of rage and grief.

Driving away from the pumps, I didn't get very far before parking and breaking down in tears. Why was my father cursing me like this? Why did he keep throwing this number in my face?

Suddenly, the answer clicked in my head. It wasn't a curse; it was him communicating with me. It was a promise he had made to me when he was still alive.

My dad's great-great-uncle was the world-renowned magician, Harry Houdini. After Harry's mother died, he was obsessed with finding a way to get in touch with her. Being a master at illusion, he quickly discovered that the methods used by mediums and psychics to pass off as making contact with those in the afterlife were merely parlor tricks.

The master magician made a pact with his wife that whoever died first would do their best to try to communicate with the other. My father and I made a similar agreement.

My dad's life-insurance money and our inheritance were used to purchase a restaurant where I worked with my family. After I told this story to one of our young employees, he was fascinated by the tale.

I couldn't help messing with the boy every time I noticed thirteen things in the eatery that were unintentional, like the number of steps leading up to the second floor, and serving thirteen lunches and dinners on the 13th.

One night, a few of his teenage friends were enjoying some soda and snacks in an area of the restaurant dedicated to my father's memory. The lad begged me to share the story about my dad being electrocuted on Friday the 13th. At the end of my tale, the boy asked, "Do you ever feel his presence here in the restaurant?"

Suddenly, the lights over our table dimmed down to near darkness and then came back to life. I glanced over to where the switch was located. No one was there. Looking back at my audience with their mouths agape, I replied, "Sometimes. Do you?"

— D.J. Sartell —

89

A Parting Gift

Flowers seem intended for the solace
of ordinary humanity.
~John Ruskin

It was one of the last conversations I had with my mother. "I left you something."

"What do you mean, Mom? Left what?"

"You'll know when you see it."

My mother was an amazing person. She was not amazing because of any major achievements, accomplishments or accolades. She was amazing because of the quiet intensity of her love for her husband, children, and grandchildren. Their needs came before her own. Like a lot of moms, at mealtime she took up sentry duty between the dining room table and the kitchen, seldom sitting or eating, but instead providing refills and top-offs between our plates and the skillets, pots and casserole dishes that never seemed to run out of food no matter how much we ate.

The one pleasure she allowed herself was her garden. It was there that she found solace and solitude. Yet, even there, the flowers, herbs, and vegetables were not for her but for others. Mom would spice up the spaghetti sauce she was making us for dinner with fresh basil and oregano, arrange an assortment of roses, lilies and daisies for a friend's wedding, and sweeten our bedrooms with a sprig of lavender.

Until the day she had to leave her garden behind.

She had been diagnosed with cancer, and while the treatment

protocol of chemotherapy had not shaken her resolve to heal, her stamina had faded until it became obvious that she could no longer live alone. As I had moved out long ago and started my own family, it was decided my mom would come and live with me, my wife and our seven-year-old daughter.

Between treatments, my mother would work in my garden, which, though not as spacious or inclusive of varietals as hers, became a source of refuge and joy. More than once, I returned from work to find that she had ordered geraniums, petunias or pansies from the local nursery, had them delivered and then planted them on every exposed piece of earth she could find. Our house became a veritable botanical garden, the envy of the neighborhood.

But as my mother's health continued to fail, she spent less and less time in the garden until, at last, she was unable to perform any of her daily gardening rituals. Even then, she would sit among the marigolds and roses, commenting on their need for water, spraying or pruning.

And then, one day, she was gone.

In the ensuing days and weeks, my family was absorbed in the seemingly endless details associated with my mother's passing. There were many tears, much laughter and nostalgic gatherings for meals, during which the chair nearest the kitchen, mom's chair, was always left empty.

Weeks passed. The pain began to slowly ebb. The coolness of the fall gave way to the richness and warmth of spring along with the promise of new beginnings.

And then something amazing happened.

My daughter noticed them first: green stalks poking through the soil in every part of the garden. Day after day, they continued their upward march, reaching toward the sky, their number too many to count. And then, almost in concert, they revealed themselves.

Daffodils! A sea of yellow and white daffodils, their bold, irresistible fragrance spilling from our house, our lawn and our garden, over the fence into the surrounding neighborhood.

And then, I remembered my mother's words.

"I left you something. You'll know when you see it."

She had planted the bulbs in the winter, knowing full well that they would blossom in the spring. When she was gone. A final gift to her children and grandchildren.

—Dave Bachmann—

90

Eternity Is in Our Nature

Look deep into nature, and then you will
understand everything better.
~Albert Einstein

"Hello?" I whisper groggily into the phone. Who could be calling at this hour? It's 11 at night.

Then I realize someone is at the door. I drag myself bleary-eyed out of bed to answer it. I open the door to two uniformed police officers with long faces. I am startled awake.

"What's going on?" I politely inquire.

It was the news that every parent dreads. My thirty-one-year-old son had passed away in a tragic accident.

Three days earlier, Aaron and I had been having dinner at our favorite pizza place, laughing and chatting about a home-renovation project he was planning. Now, I was barely able to stand up. *This must be a bad dream. I'm going to wake up, and everything is going to be like it was three days earlier,* I thought to myself.

Aaron was my first child. He was wise beyond his years and intuitive. He was witty, sensitive, and curious. He was kind, generous, loving, full of warmth and consideration for others. He had a magnetism that radiated from him. I used to say that he was an "old soul."

Aaron had completed his business and marketing degree and was working as an investment analyst. He was so excited about moving forward with his life. He inherited a talent for design and building from my grandfather and was planning to renovate a townhouse. He was skilled with his hands and had great ideas for his project. After a rough patch, he was on the road to a successful future.

And then… he was just… gone.

After the funeral and rush of condolence visits, grief began to push through my shock and disbelief. It hijacked my days and robbed me of my nights. My mind couldn't take in the fact that I had just buried my child. The reality of it seeped in, but very slowly. At times it felt difficult to breathe. My heart physically ached.

As days passed and seasons changed, life pushed on.

I'd heard that immersing oneself in nature can offer some relief to a grieving heart, so as low as I felt, I decided to pick myself up, pack whatever was in arm's reach, and head to the lake house with my boyfriend. His cottage has been a joyful sanctuary for me. Maybe it still would be.

At about an hour's drive out from the city, the hustle and bustle and pressures of life began to float away. A peaceful calm drifted in. The drone of the engine lulled me into a trance as I gazed out the window at the glory of autumn. The highway was lined with deep reds, bright yellows, and vivid oranges that looked like a painting by the hand of a greater power.

Memories of road trips just like this began to spill in. Wasn't it just yesterday when we spent hours in the car playing "I Spy with My Little Eye," Aaron's favorite road-trip game, and singing at the top of our lungs to the car radio? But it was long ago, and I missed those days.

Hot tears began to stream down my face. I couldn't stop the flood and didn't even have the strength to try. The realization that Aaron was gone hit me again. Unable to stop the avalanche of feelings, I felt myself slipping back into despair. I surrendered to the deluge, and my heart broke into a million pieces all over again.

Aaron will never see this beautiful sight again, I thought.

Then, suddenly I heard "I see it."

His voice. Aaron's voice. Clear as a bell.

I caught my breath, stopped crying, and shook my head in disbelief. *What just happened? Did I just imagine that?*

Then, he said it again, even more audibly. "I do see it, Mom. I see it."

I gasped. It was as if he were right there in the car with me. I shook like a leaf, but I felt alive with hope and possibility. Aaron's voice was loud and clear.

As I sat there holding my breath, he went on. "I know what you are seeing looks beautiful, Mom, but what I can see looks brilliant, vibrant, and glowing. Colors beyond explanation. I see the energy that the trees are emitting." I could feel him there. Right there with me.

How could this be? Was it really Aaron I heard and not my own thoughts? His voice seemed to come from somewhere outside my head. And yet, I knew that it was him. I knew by the tone and timbre of his voice, the character of his speech, the words, and the way he spoke. The things he said surprised me. They weren't things I had even thought of.

Aaron told me that I could hear him better as we left behind the jangled frequencies of the city. "The less noise, the less interference and distraction, the more clearly we can connect," he said.

This experience, this connected energy exchange with my beloved son, was the beginning of a healing balm for my wounded soul that I so desperately needed. I thought about him constantly. I was still in deep pain, sad, and exhausted, but each time I heard from Aaron, I would feel a bit better. A little bit lighter. When I felt less anxious and depressed, I would hear from him more.

Up at the lake house, I am surrounded by nature. The peace and tranquility provide me such comfort. The soothing calls of loons echo in calm breezes that float across the water. The gentle lapping of the lake against the shore sounds like a distant, mystical lullaby.

I take long walks outside every day when I am there because they are so therapeutic. The sun is warm midday. Shadows of leaves dance across the path in front of me. I take long hikes along beautiful trails that gracefully wind through forests and climb steep escarpments with breathtaking views and waterfalls. It is here, in the arms of nature, that I feel most connected to my son.

I ask Aaron questions about his afterlife, looking for reassurance that he is okay and nearby. He always answers. He tells me incredible and transcendent things about energy and the universe. He instructs me on how to maintain our connection.

Aaron told me that the universe is comprised entirely of energy. Energy can take on many forms. Love is the energy of all creation and is in constant flow and balance through space and time. In nature, we are closest to that source. Aaron said, "Everything is an extension or reflection of love."

Aaron continues to send me signs. He writes letters and words in the clouds. He plays with the electricity and the Wi-Fi. Sometimes, he sends me a series of signs and messages, kind of like a connect-the-dots-for-the-meaning game that I play with him across the veil. And we play this game together. This is how I know that he is always around me.

I keep a journal of everything I see and hear from Aaron. I want to make sure that I don't forget anything of my relationship with him... on both sides of the veil. He says, "Countless macro- and micro-incidents occur simultaneously for signs and messages to appear, and you are an integral part of it."

I will always long for my beautiful son to come walking back through the front door. I miss his big warm hugs, his radiant smiles, and his deep, loving eyes. But our spirit connection is real, and his signs and messages from heaven have shown me a whole new world. A world of unfathomable, transcendent, eternal love. It is in our nature.

— Camille Dan —

91

Rituals

A friend is a hand that is always holding yours,
no matter how close or far apart you may be.
A friend is a feeling of forever in the heart.
~Author Unknown

"What's got you so down today?" I asked my friend Rick. He'd appeared at my door unexpectedly, so I knew he must have something important on his mind.

He shrugged. "Nothing I can do anything about."

"Shall I assume you dropped in because you want to talk about it?"

He sighed. "It's Cheri's birthday today," he said. "It's the first one since she died, and I..." His voice broke.

"And you don't know how to celebrate without her?" I prompted.

He nodded. "Something like that."

"Must be time to write her a letter."

I led him down the hallway to my home office, opened up a blank document, and invited him to sit down at the keyboard.

"Tell her whatever you would tell her if she were still here. Let it all out. I'm not going to read it. It's private, just between the two of you."

"And you think it will help?" he asked.

"I'm sure of it," I said, nodding. "And when you finish, print it, fold it, and put it in this envelope." I placed an envelope next to the printer. "Feel free to take as long as you like." I left the room and closed the door behind me.

It was several hours before Rick emerged again with a bulging envelope clenched in his hand. He sat in a chair opposite mine at the dining room table and asked, "Now what?"

I reached over and patted his hand. "I'll drive."

Without a word, we got into my car and drove to the ocean's shoreline. I'd already put two lawn chairs, a garden spade, and a book of matches in the trunk.

At the beach, I instructed Rick to dig a hole in the sand about a foot deep. Then he lit the letter on fire and put it into the hole. While it burned, we sat in the chairs in companionable silence, watching the smoke "deliver his words to whatever might be up there in the sky," thinking our own thoughts about life — and death.

After the letter was incinerated, we filled in the hole and started for the car. "What's Cheri's favorite meal?" I asked.

"Hawaiian pizza," Rick answered without hesitation. So that's what we had for dinner.

Over the years, we returned to the beach time after time, as we each lost loved ones or if Rick wanted to write Cheri again. Grief relief is not a straight line of recovery.

And when it became Rick's turn to leave this life, I put my cheek against his and whispered in his ear, "Watch for your letter. But don't let Cheri read it."

He grunted, or maybe that was the best laugh he could muster. Either way, I'm grateful I had a tried-and-true ritual ready to fall back on. I wrote him the very next day.

— Jan Bono —

For the Dead

Unable are the loved to die. For love is immortality.
~Emily Dickinson

Though they are long gone, we seek their approval still.
I need to get an A, my sister-in-law swears,
Because her mother demands it.
In case her parents happen to parachute in,
My wife keeps the house immaculate.
Some days my father hovers above
As I hunch inert at my desk. He nudges me
Back to work by merely shaking his head.
Later, he reminds me not to pay full price
For the car I'd like to buy. Mornings, I dress
Under my mother's critical eye.
Until you leave your body behind,
The dead have a role to play in your life.
Would you choose to have it otherwise?

—Ed Meek—

Roses in Winter

Flowers grow out of dark moments.
~Corita Kent

I love to garden and have always enjoyed the beauty of roses in spring and summer. At my house, there is only room for a small rosebush, so I grow miniature roses.

The tradition began as I planted my flower garden in May 2004. My husband Gene surprised me with the gift of a miniature rosebush. He suggested we plant it in front of the house.

As each delicate bloom opened that summer, my husband seemed to delight in plucking one to give to me when he came home from work. He even began to take an interest in watering it as the summer went by. That spring of 2004, Gene had been especially happy due to having come through another cancer battle successfully that past winter. We were both delighted when the doctor said they had gotten all the cancer and there would be no need for further surgery or treatments.

The following March, our hopes would be quickly dashed when more cancer was discovered in a routine check-up. More surgery followed in April of that year, and this time the cancer spread quite quickly. As if to punctuate the losing battle that spring, my beautiful, miniature rosebush died. I was really not interested in gardening anyway. It was hard to think of anything except the cancer battle.

Gene struggled on, trying his best to be optimistic. For Mother's Day, he bought me another miniature rosebush to replace the one that had died. All through the summer, the bush remained green but without any sign of a rose. It was late in the month of October before the first rose blossoms appeared.

By Thanksgiving, Gene's cancer had spread and was out of control. He rapidly began to decline, and he could no longer work or leave his bed.

Early December remained mild, and that beautiful little bush just kept growing and blooming. On December 9, Gene entered the hospital for what would be the last time. Through those dark days, the little, blooming rosebush gave me comfort as I returned home each evening from the hospital. On the day before my beloved died, the weather turned cold and dark, and the roses began to die. How my heart grieved that next evening as I returned home from the hospital after Gene's death. The roses were dead and lifeless, too. It only seemed to drive home the thought that I now must face a life without my love.

On the day of my husband's funeral, we had the first snowstorm of the season. It was icy, and snow was coming down so hard that only the hardiest of souls could attend the funeral. The forty or so people who did attend remarked how even the graveside services in the snowstorm seemed as if God was surrounding us.

We were amazingly comfortable and warm as we gathered under the tent beside the grave. No one hurried away after the internment. Instead, we all stood around for about thirty minutes hugging and sharing stories, and all the mourners were given a rose in memory of my beloved.

Later that evening, after all the guests and friends had left my home following the funeral dinner, I stood for a time looking out the window at the snow that covered my little flower garden. Gently pressing a rose from the funeral to my cheek, the tears began to flow. The weight of grief felt as if it would swallow me up, and I knew that winter had truly arrived.

Winter in my garden and winter in my new stage of life… I was now a widow, and there would be no more roses of affection from Gene. I felt hopelessly frozen in that spot at the window, watching the last rays of daylight fade away. The last rays of a memory of life with my beloved had been laid to rest in that snow-covered grave.

As I stood praying and trying to gain control of my emotions, the outdoor security light came on suddenly. There, in my little front garden, a miniature rose peeked through the snowdrift, looking as alive as if it were June and not December. One last rose of summer that I like to think God allowed Gene to give me.

Today, entering the fifteenth year of my widowhood, that miniature rosebush still cheers me up each day when I come home all summer long. This past fall was once again a very difficult time, but amazingly, on the anniversary of my husband's death, the rosebush bloomed once again in a snowstorm.

— Christine Trollinger —

Creative Coping

The Magic in Christmas Photos

Christmas is the day that holds all time together.
~Alexander Smith

This was going to be our family's second Christmas without my husband being present. That first Christmas after we'd moved him into a memory-care facility, I'd wanted to hide away and skip any sort of holiday celebration altogether as the house and life felt wrong. It all felt upside down and emptied out.

But I'd managed to force myself into displaying a pre-decorated tree I'd bought at a local charity fundraiser. The kids were still coming home with their little ones, and I needed to have something up for them.

It was deeply painful for us all to realize that Grandpa wouldn't be able to build us one of his magnificent fires in the fireplace on Christmas Eve, and he wouldn't be around when we opened gifts and shared laughs over well-chosen or fun gifts for each other.

We used to play games on Christmas Day after the gifts were opened. The games made us act out silly things or showed whose memory was superior in the family.

But now, one of us was missing, and the whole family dynamic had a different feel to it. I knew I needed to work at making our family time during the holiday season special once again despite my husband's absence.

We've always taken oodles and oodles of photos, and I decided to decorate more with past Christmas family photos than figurines, candles and ceramic trees.

I sorted through my collection of black-and-white photos from my childhood years and my husband's, and then I pawed through envelope after envelope of photos we'd taken early in our marriage and through the years as the girls grew.

My shopping cart was full of frames of all sizes, shapes and colors as I worked on this old-family-photos-as-Christmas-decorations project. I didn't care; hang the cost. The older, vintage-era photos all got black matte frames. For the more recent pictures, I chose colorful or pearlized frames that would go with the dominant color in each particular photograph. This project was bringing me back to life, and I was excited to finish it so it'd be ready when the kids arrived.

I found only three photos taken in my childhood home during the Christmas season, so I framed all three. I found one of my husband at age three sitting next to his cousin of the same age, both of them laughing uproariously in the shot as they played with the Jack-in-the-Boxes they'd gotten that Christmas morning. The joy on my husband's face is priceless — no hint back then of the disease that would eventually take over his life, memories and the laughter he was so well known for.

It was fun to frame the beautiful photo of my two daughters as little girls in the dark blue velvet and taffeta dresses I'd made them for their Christmas Eve program at church one year. I'd been in a rush to finish, and the older daughter's dress was way too long that night, but she wore it anyway.

The family photo of the girls, my husband and me that we took the year before either of them had their first baby looked extra special in its pearlized red frame. It was an especially good photo of the four of us taken before everyone left to go home that afternoon. We'd had our usual noisy Christmas after a huge holiday meal.

The picture of my older daughter, age three, trying to hold her new baby sister in her lap while posed in front of our Christmas tree made me smile. The baby was slipping out of place, I remember, as I worked to capture the image that year.

Sorting through those photos of holidays past proved cathartic for me. It was good to remember how rich our life had been, how lucky we were, and that nothing could deprive us of reliving it all again by sharing these old pictures.

When the kids arrived that Christmas and saw all the photos framed and positioned around the house, they had a ball going from room to room, exploring, recalling their own stories and memories, and sharing them with their husbands.

"This was a great idea, Mom," they said.

"Oh, I remember that dress! You were still sewing it up until we left for the church that night!" (True statement. I'd run out of thread late that afternoon as I worked to finish off one of their dresses and had to make a mad dash to the fabric store before it closed to buy a new spool.)

"Look at Dad's face. Wasn't he cute?"

"Are you wearing pajamas in that photo, Mom?"

"What was your dog's name again?"

My daughters know these photos will be theirs one day, and maybe they'll remember how they helped us get through that second Christmas without Dad. The grandchildren will get to know a little about their grandparents' lives, and the family stories will live on.

— R'becca Groff —

95

Gone Fishin'

To live in hearts we leave behind is not to die.
~Thomas Campbell

M y brother, Merle, went fishing last night. He left about a quarter to 9:00, and we don't expect him back anytime soon. The cancer thinks it killed him, but I know better. He just went fishing... at least, that's how I'm dealing with it right now.

He went with our brother, Lawrence, there at Pomme de Terre. You know, there at the campsite where our family used to camp?

I watched them walk down to the boat, toward the lake all covered with warm mist. It was still dark, before sunup. Merle had on his old straw hat with a pack of cigarettes stuck in the hatband. Lawrence had a little, soft cap with some wild print that barely covered his head. They wore blue-jean cut-offs, and Merle's high-top boots squeaked as he walked. Lawrence's plastic sandals were a lot more practical. He stopped at the water's edge to shake the rocks out of them before he gave the boat a shove and climbed in.

I thought they were alone until I saw the campfire smoke twenty feet or so down the beach. Daddy was there, squatting, rolling a cigarette. He had on his tan work clothes and a brimmed hat. A blackened aluminum coffeepot sat on the stove grate over the fire, and he was watching two bank lines stretched out into the darkness of the lake. I could smell that stink bait clear upwind.

I didn't think they had seen Daddy, but then one of them said, "Hey, Dad, want to go out to the island with us?"

He said, "Naw, I'm watching these lines. Those flatheads'll be biting soon."

But they kept after him, and he finally stood up, kicked out the fire, wound up his bank lines and got in the boat with them. When they got out a few feet, Merle yanked on the motor. In the blink of an eye, its noise settled to a muffled and gentle chug.

Merle and Lawrence were already arguing about something, happy in each other's company. I heard Daddy chuckle. I couldn't remember the last time I had heard Daddy chuckle. It was a good sound.

Their happy voices drifted back across the water to me: clear and sweet the way sound comes across water.

And the misty lake top took them and their little boat in and away. But I could hear their voices for a long, long time.

—Laura Lewis—

96

No Laughing Matter

Fill your paper with the breathings of your heart.
~William Wordsworth

For the two years since my mom's cancer diagnosis, I had kept a blog of her experiences, a funny, optimistic chronicle called "Dena's Journey of Hope." In other words, I'd found humor and hope in the cracks and crevices of cancer.

The blog started as the diary of what was supposed to be a six-week stint in New York City. She had been accepted into a clinical trial that started in the spring. She needed a full-time caregiver to participate. I was thirty-two and newly married, but my Chicago-based job was flexible, so I volunteered.

We rented a 210-square-foot studio apartment in Chelsea. Until you come face-to-face with 210 square feet, you can't really understand its essence. Our "bed" was an indent in the drywall barely large enough to accommodate a mattress. To access the mattress, we climbed a ladder and slithered into place. Most nights, we giggled ourselves to sleep.

"Don't bonk your head when you sit up," Mom joked before kissing my cheek goodnight.

At first, New York overwhelmed my small-town Midwestern mom: the stench of trash, the din of car horns, the long escalators to underground subway platforms.

On our first subway ride to lower Manhattan to meet the trial coordinator, Mom gripped the silver poles as the train lurched and groaned. When the doors slid open, she barreled out as if being chased by darkness itself.

Once safe in the sunlight, we looked at each other and chuckled.

I titled the first post from New York "Holy Cannoli, What Just Happened?" Mom's friends loved our stories. "Keep 'em coming!" one said. "I can hear your laughter!"

When the researchers extended the trial through summer, we decided to stay. Mom was good, the disease stable, and I loved being with her.

We eventually learned our way around the city. We walked to Trader Joe's with our handcart; we Googled subways with shorter escalators; we finagled our schedule to make sure we'd be home for *American Idol*.

Every night after dinner, I blogged. Mom plopped into a zebra-striped beanbag chair and reviewed my drafts. The more she snorted, the better. I waited in silence for her green light: "Send it off, babe."

Each morning, we showed up for Mom's injection and then explored the city. We dropped coins into the hats of guitarists with gap-toothed smiles. We hunted down ice cream and sampled ten flavors for every scoop of butter pecan we bought. In Washington Square Park, we watched people let pigeons eat seeds from their mouths. That day, the blog post "Odd New Yorkers" wrote itself.

Some days, New York City felt like a vacation. Some days, I almost forgot my mom was sick.

But she was.

By autumn, she stopped barreling out of trains because she needed my elbow for support. We stopped walking twenty blocks to find butter pecan. We learned that "progressing disease" looked like thinning hair — the hair she'd dyed blond in New York for fun — and drooping cheeks. Headaches claimed whole days.

The blog became a sleeping potion. As long as I could call back something funny every day, I could sleep at night.

After a year, Mom quit the trial. Her disease had progressed, and she missed my dad. Until the trial, they'd spent almost every day of their forty-year marriage together.

Though humor was harder to find back home, she still insisted I blog.

"Write about the puzzle we worked," she said. "That huge stinker with the missing piece."

The puzzle showed Manhattan's nighttime skyline. It was supposed to glow in the dark, but it didn't. When she died on the Sunday before Thanksgiving — seven months after returning from New York — I packed up the puzzle and took it home. I could not have known then that I'd work the puzzle again every winter. And, every winter, I'd look for the missing piece.

The night before my mom's funeral, I sat in my dad's office — once my childhood bedroom — and tried to write a eulogy. I could not uncover anything funny. I did not have her sitting next to me, peeking over my shoulder and snorting. I would not hear "Send it out, babe" to know when my work, a reflection of her life, was ready.

But sitting there in my dad's office, staring at a blank screen, it dawned on me: I did not need to recapture the essence of my mom, her spirit, and her life. The blog already had.

Standing before her friends and family, I began, "Two years ago, Mom and I took a trip to New York City."

— Nikki Campo —

97

The Ring

No one goes on, but what we leave behind keeps us
alive for someone else.
~Adam Silvera, They Both Die at the End

"Here are your husband's personal items." The ICU nurse offered me a white plastic bag holding David's shoes and the clothing he was wearing on the night of his automobile accident. A smaller bag inside held his wallet, wristwatch and wide gold wedding band.

A shiny, steel halo, attached by bolts to his skull, anchored David's head to a bar above his bed. A white hospital gown covered his motionless body. The only movement came from his facial muscles that twitched in an attempt to smile. His voice was muted.

David would survive for two more weeks as a quadriplegic — and then his body would leave us forever.

The right side of our bed was cold and vacant after his death. My life's compass was spinning out of control as I kept looking for a path forward. During the day, I pretended to be brave for the sake of our young children. Samantha, our twelve-year-old daughter, and Richard, our ten-year-old son, deserved strength from their surviving parent. But at nighttime, I sobbed in my pillow over my loss. It was hard to let go of my wonderful partner of fifteen years.

I kept the large, plastic hospital bag with my husband's clothing hidden for many years in a corner of the garage behind sacks of soil and old garden pots. I did not know what to do with the evidence of his accident, so I avoided it. Many years later, I was able to secretly let go of it.

But David's wedding ring was sacred, and I wanted it near me as a visual reminder of our love. So, I placed his shiny band in a tiny, heart-shaped porcelain box on my nightstand. Often before I fell asleep, I would reach over and lift the lid for a reality check.

After a few months, I decided that I needed to do something more meaningful with my husband's wedding ring. Finally, an idea came to me.

One morning when the kids were at school, I wrapped the special piece of jewelry in a small, velvet pouch and put it in my purse. Then I drove to the local shopping mall. Once inside the center-court area, I checked the mall's directory. I located a familiar jewelry shop and marched directly to my destination.

The annoying lump in my throat that had been my companion since David's death expanded and pressed against my airway. I wiped away the tears from the corner of my eyes before I entered the store.

"I would like to equally divide my late husband's wedding ring," I whispered to the elderly jeweler behind the counter as I presented the velvet bag. He slipped out the ring. The bright overhead spotlight focused on the piece of jewelry, highlighting it like a valuable nugget in a pirate's treasure chest.

Without encouragement, I leaned forward and shared my story.

"My beloved husband died in a car accident, and I want to share this symbol of our marriage with our children. I want to give Samantha and Richard a tangible reminder of our love." The nice man did not know our children, but I felt an urgency to say their names.

The words continued to spill out over the glass countertop.

"'Til death do us part was what David and I had vowed, and we fulfilled that promise. Now it is time to memorialize our love." I barely took a breath between sentences.

At the end of my monologue, I left the piece of gold in exchange for a receipt for the required work. I was instructed to pick up the two gold bands in a week.

Afterward, two half-inch gold pieces filled the heart-shaped container next to my bed.

I waited six years for the second part of my plan.

On Samantha's eighteenth birthday, I presented my daughter with her half of the wedding ring. She smiled as she cradled the piece of gold in her palm.

"Can I have it engraved?" The anticipation in her voice comforted me.

"Sure, we can have it sized, and you can put whatever message you want on the inside."

The next day, off we went. Same mall. Same jewelry store. Same jeweler.

I suspected the old man remembered me by his gentle nod when I handed him the half of the gold ring.

"What would you like inscribed, dear?"

"Oh, that's easy. Daddy's Girl," Samantha chirped in response to the jeweler's question.

My tears erupted. My body quivered as my daughter steadied me with her arm around my shoulder.

"What else would I have put?" she said.

"But, of course," I murmured, "I should have known."

Two years later, it was my son's turn for his trip to the same jeweler. I braced myself. I tried to anticipate Richard's message in order to avoid another public meltdown.

RSK-DSK.

His choice was also a surprise to me. But this time, I contained my emotions. Father and son's initials would forever be linked in a circle of gold.

Grief can be counterbalanced with hope. The rings on the fingers of our children are shining symbols of hope. There is hope that their father's love is eternal. And with that hope, there is comfort.

Eighteen years after David's death, I turned my healing journal into my first book. It chronicles our love story and my grief journey. When I speak to grief-support groups, I always tell the "Ring Story." During these sessions, I know our hearts connect as heads nod in silent agreement. We pass around the tissue box to dab at our tears.

Today, Samantha and Richard are both married, and they each have a son and a daughter of their own. The legacy of their precious father stays front and center as they share stories of their own childhood with their young children.

The circle of love is resilient and everlasting. It may get stretched and tested, but it is strong—just like the two gold bands that will someday be passed on to the next generation. And on and on.

—Kim Kluxen Meredith—

98

A Promise for Someday

True friendship is a promise you keep forever.
~Sarah Desse

This was the last place I wanted to be. I was sitting on the bedroom floor next to my recently widowed friend. He had called and asked me to help him with the overwhelming burden of sorting through his wife's bureau and closet. His teenage daughter did not want the job. Neither did I. Kim had been one of my closest friends since we met in college and this was painful.

Bob took a deep breath and slowly pulled open the first drawer, the bottom one on the right. He reached for a stack of neatly folded T-shirts and lifted them out. Setting them on the floor in front of us, he began looking through them, unfolding them one at a time.

With an exasperated sigh, he said, "Why in the world was Kim saving all these old T-shirts?" He set them aside for the donation pile. I sat there stunned, because I knew what I was seeing.

Ten years earlier, I had made a quilt from some of my son's T-shirts, a record of his early childhood in fabric. I included the onesie he had worn home from the hospital following his birth and the obligatory outgrown Little League and youth-soccer shirts, as well as those collected on family trips to zoos, theme parks, and national parks. I had proudly shown it, my first T-shirt quilt, to Kim.

"Wow," she exclaimed. Then she paused before asking, "Will you make one of those for Rachel someday?"

"Sure. Just start saving her T-shirts," I replied nonchalantly, never even considering that she would be gone when "someday" arrived.

Feeling jarred by the sight of their daughter's childhood T-shirts, I heard Kim's voice in my head say, "Capi, you promised."

I responded to Bob's question. "Bob, Kim was saving those shirts for me." I gently took them from him.

Rachel's high-school graduation was less than ten months away. As I began cutting up the shirts, I realized I needed more shirts to make a quilt large enough for even a twin bed. I called Bob, and we brainstormed about others I could include that reflected her more recent activities and interests. He could not, unfortunately, start stealing clothes from her room. That might raise questions.

So, rather than resorting to petty theft, he contacted the national marketing department of the fast-food chain where she worked. They sent me a shirt. He ordered a shirt with the logo of her favorite Broadway show, the last one she had seen with her mom. He talked to her school's choir director and a pastor, enlisting their help in rounding up shirts from a choir trip to Canada and a mission trip to Peru. The manager of the hotel where their family spent their annual beach week sent me a shirt with the hotel's logo. A local printer professionally transferred a photo onto fabric, one of Kim and Rachel on their last mother-daughter trip to New York City. It is centered on the quilt, a visual reminder of her mom's great love for her.

I had always expected this quilt would be a fun, collaborative project that Kim and I would plan and enjoy together, even though her debilitating rheumatoid arthritis meant that I would do the sewing. Instead, it became a grieving quilt, every stitch and seam a tearful reminder of how much I missed my friend. Sometimes, while I sewed, I would talk to Kim in my head, wishing she could see what I was doing and hoping she would like it. When I finished the binding and the label, I said to myself and Kim, "Well, Kim, I kept my promise. Someday is today."

When Rachel unwrapped her gift following her high school graduation ceremony, she paused, looked at me and asked, "Did you finish this for my mom?"

My eyes filled with tears. "Yes, honey, I did. Your mom was saving your shirts so I could make this for you."

Whenever I think of that quilt, I feel such a sense of relief that I agreed to help Bob sort through Kim's clothing, even though it was the last place I wanted to be. Being there meant that I was able to keep my promise to Kim and give Rachel a gift filled with memories of her mom.

— Capi Cloud Cohen —

Lucky Dog

One of the joys of being a grandparent is getting to
see the world again through the eyes of a child.
~David Suzuki

It had been a gray year. Our father had died, and our eighty-five-year-old mother was having a hard time in assisted living without Dad. She begged for frequent visits, and my brother and I did our best to juggle our jobs, our mother, and our families.

Then my beloved husband, Ernie, got a cough he couldn't get rid of. After rounds of antibiotics, X-rays and, finally, a biopsy, the doctor made a statement we didn't expect. Ernie, who didn't drink or smoke, was told, "You have stage IV lung cancer. Chemo will prolong your life for a few months, but it will not save it." I gripped the gold cross I always wore around my neck until I had a cross-shaped indentation pressed into my hand.

When we got home, Ernie held me in his arms, and we both cried. Then he said, "No more tears. I want the time we have left to be as good as possible." That night, I learned to do my crying in the shower. Knowing that I could no longer keep my life in balance, I took a leave from my job.

My first marriage had produced four wonderful children, but it was difficult and ultimately ended in divorce. Several years later, I married Ernie, and for the past twelve years, I'd been learning how wonderful marriage could be. Now this precious time in my life was ending. I called each of my children and told them of Ernie's diagnosis. I saved my oldest son, Kristian, for last because his five-year-old daughter Malia and Ernie were very close.

When I called Kristian, he listened carefully and then said, "Malia's right here. I'm going to set down the phone and talk to her."

I heard him say, "Come here, honey." I pictured him getting down on her level, and then I heard him say, "Ernie's real sick, but he's going to fight."

Kristian picked up the phone again. "Malia saw the tears in my eyes and understands how serious this is. She's in her room. I'll call you back."

When the phone rang, Kristian spoke softly. "Malia came out of her room carrying her favorite stuffed animal. She said, 'This is for Ernie. It's to help him fight.' She wants to bring it to him. Is this weekend okay?"

When they arrived, Malia carried the funniest-looking stuffed animal I'd ever seen. It was about twelve inches long with skinny arms, legs, and a tail that were each at least ten inches long. Its small head had beady eyes and a huge grin.

"What is it?" I asked.

"It's a dog," Malia replied indignantly.

Soon, Malia and Ernie had their heads together, whispering furtively.

When they appeared to reach a decision, they looked at me, and Ernie spoke. "We named him Lucky Dog. He's going to make us feel better."

Then Malia piped up, "You take Lucky Dog to visit Great-Grandma, too. She needs something to help her not be so sad." At that moment, I realized that this small child understood more of our adult conversations than I thought.

Lucky Dog became my constant companion. When Ernie was having a good day, I drove the hour and a half north to see my mother. I sat Lucky Dog on the seat next to me, and I found myself talking to him so that I'd have stories to tell Malia. On Malia's monthly visit, I'd explain how Lucky Dog insisted that I drive slowly in a snowstorm, or I'd report how he liked to stop and get a hamburger and milkshake to have on the way home.

When we arrived at Mom's assisted-living home, Lucky Dog peeked out of the top of my bag. Some days, Mom would laugh when she saw him, and she'd hold him in her lap when I'd take her on wheelchair rides. When she was having a crabby day, she'd say, "Leave that silly creature in your bag. People will think I'm senile."

One week, I was able to make a second visit in the same week, but when I got to her room, it was empty. I hurried to the nurses' station and learned that she was in the exercise room. There, I found my mother arguing with the woman in charge. "I have to go to my room. My daughter is coming."

"No, Betty," the woman patiently explained. "Your daughter was here on Tuesday."

I quietly interrupted, "Here I am." Mom smiled triumphantly.

Then the women in the group turned and saw the small head sticking out of my bag. In unison, several of them exclaimed, "Lucky Dog!" Warmth rose in my chest as I realized that a five-year-old's wisdom had put smiles on these elderly faces.

Sometimes, when I left my mother and headed for home, I found myself unable to drive because of my tears. I'd pull over to the side of the road and hold Lucky Dog tight as I poured out my grief. I knew I was slowly losing two people whom I loved deeply.

Lucky Dog was also well-known at the medical center. I always packed a bag with sandwiches, drinks, and Lucky Dog to keep our spirits up during our long day. First, Ernie would visit the doctor, and then he'd go to his chemotherapy room, which looked out over Lake Superior. Lucky Dog sat on the windowsill, and the nurses delighted in addressing Lucky Dog as though he were real.

On their frequent visits, Malia held Lucky Dog close. We adults did everything we could think of to keep the atmosphere light, but Malia could see that Ernie had lost his hair and was getting thinner and weaker. On their last visit, I whispered to Kristian that the bottoms of Ernie's feet were turning black.

Kristian put his arms around me. "It means what you think it does, Mom."

The next time I called my kids, it was to tell them the time and date for Ernie's funeral.

Before the funeral, Kristian and Malia stopped at the house, and Malia picked up Lucky Dog. When we arrived at the church, Malia pulled away from her father. "Grandma needs me and Lucky Dog to sit by her." My mother had managed to join us and sat with my brother and his family.

Later, at the cemetery, the priest invited immediate family members to put something in the metal box that contained Ernie's ashes. Two of Ernie's grandchildren walked forward and dropped in letters. I lovingly slid in my gold cross, and then Malia squeezed my hand.

"Come on, Grandma. We need to put Lucky Dog in the box."

"Honey, are you sure?"

Malia was insistent. "Lucky Dog needs to be with Ernie."

The wisdom of a five-year-old and a silly-looking, stuffed animal helped get me through one of the hardest years of my life. Someday, we'll all be together in heaven. And, who knows, maybe Lucky Dog will be there, too.

— Lou Zywicki Prudhomme —

Brushstrokes of Comfort

Art is a line around your thoughts.
~Gustav Klimt

"Come sit beside me." I heard my mother's softly spoken words as I peeked into our family room, which had just been converted to an art studio. The room's dark mahogany paneling had been removed and the walls brightened with a fresh coat of lavender paint. Scattered about the room was a diverse collection of my mother's works of art in progress. There were seasonal landscapes, still-life images, portraits, watercolors painted in hues of blue and green, floral arrangements drawn in colorful pastels, and a vast array of charcoal renderings.

A towering stack of wrapped canvases and sketch pads in different sizes was positioned high atop an old bookcase. Tubes of paint, boxes of graphite pencils and erasers were haphazardly strewn. Empty, rinsed jars of Ragu spaghetti sauce lined the windowsill as paintbrush basins. Tin cans once brimming with Chock Full o' Nuts coffee now contained palette knives, calligraphy pens and nibs.

My mother had donned a paint-splattered art smock, an old white shirt of my father's, which hung loosely on her petite frame. She looked up from her easel, smiled and again suggested I join her.

I was ten years old, and I vividly recall standing in the doorway, fascinated by the contents of the room and its vibrant transformation. It had become a colorful kaleidoscope of creative chaos. However, most enduring and memorable were my mother's loving words, an expression she would repeat throughout the years, "Come sit beside me."

I skipped into the room and hopped up on the stool right next to my mother. In the decades to follow, I spent countless hours at my mother's side, learning drawing techniques, painting, blending colors, and experimenting with different media. A variety of art projects in my mother's studio provided a haven from the angst of my teenage years, a reprieve from college studies, and eventually a respite from the stress and demands of the corporate world that I joined.

However, most meaningful and significant were the conversations my mother and I engaged in. They were frequently serious, sometimes lively, and often accompanied by my mother's words of wisdom. Sometimes tears were shed, but usually our laughter reverberated down the hallway. Admittedly, my mother and I both took delight in our joint artistic endeavors, but what mattered most was that we were spending quality time together. We were strengthening our mother-daughter bond until the unimaginable occurred: My mother passed away.

I was completely devastated. My faith was shaken. I incessantly questioned and wondered how I was ever going to survive the loss of my mother. The mere thought of stepping into my mother's art studio exacerbated my grief. It was now an archive of days gone by, a snapshot of memories. I avoided the room and kept the studio's door tightly closed.

Then it happened: I had no choice. I had searched feverishly for a legal document necessary for my mother's estate. Rummaging through closets, stacks of paperwork, and bureau drawers proved futile. Then it occurred to me that the old bookcase in the art studio held a small, metal box that contained what my mother referred to as her "important papers should something ever happen."

My right hand shook uncontrollably as I fumbled with the studio's doorknob and reluctantly entered. It was exactly how my mother had left it. There were opened tubes of paint, a palette splashed in color, paintbrushes in basins, the smock on its designated hook, and her favorite teacup next to an open sketchbook. My eyes welled with tears. Just as I began to weep, sunlight suddenly filtered through the studio's window. Basking in the golden rays was my mother's tabletop easel, with her very last work of art, a nearly completed painting.

It was a majestic landscape with rolling hills, a cornflower-blue sky accentuated with patches of white billowing clouds, and a field of sunflowers. There was a single detail that needed completion. My mother had pencil-drawn directly on the canvas an outline of a single butterfly in flight. I slowly approached the easel. I was overcome by an innate need to paint the butterfly and finish the landscape for my mother. I wiped the tears from my eyes. My mother's heartfelt expression, her same four words, immediately came to mind. I said aloud, "Come sit beside me."

I took a deep breath, closed my eyes for a moment, and repeated the sentence aloud. I wondered exactly where my mother was. Was her spirit present in the studio? Was she beside me? In the weeks to follow, whenever I entered the studio, I looked for my mother's presence. I called out to her by repeating aloud, "Come sit beside me."

Late one evening, I finally completed the butterfly. I stepped away from the easel to view the painting from a distance. I walked to the opposite side of the studio and took serious note of my mother's very last brushstrokes. With deep admiration, I studied color contrasts that my mother had selected and utilized, her perceived depth and width of shadows and far-lying fields. And then it suddenly occurred to me that my mother's presence was as sweeping as her painted landscape, her final masterpiece. Not only was she beside me in the studio, she was beside me everywhere.

My thoughts then wandered to the butterfly. Why hadn't I noticed its inherent symbolism? Was I too focused on color tones and tints in my efforts to perfectly paint it? In its graceful flutter, its whimsical swirl and dance, the butterfly represented a spirit that was free, limitless, no longer subject to boundaries. Once more, I began to weep, but this time my tears were tethered to a very different emotion — a strong feeling of comfort and solace. I became firmly convinced that my mother was beside me, always and everywhere.

— Patricia Ann Rossi —

Tabi Rocks

Remember that although bodies may pass away,
the energy that connects you to a loved one
is everlasting and can always be felt
when you're open to receiving it.
~Doreen Virtue, Signs from Above

I knew it was bad when my friend Sarah texted me at 7:30 A.M. on a Saturday. Her text read, "Can you please call me?"

I quickly texted back, "Is it bad?"

"Yes."

I prepared myself for the worst. Was someone in the hospital? Had there been an accident?

She answered the phone quickly. "Tabi..." She paused to take a breath. "Tabi passed away last night."

Tabi was one of my fifteen-year-old daughter's closest friends. Keileen and Tabi had known each other since they were six. Surely, I had misheard. I asked her to repeat.

"Tabi passed away."

My brain searched for some meaning. Did she mean to say something else? Maybe she misspoke. Surely, she wasn't talking about Tabi.

"I don't know what you mean," I said as I struggled to find words.

When I heard someone crying in the background, the seriousness of the situation began to sink in.

Sarah carefully explained the events of the day before.

"Tabi and Ethan went for a bike ride."

This began to make sense to me. Tabi often went on bike rides with her brother.

Sarah continued: "They came back, and she complained about a migraine. So, she lay down for a nap."

Again, this made sense. Tabi often had headaches.

Sarah continued. "She was taking a long nap, and we thought we should wake her. It was getting close to dinner."

So far, I understood everything she said. It all made sense.

Then: "I found her. We tried our best to revive her."

To this day, I will never understand how a seizure can take a fifteen-year-old girl's life. Yes, she had had one large seizure before, but she had been under the care of a neurologist. Her seizures were under control. I had never even heard of Sudden Unexpected Death in Epilepsy. Surely, this was a mistake.

We rushed to Sarah's home with flowers after completing the horrendous task of telling my daughter. When Tabi didn't come running outside to greet my daughter, it really began to sink in.

To worsen matters, this was April 2020. The world had just been locked down due to the COVID pandemic. No celebrations of life were allowed.

We were invited to the burial plot one family at a time by appointment to bring flowers, offer up comforting words, and try to make sense of it. I couldn't look at the gravestone. I didn't want to see her beautiful name carved into it. It was impossible to understand that the girl who had just camped out on my daughter's bedroom floor was now there.

I looked over to see an older gentleman sitting on a camping chair by what must have been his wife's elaborately decorated grave. I will always remember the sadness in his face. He looked at us with such empathy and understanding, but he was older. This was how it was meant to be. We shouldn't have been standing alongside the grave of a teenager. Tabi should have been talking about proms, braces, and driving lessons.

Sarah was so valiant when she welcomed us and thanked us for the flowering, potted plant. She told us they chose the plot because it was by a tree and looked like one of our Girl Scout campsites. She explained that when they saw bunnies hopping around the tree, they knew it was the right place. Tabi loved bunnies.

"And, here, take these Tabi rocks," Sarah continued.

Sarah and her family had painted some crystal-like rocks a beautiful teal blue. Her son, Ethan, had been worried about life without his sister. He wondered how he could move on and enjoy life without her being there.

Sarah handed me a bag of beautiful blue rocks that glittered in the sun. "You can bring Tabi along with you wherever you go if you have these rocks. Leave them behind to mark that she has been there, too."

We promised we would take them wherever we went.

I put the rocks in my purse, thinking how much I wished I could bring Tabi along with me on a trip rather than a handful of painted rocks.

We did what Sarah asked, though. We began to take them along as we went on small trips.

At first, it was a trip to the beach. We brought along another close friend of Tabi's and, together, the girls left them on the beach. When we were looking for the perfect spot, we found a brightly painted shell. It had a beautiful bird painted on it.

"Tabi would love that. She loved animals."

We took a picture and left it behind. Tabi always loved the coast.

Later in the summer, we traveled out to Grand Teton National Park and found the most impressive view high on a mountain. No one was around. We took some family photos with the rocks in our pockets. It was midday, and the light was exceptionally bright. When we paused to look at the photos, we saw a beam of light coming down from the sky right beside us. In the next photo, the light created a rainbow pattern near my daughter.

"She's here! Isn't she?" The photos gave us a lot of hope.

Soon after, we entered a trinket shop and scanned the gifts, looking for something to purchase.

A bright-eyed woman approached us. "Can I help you find something?" Her demeanor was pleasant, and her face was kind. But her name tag made us pause. "Tabi," it read.

"No, thank you," I said. "I think you already helped." We left the store, leaving behind a rather puzzled saleswoman.

We continued along the road and encountered an old western town. We found a field by a barn filled with wild bunnies, and we paused to take pictures. The bunnies were amazingly tame, hopping up to us as we watched them. They continually approached us, hopping and bouncing off each other. Tabi loved bunnies so much. We decided to leave some rocks behind.

The rocks began to help ease our pain. Spreading them around allowed for the space and time to reflect upon years of friendship with Tabi. We lingered in the sweet memories and had some deep conversations about friendship. Why did Tabi leave such an enormous mark behind? What qualities made a wonderful friend? How could we demonstrate these qualities ourselves?

The rocks also helped coin a new phrase: rock-worthy. Is a moment worthy of a Tabi rock? If not, why are we spending so much time with it? What can we do to make the next moment rock-worthy?

Together, as a family, we strive to make each day worthy of a Tabi rock, and my daughters strive to be a kind friend to others, just like Tabi.

— Michele Boom —

Meet Our Contributors

John Kevin Allen is a minister and chaplain ordained by the United Church of Christ and approved for ministry with the United Church of Canada. He is a frequent contributor to *Broadview* magazine and the *Chicken Soup for the Soul* series. E-mail him at johnkevinallenwriting@gmail.com.

Monica A. Andermann is a woman of many pursuits: painting, piano, gardening, yoga and above all, writing. Her work has been included in such publications as *Guideposts*, *Sasee* and *Woman's World* as well as several titles in the *Chicken Soup for the Soul* series.

Mary Ellen Angelscribe is a pet newspaper columnist and author of *Expect Miracles* and *A Christmas Filled with Miracles*. Watch her swimming cats on Animal Planet's *Must Love Cats!* Discover inspirational pet and miracle stories on Facebook Angel Scribe and Pet Tips and Tales. E-mail her at angelscribe@msn.com.

Tonya May Avent is an engaging speaker, teacher, and award-winning author who has contributed to the *Chicken Soup for the Soul* series in addition to writing for *Guideposts* and *Stay Focused* magazines. Her first book, a devotional for young athletes, is scheduled for release in this year. Learn more at www.destined4thedub.com.

Dave Bachmann is a retired teacher who taught English to special needs students in Arizona for forty years. He now lives and writes in California with his wife Jay, a retired elementary teacher, along with their fifteen-year-old Lab, Scout.

Kathryn Hackett Bales lives in Nevada with dogs, cats, and pedigreed show rabbits. She is currently working on a series of novels with the proceeds donated to Pit Bull Rescue.

Sarah Barnum is a freelance editor with TrailBlaze Writing & Editing. When she's not writing her own narrative non-fiction or working with words, Sarah enjoys small-town life in Northern California with her husband, children, and Appaloosa horse.

Jan Bono has completed a six-book cozy mystery series set on the SW Washington coast. She's also published five collections of humorous personal experiences, two poetry chapbooks, nine one-act plays, a dinner theater play, and has written for magazines ranging from *Guideposts* to *Woman's World*. Learn more at www.JanBonoBooks.com.

Michele Boom has taught elementary school, both in the traditional setting as well as online, for twenty years. She also works as a freelance writer and is a frequent contributor to the *Chicken Soup for the Soul* series. She lives in Bend, OR with her family and pets.

Beth Bullard is an author, an award-winning photographer, a budding interior designer and an amazing personal shopper for her family and friends. Beth lives on a small acreage in Northern Colorado with her two children and their menagerie of animals.

Nancy Burrows is a former television promo writer who pivoted when her son was diagnosed with autism. Co-author of *Chicken Soup for the Soul: Raising Kids on the Spectrum*, Nancy relishes writing that taps into her passion for storytelling and creating a more inclusive world. She lives in Baltimore, MD with her husband and two children.

Nikki Campo is a mother to three young children and works as a writer in Charlotte, NC. She has published true stories and humor in *The New York Times*, *The Washington Post*, *McSweeney's Internet Tendency*, and *Good Housekeeping*, among other publications. Right now, she's probably eating chocolate.

Nebula Award–nominated **Beth Cato** is the author of the *Clockwork Dagger* duology and the *Blood of Earth* trilogy from Harper Voyager. She's a Hanford, CA native transplanted to the Arizona desert. Follow her at BethCato.com and on Twitter @BethCato.

Rachel Chustz earned her bachelor's and master's degrees at Louisiana State University. She was an elementary teacher until the birth of her first child. Rachel and her husband, Michael, now have three children: Tripp, Charlotte, and Joseph. Recently, Rachel wrote and illustrated her first children's book, *The Bubble's Day at LSU*.

Capi Cloud Cohen crafts stories, quilts, clothes, and cookies in Tennessee. She's now happily married to the Bob in her story and loves spending time with her mom, children, and grandchildren, in-person or on FaceTime. A Penn State grad, she yells at the TV during football games. Find her on Instagram @sewcloudy.

Julie Cole is a wife, mother, and grandmother of nine very loved and spoiled grandchildren. She and her husband reside in the Big Rapids, Michigan area, where Julie is a receptionist for a pregnancy resource center. Her hobbies include journaling, crocheting, reading, raising chickens, and spending time with her family.

Camille Dan is the mother of Aaron, his two brothers and one sister. She received her BScNursing from University of Windsor in 1982. She is president of a private investment management firm she founded in 2004. Camille has authored books on grieving and afterlife. She enjoys reading, bicycling, tennis, and time with her kids.

Kerri Davidson is a writer based in New York City. Her non-fiction and poetry pieces have appeared in several national publications and her poetry chapbook, *How to Fly*, was published by Finishing Line Press. In her free time, she loves to dance. Learn more at www.kerridavidson.com.

Susan Evans is a lifelong practitioner of journaling, which led her to writing memoir pieces. In addition to a family history and biographies of her children and grandchildren, she has written a book chronicling the first year after her daughter's death titled *Later Courtney*. It is available on Amazon.

Kate Fellowes has published six mysteries, most recently *A Menacing Brew*. Her short stories have appeared in many publications, from *Woman's World* to *Crimestalker Casebook*. Working in a public library, every day is a busman's holiday for her. She blogs at katefellowes.wordpress.com/.

Marianne Fosnow lives in Fort Mill, SC. She enjoys reading and learning and is currently obsessed with jigsaw puzzles. She loves reading *Chicken Soup for the Soul* books and is very proud to be a contributor.

Denise R. Fuller became a widow in 2012 at the age of forty-one.

She has learned how to conquer grief and loneliness and how to forgive and live each day with purpose. She is an esthetician and her ferocious love for aesthetics prompted her to create the National Aesthetic Spa Network for salons and spas.

Mackenzie Gambrill is currently a senior in college and is planning to attend law school in 2022 to become a criminal defense attorney. In her free time, Mackenzie loves spending time in nature, hanging out with her two orange cats, enjoying the company of family and friends, and listening to music.

Amanda Gist is an author, professional copywriter, and dog mom. Her first book, *10 Reasons Dogs Are the Absolute Best*, won the honor of becoming an Amazon #1 New Release. When she's not writing, she enjoys spending time with family, listening to music, reading, and expressing her creativity.

Bracha Goetz is the Harvard-educated author of forty books that help children's souls shine and *Searching for God in the Garbage*, a candid memoir for adults on overcoming food addictions joyfully. Her books can be found on the Bracha Goetz Amazon Author Page and at the website created by her children: www.goetzbookshop.com.

Deb Gorman, owner of Debo Publishing, is the author of three creative non-fiction devotional books available online. Deb lives in the Pacific Northwest with her husband. Together they have seven children and numerous grandchildren, plus their German Shepherd, Hoka. Deb is currently working on publishing her first two novels. Learn more at debggorman.com.

R'becca Groff lives and writes in eastern Iowa. She enjoys a wide variety of interests that include culinary expertise, flower gardening, and spending time with grandchildren and her zany collection of friends. She gladly shares her experience and insight into dealing with her husband's dementia to assist others.

Robin D. Hamilton is the author of *Shedding Negativity, Gaining Grace*. She enjoys writing books, stage plays, and screen plays. When not writing, Robin enjoys spending time with family and friends.

Christy Heitger-Ewing pens human interest stories for national, regional, and local magazines. She has contributed to twenty-four anthologies. This is her fourteenth contribution to the *Chicken Soup for the Soul* series. She writes to bring readers joy, peace, and hope. She runs five miles a day and believes pets are the key to happiness. Learn more at www.christyheitger-ewing.com.

Kayleen Kitty Holder is the editor of *The Devine News* and a children's book writer. Follow her on Facebook for more stories or to help with a gift drive. She dedicates this story to her grandma's unending love, and to her daddy for showing her how to chase dreams and teaching her the most important thing in the world is to simply "be nice" and help others.

After twenty-five years as a corporate executive, **Kathy Humenik** returned to her love of writing. In addition to memoirs, she has written short stories, novels, and several children's books. She enjoys traveling, cooking, and spending time with her grandchildren.

Stephanie Tolliver Hyman received her Bachelor of Arts in English Literature and a Master of Arts in English. A lifelong academic, she serves as Dean of Arts and Humanities at a community college. She enjoys spending time with her husband, Cory, daughter, Harper, and two spoiled cats: Remi and Tess.

Sally Jadlow has published thirteen books of historical fiction, true inspirational short stories, poetry, and devotionals. She is a mom of four, grandmother of fourteen and great-grandma of three. Sally loves to write, cook, and garden in her home in Overland Park, KS. She teaches writing for the Kansas City Writers Group.

Pamela Jane is an author of over thirty children's books, and an essayist whose work has appeared in *The New York Times*, *The Wall Street Journal*, *New York Daily News*, *Writer's Digest*, *The Independent*, and *The Writer*. Pamela is also co-author of *Pride and Prejudice and Kitties*.

Kim Johnson is a southern girl who has always loved to write. From doodling on the back of napkins to the bottom of receipts, her creative juices are always flowing. She derives the inspiration for her stories from life's little ironies and the antics of her family — especially her young grandsons.

Mariah E. Julio has published stories and articles in newspapers, periodicals, and general interest publications. Several stories placed in international contests. A retired nurse, Mariah spends her time writing, painting, traveling and in futile attempts to outwit her cat.

Nick Kachulis is a writer, storyteller, musician, and composer. His music has been featured on broadcast television on five continents and his writing has been published in several periodicals. He is currently writing a novel and a memoir about his father. E-mail him at njkachulis@gmail.com or visit his website at NickKachulis.com.

A University of Michigan liberal arts graduate, **Barbara Rady Kazdan**, non-profit founder and lifelong change agent, enjoys back-roads travel and forward thinking. Between visits to far-flung family, find her with open-hearted friends and in writing workshops in Silver Spring, MD. Drawn from personal experience, a book on widowhood is in the works.

Joyce R. Kebodeaux lives in Lake Charles, LA and is a graduate of Sowela Tech. Her husband, Clyde, died in 2007. They have four children and thirteen grandchildren. Joyce retired from Market Basket food stores in 2007 after thirty-two years. She enjoys writing, crafting, baking, and visiting with her family and friends.

Shannon Kernaghan writes and creates visual art from Alberta. She enjoyed life as a digital nomad for many years, traveling and writing poetry, fiction, and everything in between from her RV. She continues to tell her stories at ShannonKernaghan.com.

Jamie Korf is forever on the lookout for the odd detail. Her past public-facing gigs exposed her to every personality trait and tic, giving her fodder for future character development. She's a Twin Cities-based editor and writer, glutton for digital news and media, and newly anointed mama.

Evelyn Krieger is the author of the award-winning young adult novel *One Is Not a Lonely Number*. Evelyn works as a private tutor and college advisor, is the founder of the Byron Krieger Athletic Scholarship in honor of her father's legacy, and writes a blog on living the creative life at EvelynKrieger.net.

Trish L. spends her time teaching yoga and with her three grown children. Through difficult life journeys she hopes to shine a light on the path for others through a genuine belief that life is a beautiful adventure.

Angela Larks received her Bachelor of Arts in Communications in 2016. She has two daughters and four grandchildren. Along with writing, she enjoys crocheting, reading, and traveling with her husband, Mike. Angela plans to complete her memoir, with an emphasis on love and loss.

Marlys Johnson Lawry is an award-winning writer and speaker. She enjoys hiking tall mountains, snowshoeing through powder, and knitting warm, fuzzy things for the people she loves. Marlys is a chai snob, enjoys repurposing old junk into cool new stuff, and blogs about living well through life's hard and holy moments.

Laura Lewis is retired with a B.S. in Communications and Public Relations from CMU at Warrensburg. Her work has been published in two anthologies: *Kaleidoscope WoJo* and *More Voices of The Willows*. She has self-published a historical novel titled *Where Roses Grow*.

Marcia McGreevy Lewis lives in Seattle, WA and is a retired feature writer for a Washington newspaper. In 2020-21 her stories appeared in the literary journals *F3LL Magazine, Life in Lit* and *Freshwater* as well as the magazines *Go World Travel, ROVA* and *Third Act*.

Natasha Lidberg received her Bachelor of Arts degree in Human Development from California State University San Marcos. She lives in Southern California and enjoys long walks and deep talks. This story is dedicated to Lenae and to those who have experienced the pain of loss. For prayer, hope, or connection visit www.coastcitychurch.com.

Queen Lori, aka Dancing Grammie, is ninety-three, a mother of seven, grandmother of twenty-two, and three-time contributor to the *Chicken Soup for the Soul* series. She began writing after being crowned queen of the 2016 Erma Bombeck Writers Workshop. Lori leads and tap dances with the Prime Life Follies. Follow her at DancingGrammie.com.

Diane Helmken MacLachlan is a graduate of Hope College and a student of life. With three outstanding adult children, she now pursues her passion to read and travel the world. Still on her to-do list is finishing a non-fiction novel and developing a series of children's books.

Dr. Christine Malone has worked in healthcare and taught in higher education for over twenty years. Christine and her husband live in Ocean Shores, WA. Though she has published a number of textbooks, she is currently working on her autobiography.

Maegann Mansfield received her Bachelor of Arts in English and Professional Writing, with honors, from Pensacola Christian College in 2021. Currently, she is a copywriter for Ramsey Solutions in Tennessee. Maegann enjoys traveling, hiking, swimming, calligraphy, and writing creative non-fiction.

DaNice D. Marshall is an established writer and artist. She was published in *Chicken Soup for the Soul: I'm Speaking Now* in 2021. Her paintings have been on exhibit at Piano Craft Gallery in Boston, and her art is included in Forbidden Fruit I Like Your Work fall 2021 art catalog. She had a solo exhibit at Billboard Hope in Boston. She and her husband happily live in Massachusetts.

Tim Martin's work has been featured in over two dozen *Chicken Soup for the Soul* books. He is the author of *There's Nothing Funny About Running*, *Wimps Like Me*, *Summer With Dad*, *The Legend of Boomer Jack* and *Why Run If No One Is Chasing You?* E-mail Tim at tmartin@sitestar.net.

Mark Mason has written on a variety of non-fiction topics. This has been by far the most challenging. But it is hoped, that by sharing about his grief journey, others who are traveling their own unique path will be able to connect and know a measure of peace. E-mail him at got.mark@verizon.net.

Sara Matson is a freelance children's writer who lives with her husband and daughters (who are now in college) in Minnesota. Learn more at www.saramatson.com.

Ed Meek writes poetry, fiction, and book reviews. His book, *High Tide,* was released last year. *Luck: Stories* came out in 2017. He enjoys softball, cycling, walking and travel. He lives in Somerville, MA with his wife Elizabeth and dog Mookie.

Cynthia Mendenhall, an author of three books, is an engaging speaker, audacious adventuress, and loves meeting friends for meaningful cups of coffee. Her latest manuscript (which is looking for an agent/publisher) is titled *Mugs of Mojo: When Coffee Enlightens Your Way*. Cynthia contributes monthly to www.vinewords.net.

Kim Kluxen Meredith, a multiple contributor to the *Chicken Soup* *for the Soul* series, is a retired Spanish teacher. She resides in central Pennsylvania. Kim has four published books in various genres and numerous other published stories and articles that can be found on her website www.kimkluxenmeredith.com.

Michelle Close Mills has been a frequent contributor to the *Chicken Soup for the Soul* series as well as many other anthologies. She and her hubby Ralph, kitty Maggie and bird Lucy are lifetime Floridians. Michelle is also a vocalist and sings with her church worship team. Learn more at www.authorsden.com/michelleclosemills.

Dr. Melissa B. Mork is a professor in the Department of Psychology, Criminal Justice and Law Enforcement at the University of Northwestern, St. Paul. She is also a certified humor professional through the Association for Applied and Therapeutic Humor. She enjoys throwing pottery, SCUBA diving, and laughing at her own jokes.

Mary Lee Moynan is the published author of short stories and the inspirational book *Get Off Your Knees*. A devout Christian, she believes there's a time to pray and a time to get on with life. She recently completed a war time screenplay entitled *Wanted: The Unknown Woman*. E-mail her at moynan-marylee@hotmail.com.

Gail Nehamen became a widow after forty-four and a half years of marriage. She is learning how to live with grief.

Florence Niven lives in Kingston, Ontario with her husband Don. They have two grown sons, Chris and Ben. This is Florence's second story in the *Chicken Soup for the Soul* series. The first, "Company Along the Way" can be found in *Chicken Soup for the Soul: Age Is Just a Number*.

Charlotte Louise Nystrom is a historical fiction author and poet from the rocky coast of Maine but currently settled further inland. Her works are thought-provoking and filled with visceral imagery. Charlotte strives to capture words that make the world a little softer by celebrating its beauty and bridging connections.

Linda C. Olaveson's passion for writing was sparked in grade school when her teacher read *Taffy's Foal* to the class each day after their desk work was completed. Through her writing, Linda presents the rich and subtle nuances of everyday interactions, finding meaning in life's small moments.

Anne Oliver, a native of West Virginia, holds bachelor's and master's degrees from the University of Georgia. She and her husband George reared three Army brats during his thirty-one years with the Army. (HOOAH!) She enjoys volunteering, reading, writing, and is looking forward to future adventures. E-mail her at armygrl74@aol.com.

Nancy Emmick Panko is a retired RN from North Carolina who has contributed many stories to the *Chicken Soup for the Soul* series. Award-winning author of *Guiding Missal*, *Sheltering Angels*, *Blueberry Moose*, and *Peachy Possums*, Panko is a member of NC Scribes and The Military Writers Society of America.

Tammy Parker is a long-time telecom analyst and trade journalist. Her first published work was a short poem that her second-grade teacher submitted to the elementary school's newsletter. She has had two other stories published in the *Chicken Soup for the Soul* series.

Andrea Peebles lives in Pendergrass, GA with her husband of forty-five years. She has had multiple stories published in the *Chicken Soup for the Soul* series since her first story in 2007. She retired after thirty-five years in the commercial insurance industry and now spends her time traveling and volunteering for Agape Hospice.

Ava Pennington is a freelance writer and speaker and has contributed to magazines and thirty-four anthologies, including twenty-six titles in the *Chicken Soup for the Soul* series. She also authored *Reflections on the Names of God: A Devotional*, endorsed by Kay Arthur. Ava is also a freelance editor and writing coach. Learn more at www.AvaPennington.com.

Rita Plush is the author of the novels *Lily Steps Out* and *Feminine Products*, and the short story collection *Alterations*. She is the book reviewer for *Fire Island News* and teaches memoir at Queensborough Community College and the Fire Island School, Continuing Ed.

Lou Zywicki Prudhomme earned a B.A. and two M.A.s from the University of Minnesota, Duluth. She is the mother of four children and taught high school English for more than thirty years. She and her husband Fred are enjoying retirement in Cocoa, FL and Duluth, MN.

Toya Qualls-Barnette holds a Bachelor of Arts in Communications/Public Relations from Pepperdine University, Malibu. She has two sons and works as director of sales in Northern California. She enjoys writing, singing, and traveling. She is writing a memoir.

Nicholas R. lives in California where he uses his current home as the base for his work as a tour manager for artists and musicians. He is the youngest of three sons to his mother and late father. He enjoys music, traveling, adventures with friends and family, and attempting to better himself each day with good influence from his peers.

Wayne Rapp holds a Bachelor of Arts degree from the University of Arizona. He has written two books and numerous fiction and non-fiction pieces for publication. A short story, "In the Time of Marvel and Confusion," was nominated for a Pushcart Prize. His writing has twice been honored with grants from the Ohio Arts Council.

Sheila Roe is an award-winning author whose work has been published in newspapers, magazines, anthologies and books in the United States and the United Kingdom. She has facilitated grief recovery groups and written grief-related material since 2003. Sheila is a graduate of the University of Southern California.

Patricia Ann Rossi is an avid reader, writer, and runner. For over a decade she has facilitated writing to heal workshops for cancer survivors. She has also facilitated writing workshops for bereavement groups. She is an active member of her community. Patricia serves on local boards including her college alumni board.

Diane Rumbo graduated from Northeast Missouri State University in 1991. She has been a Realtor since 1997. She married a man who also lost his spouse to cancer, and they stay busy with six children and one granddaughter. Diane also enjoys being with family and friends, traveling, boating and golf.

Katy Ryan is the author of a forthcoming memoir about her squatter upstairs, a brain tumor that unraveled the life that she knew. Her writing explores the humorous and heartbreaking sides of parenting. When she's not with her three spunky children, she can be found swimming, hiking, or trying to up her pickleball game.

Beth Saadati is a high school English teacher with an MFA in creative writing. She shares stories at bethsaadati.com that offer insight, understanding, and hope to those who weather the storms of suicidal thoughts and suicide loss... and to those who simply know how bittersweet life can sometimes be.

A lifelong writer, long distance runner and community advocate, **Sue-Ellen Sanders** lives with her husband and two rescue pups, while trying to micro-manage — without success — two young adult children. She's published essays and stories and hosts a radio talk show.

Patti Santucci is an emerging writer in Fair Oaks, CA. Her work has been published in *Stories on Stage Sacramento*, *American River Review*, *Dime Show Review*, and others. Her non-fiction story, "Looking for Signs," won first place (Pacific West Region) in the CCHAs Literary Magazine Competition.

D.J. Sartell is a freelance author and content creator who lives in Roseville, a quaint suburb of Sacramento, CA. As a two-time contributor to the *Chicken Soup for the Soul* series, this is one of her favorite platforms as a writer.

Loretta D. Schoen grew up in Brazil and Italy and now resides in sunny Florida. She loves spending time with her husband, grandsons and dog Liesl. Having spent a lifetime surviving medical adversity she has written a book, *Surviving Medical Mayhem: Laughing When It Hurts*. Learn more at www.SurvivingMedicalMayhem.com.

Deborah Shouse is a writer, speaker, editor, laughter facilitator, and dementia advocate. She is the author of *Love in the Land of Dementia: Finding Hope in the Caregiver's Journey* and *Connecting in the Land of Dementia: Creative Activities to Explore Together*. She is using her writing as a way to understand and heal from her adult daughter's sudden death.

Marianne Simon was born to a family of artists and has spent her life exploring creativity in its many facets. She has worked as an actress and director for twenty years and has been writing for longer than that. She also discovered a passion for nature that inspires her writings. E-mail her at Marianne@poeticplantings.com.

Diane Stark is a wife, mom, and writer. She is a frequent contributor to the *Chicken Soup for the Soul* series. Diane loves to write about the important things in life: her family and her faith.

John Stevens is a proud resident of St. Marys, Ontario. He has led a charmed life in TV, with Softball Canada and the Canadian Association of Journalists, in administrative roles, teaching computer courses and teaching ESL. He has worked in many countries in the world, living in London, Jeddah and Istanbul.

Julie Stielstra lives in the Chicago suburbs but escapes regularly to central Kansas. She is the author of over a dozen published short stories and essays, and two award-winning novels: *Pilgrim* and *Opulence, Kansas*. She blogs on animals, books, writing, the prairie and whatever else strikes her fancy at juliestielstra.com.

Shannon Stocker believes that people are stronger at their broken places. She authored a picture book titled *Listen, Can U Save the Day*, and is a memoir author, coma, abuse and rape survivor, mother to a brain cancer warrior, and frequent contributor to the *Chicken Soup for the Soul* series. Her world revolves around Greg, Cassidy, and Tye. Learn more at www.shannonstocker.com.

Jennifer Stults grew up in a suburb of Portland, OR. She has one daughter and a very supportive extended family. When tragedy struck, she found writing to be the only way out. She has written and self-published a book about her grief entitled *Carry on Castle* that is available online.

B.J. Taylor loves being a great-grandmother and relishes every moment with her family. She's an award-winning author whose work has appeared in *Guideposts*, many titles in the *Chicken Soup for the Soul* series, and numerous magazines and newspapers. You can reach her through her website at www.bjtaylor.com and check out her dog blog at www.bjtaylor.com/blog.

Bob Thurber is the author of six books, including *Paperboy: A Dysfunctional Novel*. Regarded as a master of Flash and Micro Fiction, his work has received a long list of awards, appeared in *Esquire* and other magazines, and been anthologized sixty times. He resides in Massachusetts. Learn more at BobThurber.net.

Luanne Tovey is a writer from western New York who has published stories in five titles in the *Chicken Soup for the Soul* series. She is retired from a twenty-five-year career as community outreach coordinator for a New York statewide education agency. She loves spending time with her eight grandchildren most of all.

Aimee C. Trafton is an e-learning specialist and writer from Fredericton, New Brunswick, Canada. Her first children's book, *Amber Tambourine and the Land of Laugh-a-Lot*, was published in May 2021 (Austin Macauley Publishers USA).

Christine Trollinger likes potlucks and bingo. Christine is a retired insurance agent who enjoys writing and reading, spending time with her children and grandchildren, and now great grandchildren. She has written many stories for the *Chicken Soup for the Soul* series over the last twenty years.

Miriam Van Scott is the author of *Encyclopedia of Heaven*, *Encyclopedia of Hell*, *Boomer's Criss-Cross Christmas*, *Song of Old* and the fact-inspired ghost story *Bandun Gate*. She has provided content to *Good Housekeeping*, The History Channel, ABC News, Paramount Entertainment Group, TLC, Sy-Fy and many other media.

Raymond M. Wong draws inspiration from his wife, Quyen, and their two children, Kevin and Kristie. He is grateful for the opportunity to make a difference through his writing. "The Truest Thing" is dedicated to his wife, Quyen, and her father, De Huynh. Learn more at www.raymondmwong.com.

Meet Amy Newmark

Amy Newmark is the bestselling author, editor-in-chief, and publisher of the *Chicken Soup for the Soul* book series. Since 2008, she has published 179 new books, most of them national bestsellers in the U.S. and Canada, more than doubling the number of Chicken Soup for the Soul titles in print today. She is also the author of *Simply Happy*, a crash course in Chicken Soup for the Soul advice and wisdom that is filled with easy-to-implement, practical tips for enjoying a better life.

Amy is credited with revitalizing the Chicken Soup for the Soul brand, which has been a publishing industry phenomenon since the first book came out in 1993. By compiling inspirational and aspirational true stories curated from ordinary people who have had extraordinary experiences, Amy has kept the twenty-eight-year-old Chicken Soup for the Soul brand fresh and relevant.

Amy graduated *magna cum laude* from Harvard University where she majored in Portuguese and minored in French. She then embarked on a three-decade career as a Wall Street analyst, a hedge fund manager, and a corporate executive in the technology field.

Her return to literary pursuits was inevitable, as her honors thesis in college involved traveling throughout Brazil's impoverished northeast region, collecting stories from regular people. She is delighted to have come full circle in her writing career — from collecting stories "from the people" in Brazil as a twenty-year-old to, three decades later, collecting stories "from the people" for Chicken Soup for the Soul.

When Amy and her husband Bill, the CEO of Chicken Soup for the Soul, are not working, they are visiting their four grown children and their four grandchildren.

Changing your life one story at a time®
www.chickensoup.com